# Cultural History of Modern India

# Cultural History of Modern India

Second Edition

Dilip M. Menon

Orient BlackSwan

CULTURAL HISTORY OF MODERN INDIA (SECOND EDITION)

ORIENT BLACKSWAN PRIVATE LIMITED

*Registered Office*
3-6-752 Himayatnagar, Hyderabad 500 029, Telangana, India
Email: centraloffice@orientblackswan.com

*Other Offices*
Bengaluru, Bhopal, Chennai, Guwahati, Hyderabad, Jaipur, Kolkata, Lucknow, Mumbai, New Delhi, Noida, Patna, Vijayawada

*First published in India by*
Social Science Press 2006


First published 2017

ISBN 978-93-86392-60-2

025184

23022017

Typeset in Minion Pro 10/11.9 by
OSDATA, Hyderabad

*Printed in India at*
Yash Printographics
Noida

*Published by*
Orient Blackswan Private Limited
3-6-752, Himayatnagar, Hyderabad 500 029
Email: info@orientblackswan.com

# Contents


*Preface and Acknowledgements* *vii*

*Introduction* *ix*

1. Cricket and Caste: The Heroic Struggles of the Palwankar Brothers 1
RAMACHANDRA GUHA

2. A Book of Her Own, A Life of Her Own: The Autobiography of a Nineteenth-Century Woman 33
TANIKA SARKAR

3. The Past in the Present 66
RUSTOM BHARUCHA

4. National Identity and the Realist Aesthetic 83
SUMITA S. CHAKRAVARTY

5. 'Unity in Diversity?' Dilemmas of Nationhood in Indian Calendar Art 115
PATRICIA UBEROI

6. Guru and Gramophone: Fantasies of Fidelity and Modern Technologies of the Real 156
AMANDA WEIDMAN

7. Things Fall Apart: The Cinematic Rendition of the Agrarian Landscape in South India 179
DILIP M. MENON

*Notes on Contributors* *211*

# Preface and Acknowledgements

THIS READER WAS CONCEIVED TO MEET THE DEMANDS OF THE NEW B.A. CONCURRENT Course in History at the University of Delhi designed for Honours students in social sciences and humanities who opt to do a concurrent course in History. However, it is also aimed at a general readership interested in the most recent research on issues of culture in modern India. One way of doing this reader would have been to put together the work of historians engaged in writing on issues of culture broadly defined. Given the fact that we are all interdisciplinary nowadays, it seemed to be an interesting enterprise to actually collate works done by sociologists, art historians and music theorists working within a historical paradigm. This means that the essays occasionally have a technical vocabulary particular to a discipline. However the quality of thinking and speculation in these essays is of such an order that we hope that general readers will be adventurous and strike out on their own. In the classroom this may allow a fruitful exchange between teachers of history engaging with students primarily specializing in literature, sociology and other disciplines.

As Convenor of the B.A. Concurrent course committee for the University, I had the opportunity of engaging with some of the best teachers and scholars in deciding on readings. Our meetings over a period of a few months were challenging and opened up many issues as also exposing us to cutting edge scholarship from all over the world in many disciplines. If we had had our way, students would be reading volumes of a few thousand pages each! In the interests of teaching and comprehension as well as the time constraints on teacher and students we opted for a minimal format of not more than 250 odd pages of readings. I would like to thank, in particular, Sunil Kumar, Shahid Amin, Upinder Singh and Meenakshi Khanna. In Tagore's words, 'you have made known to me things that were unknown' (*koto ajaanare janaayile tumi....*)

A special thank you to the several authors featured in this volume and their publishers who rallied around so that the volume could be brought out with minimum bother. Ram Guha, Amanda Weidman, Tanika Sarkar and Patricia Uberoi in particular did not mind my presuming on our friendship and making demands on their generosity.

Dilip Menon
Mellon Chair in Indian Studies and Professor of History,
University of Witwatersrand,
Johannesburg

# Introduction

IS CULTURAL HISTORY MERELY HISTORY WITH THE POLITICS LEFT OUT? THIS QUESTION is not as simple as it may seem. It has been argued by many scholars of modern India that one of the strategies adopted by Indian intellectuals and reformers in colonial India was to remake the space of culture and tradition, since involvement in formal politics was either interdicted or curtailed by the British government. The retreat as it were, into the space of culture, reflected an attempt to create both a sense of autonomy as well as agency. Many of the social projects under colonialism were about reconstituting gender relations, family and social hierarchy arguing along the lines of the distinctiveness of Indian civilization. The ideal Indian woman; caste as an expression of a benevolent division of duties that kept society together; and, the family under the patriarch as the source of stability and order were some of the themes through which an idea of Indian culture was invented. These ideas were reflected in popular press and art, in paintings, in literature and the political rhetoric of the period. This contemporary invention was presented as features of an ageless Indian culture, time out of mind, and a civilizational mode of thinking emerged. This meant a reaching back in time to look for spaces of cultural and political efflorescence (the "golden age of the Guptas" for example) and a difficult relation with history and the contemporary.

Ironically, the idea of a homogeneous, unchanging civilizational mode tended to be parasitical on the colonial representation of the past. The periodization of history that emerged under colonialism into Ancient (Hindu), Medieval (Muslim) and Modern drew upon European characterizations of their own modernity as distinct from a medieval dark age. The past became a solace for most nationalists and the medieval period came to be presented as a period in which many of the glories of an ancient period were attenuated. A certain brand of nationalism took up this civilizational paradigm to argue that independence for India meant a leap forward while looking back. The politics of the nation would be future oriented but its cultural orientation would be restorative, burnishing values developed and presumably nurtured over millennia. Such a writing of history had little time for the miscegenated nature of Indian history with the multiple influences of Buddhism, Jainism, Sufism, Christianity, Zoroastrianism, Judaism. The search for purity made the idea of history a problematic one. The idea of tradition came to stand against the idea of history and classicism, civilization and ancientness were valued. There were multiple critiques of these views that emerged from the foremost intellectuals and leaders of the 20th century. Tagore rejected the idea of national chauvinism which would put one's nation above others without reflecting on the inequalities that made up society. Gandhi's critical traditionalism made truth, justice and ethics the touchstones for the evaluation of any national inheritance. Nehru sought to break away from the coils of tradition and longing for a glorious past to address the question of a radical modernity for India. And Ambedkar relentlessly argued for universal equality showing how the idea of civilization was premised on brutality towards the many.

Over the last two decades the writing of cultural history has meant rendering the very idea of culture historical. Asking the questions whose culture and whose tradition has inaugurated two kinds of intellectual enquiries. The first queries ideas of classicism and civilization and asks when these ideas came into existence, which social groups were invested in them, and the purpose that these concepts served in exalting the culture of a few over the many. The second kind of enquiry has looked outwards from art, painting and music to popular forms like cinema, cartoons, woodcuts, photographs, folksongs, calendars—in short a wide range of visual and aural material. This has meant a scepticism towards the idea of culture as a monolithic entity as much as a questioning of the centrality of the historical discipline and its formation. Much cultural history, premised as it has been on the interrogating the politics of culture, has also argued that ideas of history, self, ethics and community are dispersed through popular forms and imaginations. The historical imagination is present in representations from outside the academy, however contentious and baroque these imaginations may be. What we need is a dialogue and an engagement across many forms rather than gatekeeping by an establishment. Nationalism and patriotism need not descend into chauvinism as Tagore warned, but rather nations should be premised on argument, debate and constructive disagreement. The "argumentative India" as Amartya Sen put it lies at the very heart of our conception of culture and politics.

The history of modern India has been written largely as the history of the coming into being of the Indian nation. Over the conventional two hundred year time span from 1757 to 1947, India is seen as emerging from subjection to its tryst with destiny with other nations of the world at the stroke of midnight. Salman Rushdie's evocative phrase, midnight's children, captured the self perception of a generation who saw their lives and fortunes as twinned with the destiny of the young India. There was a sense of newness as also arousal; it was as if like the sleeping beauty at the kiss of the prince, the nation too had awoken to a sense of itself. Nehru's *Autobiography* as well as *The Discovery of India* spoke of nationalist politics as the unearthing of a sentiment and an actuality that was already there; hence the word discovery rather than invention. The nationalist movement had had to work hard in creating a sense of a territorial and cultural unity (large parts of India did not concur with the Congress understanding of national geography). Debates continued in the public sphere, even after Independence, as to how deep-rooted was the idea of India, rather than of region, ethnicity or religious affiliation. However, political exigencies and the necessity of governance meant that the 'unity' of India had to be presented as a self evident truth. One of the effects of this was that the history of 15 August 1947 came to be written about by a generation of historians as the glorious story of independence gained. Other possible narratives, particularly the tragic history of a nation partitioned, were sidelined. The fratricidal violence attending Partition seemed to fundamentally question the smooth narrative of non-violence, and the unity of both people and territory that nationalist ideology had generated. It is only 50 years after the fact that history writing has begun to engage with the trauma of what the Partition meant for the psyche of the young nation and its people.

## I

Increasingly, a newer generation of historians has begun to ask questions about the silences, evasions and seemingly self-evident truths that are part of the writing of history. History is as much about what happened as it is about the selective narration of those events. As Shahid Amin puts it, the historian's concern has come to be about 'how nationalist history is made and remade' and revealing 'the strategies—narrative or otherwise—which go into its making.'[1] The writing of the history of modern India is evidently as much about inclusions as exclusions. The primary criterion for inclusion was participation in the nationalist movement within the paradigm of a non-violent Gandhian politics (what Amin has memorably termed as the *yogdaan* perspective). Hence, political activity that resorted to violence and challenged the authority of the Congress ideology like the Mappila rebellion or Chauri Chaura in the 1920s, or the activities of Subhas Chandra Bose's Indian National Army and the Royal Indian Navy mutiny in the 1940s were seen as anomalies. They were to be explained away, not merely accounted for in the paradigm of *De di hamen aazadi bina khadg bina dhal/Sabarmati ke sant tune kar diya kamaal* (to borrow the words of a popular Hindi film song of the 1960s). Political opponents of the Congress's self representation as speaking for all Indians like Ambedkar, Jinnah and Savarkar with their different ideological positions could not find a place in the history textbooks except as failed opponents. More important, the history of regions like the north-east, southern India and over 500 Princely states where Congress activity had been minimal or indeed absent were excluded from mainstream historical memory as embodied in textbooks and pedagogy. We have to ask ourselves the fundamental question: can a narrow history of modern India written from the standpoint of nationalism alone stand in for a more complex narrative of multiple and dissenting histories within the nation? How can we begin to think about a history of modern India that is more inclusive of questions of difference? How do we engage seriously with dissenting strains in political conceptions in a way that transcends the textbook formula of unity in diversity?

Earlier nationalist narratives emphasized the creation of larger political unities: the idea of India and the Indian. The creation of a modern Indian citizen was counter-posed to what were seen as atavistic and non-modern identities of caste, religion and ethnicity. So for instance, movements and ideologies that raised issues of caste difference were presented as divisive in nature and detracting from the main task at hand. Whether it was the non-Brahmin movement in Tamil Nadu or Ambedkar's questioning of the Congress claim to represent all putative Hindus, the question of how some Indians were more equal than the others was deferred in the politics of creating a united India. While this may have been necessary as an anti-colonial political strategy, historical writing took on the presuppositions of nationalist activity uncritically. Following the imposition of the Emergency in 1975, and a growing sense of disillusionment with the nation-state, some historians tried to look beyond the activities and the self presentation of the Indian National Congress. For instance, in an early work the historian Gyanendra Pandey showed that there may have been a direct relation between the strength of Congress organization and curbs placed on popular political initiatives. The growth of nationalist activity meant a disciplining of other political activities that addressed local concerns in a more confrontational idiom.[2] Pandey simultaneously questioned the equation of nationalism with the Congress and the idea that the Congress promoted all local political activity that was nationalist. The emergence in the 1980s of what came to be called Subaltern Studies[3] created a body of work that tried to move away from a concentration on elite and organizational politics. It focused on movements by peasants, tribals and other subordinated or 'subaltern' groups and argued that these may have constituted a parallel national politics. While there may have been an attempt to challenge the conflation of Congress politics with all political activity in India, the understanding of what constituted politics remained rather limited. Subaltern Studies concentrated on challenges to the authority of the state, and interventions within a public sphere constituted by the state's activities whether of revenue collection or the legal framework.

Part of the problem lay with the use of sources. Historical practice since the late 19th century had stressed the importance of state generated archives for writing the histories of nations. And indeed histories came to be about the biography of the states as they evolved over time. If an earlier colonial historiography had emphasized the various Charters and Acts and institutions of government that had come into being over the 19th and 20th century, nationalist historiography spoke about the winning of state power from the British, culminating in the transfer of power in 1947. There was no space for the people here except inasmuch as the state chose to define them or as they entered into conflict with the state under the leadership of nationalist stalwarts. One significant example of this is the characterization of nationalist activity in the period of the *swadeshi* movement as 'revolutionary terrorism'; a statist label which survives in our historical imagination. The Subaltern Studies enterprise sought to read the archival records 'against the grain', that is to say in opposition to the meaning that the records sought to convey. Descriptions of groups of people and activities as criminal or terrorist could well be seen as the state's interpretation of acts antagonistic to its existence, and the historian could argue that social justice or national freedom was at stake here. However, there are limits to the inversion of characterizations. While the state's criminal could well be the historian's social revolutionary, sometimes, to put it simply, a criminal was merely a criminal. In order to write the history of popular politics it was necessary to move beyond the state archives and search for newer sources.

Three essays within the subaltern collective constituted a departure in rethinking the question of sources as much as the nature of politics and the political imagination. Ranajit Guha in his essay titled 'Chandra's Death'[4] rescued from the archive the story of a lower caste widow named Chandra, who died in the course of a badly performed abortion. Her otherwise unremarkable life came to the attention of the state through the possibility that she may have been murdered. Guha made this incident the point of entry for an enquiry into the status of widows in traditional Bengali society as also patriarchy and the regulation of female sexuality. He explored in nuanced detail the politics of community, gender and the individual. It was not a story of nationalist heroism, of an extraordinary individual or indeed of an event that transformed notions of legality in the public sphere. It was rather an act of writing, that, to paraphrase the words of the English social historian E.P. Thompson, rescued the lives of the ordinary human being from the condescension of posterity. By looking at the domain of the private, Guha showed how even intimate spaces like the family were suffused with the working out of social power.

Sumit Sarkar in another cameo piece, 'The Kalki avatar of Bikrampur',[5] picked out of obscurity the events at the turn of the 20th century on a bizarre night in the life of a small town Bengali family. A domestic servant claiming to be the Kalki *avatar* turned the well regulated home upside down and subjected his employer and wife to ritual humiliation. Through this event, Sarkar looked at emerging definitions of family and household in colonial Bengal and the construction of the authority of the *karta*, or male head of the household, vis-à-vis domestics and women. The events of a night in a home were pieced together from archival sources, newspaper reports, police records and popular pamphlets. In the historian's hands they were woven into larger speculations on the significance of millenarian myths like the belief in the advent of Kalki *avatar* signifying the end of *Kaliyug* with the coming of the 20th century. A window was opened into conceptions of mythical time and history which coexisted alongside the secular time of colonial modernity. Here again ordinary lives were the focus of the study and the politics of hierarchy and the household were central to an understanding of the working of a wider social structure.

Finally, Shahid Amin's classic essay 'Gandhi as Mahatma',[6] tried to move away from the historical record of Gandhi the individual, to understand how he came to be venerated as a *mahatma* in the countryside of eastern U.P. in the 1920s. Trawling through Hindi newspapers and archival records of the period, Amin studied in detail the circulation of rumours about the magical powers of Gandhi and the growing belief among peasants that to oppose Gandhi would invite his divine wrath on them. The name of Gandhi increasingly came to be invoked in local conflicts and resolving local hierarchies. In the famous instance of the burning of a police station at Chauri Chaura in 1922, which brought to a halt the non-cooperation movement, the crowd of people who engaged in the act saw Gandhi less as a prophet of non-violence and more as a divine figure who sanctioned violence against injustice. In all of these essays, the idea of both politics and political imagination had been expanded beyond the story of nationalism and of the politics of the state. These historians questioned the idea that events in the public realm were of greater consequence than the actions of individuals in the private sphere of community or family. Moreover, they tried to understand popular culture—whether the belief in the magical powers of Gandhi or widespread panic about the coming of the end of *Kaliyug*—on its own terms rather than by the demands of a modern rationality. There was a move out of the state archives in order to capture the intimate details of ordinary lives and their extraordinary manifestations. The meaning of the political was expanded far beyond organized political activity to the micro-politics of gender, home and community.

## II

The writing of the history of modern India has moved towards new sources, new definitions of the political, and an engagement with issues of culture and community. We need to stay with the nebulous idea of culture a while, in order to understand what a cultural history of modern India may involve. A rather simple minded cultural history might be one, with culture imagined as an apolitical space. So for instance, philosophical traditions, art, architecture, could be studied without asking the larger question of the social matrix within which these are generated. However, issues of the disposition of power within a society and questions of labour and wealth are crucial to engage with seemingly abstract issues like philosophical ideas as much as concrete themes like architecture. So, for example, modern day celebrations of a glorious Vedic culture, do not address the question that Uma Chakravarty raises: 'whatever happened to the Vedic *dasi*?' Questions of both servitude and gender difference become crucial.[7] Partha Chatterjee offers a possible explanation for why a characterization of culture and tradition as located in a timeless, apolitical space emerges within colonized societies. Under colonialism, Indians were subjects not citizens. The possibility of their acting as political agents was curtailed by restrictions on the freedom of speech, assembly and representation. Deprived of agency in the political and material realm, native intellectuals turned towards the construction of an inner space of culture ostensibly uncorrupted by colonial modernity and the politics of subjection. If the west was politically superior, well, then the Indians were spiritually and culturally superior, or so the argument went. Historical constructions of a golden age and an obsession with the ancient past as a compensation for a bleak present are typical features of the colonized imagination.[8] Timelessness, purity and unbroken continuity come to be the required hallmarks of culture as the idea comes to be collapsed into the conception of a national tradition that is unitary in nature. Should one not accommodate the presence of other religions, multiple ethnicities and diverse regional traditions within the idea of a 'national' culture? May not the idea of a plurality of traditions within the nation be a more democratic one?

Tapati Guha-Thakurta has argued that when the National Museum was opened in Delhi in 1949, the collection of 'masterpieces' of Indian art was very clearly associated with achievements in early Indian sculpture. The veneration of the ancient origins, as it were, of Indian art came to express also a static opposition derived from a contemporary social and political perception. 'Western' realism was characterized as expressing a narrow material reality while 'Indian' idealism supposedly embodied a spiritual, transcendental, civilizational spirit. We are back within the space of Chatterjee's argument spelt out earlier. Historians of art like E.B. Havell and A.K.Coomaraswamy had preferred to look back to early Buddhist art in India to sidestep the uncomfortable issue of Greek influences on an 'Indian' art following Alexander's invasion and subsequent cultural traffic. The curators of the National Museum too preferred an all-embracing notion of what was Hindu, as the master tradition of Indian art, engulfing Buddhist and other genres in the idea of a great Indian synthesis. The Mathura school of sculpture was chosen as most representative of 'Indian' art since it was perceived as being most free of 'foreign' influence.[9]

Another definition of cultural tradition involved the severing of artifacts from any connection with living traditions of work, prayer and community. Culture was seen in definite ways as the glory of the past. Nowhere is this more evident than in the ironic story of what Guha-Thakurta terms the 'museumisation' of the Didarganj Yakshi from Bihar. The Yakshi, was the object of popular worship, and occupied a makeshift shrine where devotees went to pray. Once identified as an object of art, and an icon of India's civilization, she was plucked away and planted in Patna museum; a journey that was to end in the National Museum, Delhi. Over the next few decades icons were recovered from 'inappropriate' uses and locations and 'rescued' from popular village worship. The glorious past had to be excised from the fallen state of the present and from the people, who came to be seen as the inappropriate guardians of a national tradition that had to be nurtured by the state. Ideas of culture are historical constructions and reflect the politics and relations of power at any given time. And certainly the idea of a national culture is exclusive as much as inclusive, depending on who and what are seen as comprising the nation. What comes to be presented as national culture may be, in fact, a representation of the customs of a perceived majority whether religious, regional or ethnic. What would the idea of national culture look like from the point of view of minority groups like Jains, Buddhists, Sikhs and Muslims? Or indeed, from the standpoint of those living in Manipur, Nagaland, Tripura, Kashmir or Kerala? Development projects in independent India have often involved the displacement and dispersal of people whose local cultures have perished as they moved into a new identity as uprooted migrants. How do we account for the worlds that we have lost and the shrinking of our horizons of understanding?

This is but one example of the new kind of cultural history that asks questions about what a people see as their culture and how definitions change over time. For instance, while looking at traditions of Indian classical music, we can ask when the idea of a 'classical' form emerged. When did a certain form of music move beyond confines like courts and temples and come to be perceived as something an ordinary individual could have access to? What were the changes in what was sung, who was allowed to sing, and how training was imparted? Janaki Bakhle in her work on Hindustani music looks at the influence of two men in the early 20th century, V.D. Paluskar and V.N. Bhatkhande, who defined what Hindustani classical music means to us today. In their different ways, they systematized *ragas*, innovated methods of teaching, structured the format of public concerts and introduced musical notation so that textbooks could be created for teaching complex structures of music on a larger scale in schools. Lakshmi Subramanian has argued for similar developments in Carnatic music also showing that there was a 'purification' of lyrics so that devotional and formal aspects came to be emphasized over erotic songs which were seen as unacceptable by the listening standards of an emerging middle-class. Thus, the creation of a 'canon'—a defined corpus of songs and the manner of their singing—was central to the 'invention' of Indian classical music in the early 20th century.[10]

The essays in this collection present original and pioneering forays in the cultural history of modern India, ranging over diverse themes such as cricket, oral history, gender studies, film, popular culture and Indian classical music. Whether looking at issues of caste on the seemingly level playing field of cricket in early 20th century India; or how a 19th century housewife comes to pen the first autobiography by an Indian woman; calendar art reflecting deeper notions of religion and community; or how an idea of 'pure' classical music faces the challenge of technology, these essays show how ideas of self, community and art are formed within a larger politics. Moreover, culture far from being a refuge from the political is also the space within which politics comes to be worked out. This reader hopes to raise issues about modernity, culture as also Indian-ness. None of these categories can be taken as self-evident as we look historically at constructions of culture.

We tend to understand sport as either occupying one's moments of leisure, or in these days of highly competitive and professionalized organization, as a profession in itself. Studying sport historically means looking at changing notions of work and leisure as much as the emergence of the idea of sport as a primary profession. We could also ask about the role that different sports play in different societies. Why, for example, do England, West Indies and India play cricket, but the United States of America and Japan play baseball? Ashis Nandy, opens his memorable book on cricket with the sentence, 'Cricket is an Indian game accidentally discovered by the British.'[11] He goes on to argue that the nature of cricket as a game reflects the obsession in both societies with class, gradation and the containment of social conflict. The emphasis on sportsmanlike behaviour amidst controlled aggression and an informal hierarchy between batsmen, bowlers and fielders symbolized expectations of social behaviour as also issues of rank. For example, in the early days of Indian cricket, when princes used to play the game in imitation of their colonial masters' lifestyles, they were more inclined to take the crease than run around the field chasing the ball. Fielding was seen as equivalent to manual labour. In England too, the pace bowlers tended to come from the working classes while the specialist batsmen were gentlemen who had attended public schools. Ramachandra Guha takes up an unusual biography to enter into the culture that underlay cricket in colonial India. Three representatives of the

Depressed Classes attended the Round Table Conference held in London after the cessation of the civil disobedience movement: B.R.Ambedkar, M.C.Rajah and Baloo Palwankar. The first two names are known to historians as political leaders. However, Palwankar acquired fame through being a bowler and a very good one at that. In the first decades of the 20th century, cricket was organized around communities rather than regions (as the Ranji trophy is now) and Parsis, Hindus, Muslims and Europeans played against each other in tournaments. The victory of an Indian community over the Europeans was a matter for general rejoicing under conditions of colonialism where cricket became the practice of politics by other means. However, other divisions ran deep in Indian society

Baloo was of the Chamar caste, and his cricketing skills were in great demand, however his fellow caste Hindu players would not sit or eat with him during tea breaks. While his fame spread among cricket lovers in Bombay and Maharashtra, within the Hindu team, his caste was what distinguished him and he never got to be captain of the team that he bowled to victory on several memorable occasions. When his youngest brother Vithal, finally got to captain the team, this was seen by several social commentators as nothing short of the culmination of a social revolution inaugurated by Gandhi's attack on Untouchability. This essay opens up issues of the seemingly level playing field of sports and shows how social hierarchies and prejudices may continue to structure spaces which seem to be built on notions of merit. Cultural history encourages us to ask questions about the cultural matrices within which all human activity functions: we are created by culture as much as we create culture. We might go on to ask questions about the social background of players of chess, football or those who are boxers or practice archery for that matter. Why are the most popular sports in India the ones that avoid bodily contact between players: why cricket and not football? Why is football the most popular game in Bengal and Kerala, two regions which have seen a collapse of a hierarchical caste order and its ideology? Why do cricket tests and hockey matches draw large audiences and sponsorship but only when men's' teams play?

Playing the Englishman at his game and beating him meant much more under colonialism than a simple victory. It was about an assertion of manliness in response to colonial characterizations of Indians as effeminate and not given to physical exercise. Colonial history writing had built a stereotype of Indians as a nation given to defeats by foreign invaders because of their tendency to intellectualism and other worldliness. Ashis Nandy has argued that one of the ways in which native intellectuals reacted was to create a culture of masculinity. Nandy reads Swami Vivekananda's recasting of Hinduism in a muscular mode emphasizing sports and physical development as much as spirituality as being exemplary in this respect.[12] The *swadeshi* movement in Bengal (1905–08) with its emphasis on physical culture and the cult of violence can be seen as the political expression of this reassertion of masculinity. Chris Pinney has pointed to contemporary pictorial depictions of the revolutionaries in which Chandrasekhar Azad and Bhagat Singh were shown as models of masculine virtue.[13] This recovery of masculinity was a protection of tradition from the onslaught of colonialism and entailed a defence of Indian customs like child marriage and interdictions on widow remarriage for better or for worse. Tanika Sarkar has argued that patriarchy may well have been strengthened under colonialism as native male elites constructed the home in opposition to the world.[14] How do we recover the lives of women under colonialism trapped as they were within structures of domesticity with men taking on the task of representing them in public as embodying traditional virtues? Rashsundari Debi's *Amar Jiban* [My life] published in 1876 in Bengali, is arguably the first autobiography in an Indian language written by a woman. What makes this text even more remarkable is that it was written by a housewife stealing time from her household chores to do a bit of reading and writing. This raises the important question of the value of a woman's life under the requirements of silent self-effacement and performing of duties required of a wife and a mother. Why did Rashsundari write her life? What gave her the courage and what models did she draw upon for inspiration? Tanika Sarkar shows how Rashsundari framed her life within the parameters of religious hagiography drawing upon the life of the Vaishnava saint Chaitanya as a model. From within a culture of patriarchy there were resources that she and other women like her could draw upon. From within a religious paradigm Rashsundari created a secular narration of an ordinary life. This essay raises fundamental questions of patriarchy, selfhood and the intellectual wherewithal available to women in order to impart order and dignity to their lives. Not everyone who lives need feel the necessity to narrate their life; Rashsundari's autobiography is an assertion of defiance in the face of a masculine order which renders women as faceless and voiceless.

Rashsundari's life, the extraordinary life of an ordinary woman, raises questions of the sources for the writing of history. Neither state records nor nationalist accounts would have found her life worth recovering or telling. What about lives even more obscure, of nameless peasants and productive groups all over India? How do we even begin to tell their stories if we rely on written narratives alone? Rustom Bharucha, in an extraordinary book *Rajasthan: an Oral History* draws upon extensive interviews and conversations with Komal Kothari, the late folklorist and preserver of the performative traditions of Rajasthan. Kothari summons up from personal memory, experience, and interactions with diverse groups of people a wide range of stories, legends, and traditions. We get insights into notions of time and history, classifications of landscape and ways of remembering. One of the important issues raised in this chapter is that of history. Tending as we do to equate the historical record with written sources we are skeptical about word-of-mouth transmission: how reliable is it, we ask? The question is not so much one of reliability alone but the questions that we are seeking answers to. Oral history cannot be seen as merely something that we turn to when written records are not available. Very often, issues of local knowledge of agrarian traditions, bio-diversity and the like are embodied in stories, proverbs, and anecdotes. We need to work with the idea of social memory which encompasses both the written as well as the oral. The historical imagination is much larger than the limited procedures and questions raised by the historical discipline. Moreover, Komal Kothari draws our attention to performances of culture—rituals, festivals and songs—which too embody local knowledge. Finally, there is the question of memory and remembering. Ajay Skaria in his work on the Dangs region in Gujarat compares the *goths* or the oral traditions of the Dangi *bhils* with the archival record of the late Mughal and colonial period. He creatively explores the similarities and differences to show how both sources may have their particular silences and what we need to understand as well is the question of strategic memory.[15] Why do we remember what we do? Do we remember everything of the past? Is it necessary? The creation of records can be as much about erasing particular pasts and memorializing a certain version of the past. Oral history as much as written sources may be culpable of the same strategies.

Societies have particular collective myths about themselves and performative traditions project these in apparent and veiled ways. Cinema is one such projection of the self-image and desires of a collective unconscious; it is not just about mere fantasy even though the average Bollywood film may lead one to think so. Cinema can be studied as embodying within itself the contradictions, aspirations and conflicts within any society. In the first decade of independent India many Hindi films sought to depict the hopes of the new nation through an attempt at portraying social realities in their rawness. Film directors dealt with issues of poverty, inequality and the survival of decadent values cast within familiar plotlines of love lost and regained. Realism was the keyword as the leading figures in the industry tried to move away from costume dramas and mythological films in order to show the gritty texture of everyday life. However, it must be remembered that the representation of reality is not unmediated; it is not just the putting of a camera before something called 'life'. The camera and technology as much as plot and artifice mediated between reality and its depiction. We have to understand realist cinema as expressing a particular view of the world. Sumita Chakravarty uses the term 'morbid realism' to show how reality was exaggerated for purposes of generating empathy towards a distinctive view of what a new India should look like. While one can study cinema as representative of its times, we must also remember that works of art have a certain autonomy of their conditions of production. There is both an internal history of cinema (the fact that Indian realism was influenced to a great extent by the neo-realist movement in Italy) as also the fact that viewers of cinema generate their own understandings. Any work of art is a triangular relation between a reality (perceived conditions of living); its representation (in cinema or the novel); and its understanding (by the viewer or reader). The relation between cinema and social history is a difficult one. We cannot reduce films to the merely social, i.e., representing the politics and social conditions of the time of its production. On the other hand cinema does not occupy a space of pure autonomy and we have to pay attention to the conditions of production: financing, producing, distribution and so on.[16] The question is moot as to whose point of view the Hindi film represents: the elements internal to the Bollywood industry; external elements like the Indian state or vested social interests; or the fans and the audience? And what is the space that it occupies? Ashis Nandy, for instance argues from the point of view of the audience that both the 'cinema and the slum in India show[ed] the same impassioned negotiation with everyday survival, combined with the same effort to forget that negotiation, the same mix of the comic and the tragic, spiced with elements borrowed indiscriminately from the classical and the folk, the East and the West.'[17]

The last two essays deal with different issues but have a thread in common. We take up the issue of calendar art and of classical music and explore the history that attempts to create strict demarcations between popular and elite culture. When we hear the word 'art', we generally tend to associate it with a high culture and a world of meaning accessible to few. Those who possess 'culture' are those who appreciate 'art'. How do certain artifacts, persons and institutions come to acquire value and distinction in any society? Is this the recognition of something intrinsic to great works and inspiration or is there a social process of the accruing of worth which once started is self sustaining? To know for example, that the Mona Lisa is a great work of art, or to appreciate the singing of Bhimsen Joshi could also be seen as part of the acquiring of a notion of culture over time, as it were: guaranteeing recognition of one's belonging to an aesthetic and social elite. However, there is also a larger public domain where artifacts like pictorial calendars, posters of film stars, pictures of gods and goddesses are seen as aesthetic and possessing a significance that transcends their cash value. The calendar, for example, is a ubiquitous object present in every home signifying multiple and coexisting ways of reckoning the passing of a year (the Vikram Samvat, the Georgian year, Al Hijra, the Nanakshahi era and so on). The pictures on calendars range from the hand painted to the photograph; religious to secular figures; allegories to realist depictions; each of them catering to a particular constituency and appealing to a different aesthetic. Some of them are obviously about nation-building (Jai Jawan Jai Kisan or speaking about the equality of all religions). Some have religious functions and double as objects of worship. The calendar on the wall of a home is a window to conceptions of art, religion, and politics in the everyday life of a nation. If the calendar is about infinite reproducibility and quicksilver responses to changing politics and fashions, classical music represents what is unchanging and 'pure'. Or does it? We have seen earlier how traditions of 'classicism' came to be constructed in the early 20th century. One of the challenges to this idea was of the possibility of reproduction and circulation of music with the coming of the gramophone industry. It moved music beyond the circles of supposed cognoscenti and democratized access to it. It pitted the guru against the gramophone; unbroken, carefully guarded traditions in opposition to the idea that art and culture were open to all. On the other hand it brought peculiar problems of the marketplace as well. *Ragas* could not be sung at leisure; there was just so much music that a 78-rpm record would hold. Conventions like the singing of particular *ragas* at certain hours could not be adhered to since recordings could not be done at midnight to accommodate the mood of a particular song. The 'purity' of a high tradition had to be diluted, or was it democratized? What these two essays do is to raise the central issue of the actual production of the cultural: the economics behind it as also the productive networks.

The final essay addresses some conundrums of the imagination. If the production of culture is also a matter of location (urban societies having distinctive forms of imagining social life and space), what would explain the absence of the sea in the imagination of those living by the coast? Why does literary and filmic production in Kerala, on the southwestern coast of India, not reflect on the ocean? By looking at the literary and cinematic oeuvre of M.T. Vasudevan Nair, arguably one of the towering figures of Malayalam, Menon tries to understand the history of Kerala over a 300 year period. The history of Kerala was over millennia part of the maritime history of the Indian Ocean. Muslims, Jews, Christians and Hindus created a cosmopolitan culture along the coast. With the coming of the English East India Company in the 18th century two things happened. First, the long distance maritime trade came to an end as did the fortunes of those associated with it, as the Indian Ocean became a "British lake". Second, the East Indian Company through land settlements created a landed elite that acquired power as revenue collectors and the guarantors of law and order. There was a turn inwards as land became the guarantee of status and domination. The history of trade and travel on the coast was diminished to a story of fishermen eking out a livelihood and the merchant princes were no more. M.T. Vasudevan Nair's stories and films reflect this landed imagination as also its fraying in the 20th century. Social reform movements and Communist mobilization against the landed elite, as also the migration of the underclasses to the Gulf from the 1970s, created a dark, brooding, pessimistic imagination centred on the Hindu upper caste household, the temple and the temple pond. This shrinking of the imagination from the ocean to the pond is also in some senses the story of the region.

In the journey through this book, readers will hopefully begin to engage with the fact that culture, tradition and art are historical constructions and reflect the balance of forces in any society. We need to cultivate an intelligent skepticism towards ideas and objects that are seen as coming down to us from a distant unknowable past and understand that the present invents pasts for its own purposes. George Orwell observed that he who controls the present controls the past and he who controls the past controls the future. Any appeal to the timelessness of any idea or artifact is an invitation to suspend our historical imagination. Culture is a historical, social and economic phenomenon located in structures of production, the exigencies of politics, and shifting perceptions of value. Understanding the formation of ideas of the cultural allows for a open, democratic and inclusive space for everyone.

## NOTES

1. Shahid Amin, *Event, Metaphor, Memory: Chauri Chaura 1922–1992* (Delhi: Penguin Books, 2006), p. xxi.

2. Gyanendra Pandey, *The Ascendancy of the Congress in the United Provinces, 1926–34: A study in imperfect mobilization* (Delhi: Oxford University Press, 1978).

3. Between 1982 and 2006 twelve volumes of the Subaltern Studies have appeared. The initial volumes were edited by Ranajit Guha, the centre of the collective who also wrote the classic programmatic study *Elementary Aspects of Peasant Insurgency in Colonial India* (Delhi: Oxford University Press, 1983) which created a typology of subaltern political action.

4. Ranajit Guha, 'Chandra's Death,' in Ranajit Guha ed. *Subaltern Studies V* (Delhi: Oxford University Press, 1987).

5. Sumit Sarkar, 'Kalki Avatar in Bikrampur: A village scandal in early twentieth-century Bengal,' in Ranajit Guha ed. *Subaltern Studies VI* (Delhi: Oxford University Press, 1989).

6. Shahid Amin, 'Gandhi as Mahatma: Gorakhpur district, eastern U.P., 1921–22,' in Ranajit Guha ed. *Subaltern Studies, III* (Delhi: Oxford University Press, 1984).

7. Uma Chakravarty, 'Whatever Happened to the Vedic *dasi*', in Kumkum Sangari and Sudesh Vaid ed. *Recasting Women*.

8. Partha Chatterjee, *The Nation and its Fragments: Colonial and post-colonial histories* (Delhi: Oxford University Press, 1995).

9. Tapati Guha-Thakurta, 'Marking Independence: The ritual of a national art exhibition', *Journal of Arts and Ideas*, numbers 30–31, 1998.

10. Janaki Bakhle, *Two Men and Music: Nationalism in the making of an Indian classical tradition* (Delhi: Permanent Black, 2006); Lakshmi Subramanian, *From the Tanjore Academy to the Madras Music Academy: A social history of music in south India* (Delhi: Oxford University Press, 2006).

11. Ashis Nandy, *The Tao of Cricket: On games of destiny and the destiny of games* (Delhi: Oxford University Press, 2000).

12. Ashis Nandy, *The Intimate Enemy: Loss and recovery of self under colonialism* (Delhi: Oxford University Press, 1983).

13. John Rosselli, 'The Self-image of Effeteness:Physical education and nationalism in nineteenth century Bengal', *Past and Present*, 86 (1980); Christopher Pinney, *'Photos of the Gods':The printed image and political struggle in India* (London: Reaktion Books, 2004).

14. Tanika Sarkar, *Hindu Wife Hindu Nation: Community, religion and cultural nationalism* (Delhi: Permanent Black, 2001).

15. Ajay Skaria, *Hybrid Histories: Forests, frontiers and wildness in western India* (Delhi: Oxford University Press, 1999).

16. Madhava Prasad, *Ideology of the Hindi Film: A historical reconstruction* (Delhi: Oxford University Press, 1998).

17. Ashis Nandy, 'Indian Popular Cinema as a Slum's Eye View of Politics,' in Ashis Nandy ed. *The Secret Politics of our Desires: Innocence, culpability and Indian popular cinema* (Delhi: Oxford University Press, 1998).

# 1.

# Cricket and Caste

## The Heroic Struggles of the Palwankar Brothers

RAMACHANDRA GUHA

V.S. NAIPAUL ONCE WROTE OF HIS NATIVE TRINIDAD THAT 'WE WERE A SOCIETY WITH no heroes—except cricketers'. In other times and other places, too, it is sportsmen who have often most fully embodied the hopes of the lowly and dispossessed. Naipaul's sentiments shall be recognized by blacks in the Chicago ghetto, who honour no hero other than Michael Jordan, and by mulattos in the slums of Buenos Aires, devotees of the deity Diego Maradona. They would also have been appreciated by an Indian not generally known for his interest in sport, Dr B.R. Ambedkar.

As an Untouchable boy placed by the accident of birth at the bottom of the Hindu hierarchy, the future draughtsman of the Indian Constitution took as his role model a slow left-arm bowler named Palwankar Baloo.

Year after year, Baloo dominated the Bombay Quadrangular, at the time the showcase cricketing tournament of India. He was the first great Indian cricketer, and also among the first public figures to emerge from the ranks of the Untouchables.

Now almost wholly forgotten, while he lived Palwankar Baloo commanded enormous respect within and outside his community. Consider thus a little, thirty-page biography published in Poona in 1959 as part of a series of Marathi tracts with the running title 'Kahintari Navech Kara!', or 'Do Something Distinctive!' Priced at half-a-rupee, these booklets were aimed at school and college kids presumed to be in search of role models. The subjects were chosen for having 'gone outside the rut of normal life', for making a name through courage and innovativeness. The tracts were short enough to be read within thirty minutes. Of the forty titles listed in the series, twenty were of Maharashtrians, twenty of people from other parts of India or the world. The publishers did not, of course, commission tracts on men like Shivaji or Tilak or Gandhi or Einstein, whom one could worship but certainly not emulate. The subjects actually written about included Marathi pioneers of theatre, printing, education, history, and the cinema. They included a progressive Marathi poet, a wealthy and successful Marathi lawyer, and the first circus promoter in

Maharashtra. From elsewhere in the sub-continent came the hockey player Dhyan Chand, architect of India's Olympic victories in 1928, 1932, and 1936; the first of our great modern painters, Raja Ravi Varma of Kerala; and the myriad-minded Bengali, Rabindranath Tagore.

More interesting perhaps was the choice of foreigners. There was Spartacus of Rome, described simply as 'A Slave who Revolted'. There was Michaelangelo, the 'Unequalled Sculptor', and Benjamin Franklin, the diplomat and scientist remembered also for 'The Art of Cultivating Good Qualities'. There was a pamphlet on Captain Cook, 'Girdling the Oceans for his Country', and another on Lawrence of Arabia, that 'Great Organizer of Military Campaigns'. From the world of technology came the builder of the Suez Canal, the 'Monumental Architect' Ferdinand Lesseps. And finally, moving from the heroic to the pragmatic, there was a study of Woolworth, the founder of the supermarket, titled 'Buy Anything Here'.

In this exalted company was to be found the name of Palwankar Baloo. The pamphlet on him, written by the Poona cricketer and broadcaster Bal J. Pandit, was titled 'Khada Kheladu', or 'True Sportsman'. Palwankar Baloo was born in July 1875, in the town of Dharwad, deep in the Deccan Plateau. His father worked there, but soon after his birth appears to have taken a job in Poona. They were Chamars, from a caste that lies almost at the bottom of the Hindu social hierarchy. The caste's name comes from the Sanskrit word for leather, 'charman', and the people of the caste work with leather, as tanners and dyers, and as the makers of shoes, bottles, tents, and saddles.

The Chamars, wrote one authority, 'are by birth doomed to illiteracy' and a 'lamentable and abject poverty'. They undertook tasks vital to the clean castes, yet were despised by them. 'Economically the Chamar is a most valuable element in the population, and his function is the rough toil and drudgery of the community'. In the 'traditional' Indian village the Chamar is

> regarded with loathing and disgust by the higher castes.... Except when it is absolutely necessary, a clean-living Hindu will not visit his part of the village. The author of *Hindu Castes and Sects* says that the very touch of a Chamar renders it necessary for a good Hindu to bathe with all his clothes on. The Chamar's very name connects him with the carcasses of cattle. Besides, he not only removes the skins from the cattle that have died, but also he eats the flesh. The defilement and degradation resulting from these acts is insurmountable.[1]

For the Chamars, as for other Untouchable castes, the advent of British rule allowed a means of escape. The adventurous and skilled among them could abandon the village to seek employment in the towns and cities of the Raj. In some professions, indeed, their past was an advantage. Caste

Hindus would not work in ammunition depots and gun factories, whose bullets might use the grease of the sacred cow. But the Chamars had no such inhibition. They would, when they could, flock to the cantonments and factories set up by the British in western and southern India after their defeat of the Peshwas in 1818.

Baloo's own father was employed in the army. One account suggests that he worked in the ammunition factory in the suburb of Kirkee, another claims that he was a sepoy in the 112th Infantry Regiment.[2] It was in Poona that Baloo and his younger brother Shivram learnt to play cricket, with equipment discarded by army officers. The boys also went, briefly, to school, but were soon withdrawn to help augment the family income. Baloo's own first job was at a cricket club run by Parsis. Here he swept and rolled the pitch, and occasionally bowled to the members at the nets. For this work he took home three rupees a month.[3]

In or about the year 1892 Baloo moved a step upwards, from the Parsi cricketers of the city to their European counterparts. These were congregated in the Poona Club, begun a few years previously in a wooded estate known as the Edwardes Gardens.

At the Poona Club Baloo had his salary increased to four rupees a month. His duties included rolling and marking the pitch, erecting the nets and, when required, marking the tennis courts as well. To these routine tasks was later added an altogether more pleasurable one: bowling to the members. It was, it seems, a Mr Tross who first encouraged Baloo to bowl to him. He might, after play ended, have seen the ground boy bowl a ball or two into an empty net, and recognized his talent. Baloo had taken as his model a Captain Barton, a left-arm bowler with a smooth, flowing action. Soon Baloo was bowling on a more-or-less regular basis to the members of the Club, valuable practice for the matches they would play against other teams of expatriates.[4]

At this time, the leading English cricketer of Poona was Captain J.G. Greig. He was known as 'Jungly', because that was how his forenames, 'John Glennie', sounded if spoken quickly.[5] Greig was a small man with supple wrists and quick feet. A master of the square cut, for years he was regarded as the best white batsman in India. Like other little men—Don Bradman and Sunil Gavaskar most obviously—he had an appetite for runs that was gargantuan.

Every day, Greig would arrive at the Poona Club an hour before anybody else, and command Baloo to bowl to him. Thus he would perfect his technique, and thus would the Indian improve his bowling. There is a nice story, undocumented but therefore all the more appealing, that Greig paid Baloo eight *annas* for every time he got him out. At this rate, if the bowler was successful once a week he would have doubled his salary every month.

Baloo once told his son that although he had bowled for hundreds of hours at the Poona Club, not once was he given a chance to bat.[6] In India, as in England, batting was the preserve of the aristocratic élite. One consolation was that by adding bowling to his other duties Baloo had his salary tripled. And his control of spin and flight was honed to perfection by the thousands of balls bowled to Jungly Greig and his less gifted colleagues.

Like his ancestors, Palwankar Baloo came to make a living working with skill and care upon a piece of leather.

Slowly, word of his talents with the cricket ball reached the 'native' part of the city. There was a pioneering Hindu club, which sought to challenge the Europeans of Poona. Should they call upon the services of the Chamar bowler? The question divided the Hindu cricketers. Some Telugu members were keen to include Baloo, whereas the local, Marathi-speaking Brahmins were not. At this stage J.G. Greig jumped into the fray. He gave an interview to the press suggesting that the Hindus would be fools to deprive themselves of Baloo's services. It was not that Greig had the instincts of a social reformer—his commitment to his race was scarcely less strict than the Poona Brahmin's commitment to his caste—but, rather, that he wished to test his skills against his net bowler in the fierce heat of match competition.

In the event, Baloo was invited to play for the Poona Hindus, but at a price. On the field the upper caste cricketers touched the same ball as he, but off it they observed the ritual taboos. At the tea interval, that ceremony sacred to cricket, Baloo was served the liquid outside the pavilion, and in a disposable clay *matka*, while his colleagues drank in white porcelain cups inside. If he wished to wash his hands and face, an 'untouchable' servant of the club took a kettle out into a corner of the field, and poured water from it. Baloo also ate his lunch off a separate plate, and on a separate table.[7]

But he took plenty of wickets all the same. Due chiefly to Baloo's bowling the Poona Hindus defeated the Poona Europeans, and other local sides as well. On a celebrated occasion they visited the inland town of Satara, to play against its white-only Gymkhana. The hosts had instructed their groundsman to roll the wicket for a week, so that it would blunt Baloo's spin. Baloo still took seven wickets, and his team won easily. In one account the bowler was then serenaded on a elephant through the streets of Satara. In another account he was garlanded at a public function on his return to Poona, the garland lovingly placed around his shoulders by the great scholar and reformer Mahadev Govind Ranade. It was also Ranade who told his fellow Brahmins that if they could play with Baloo, they must drink tea and break bread with him too.[8] A little later, Baloo was praised at a public meeting by a Brahmin nationalist even more celebrated than Ranade, Bal Gangadhar Tilak. This, writes one chronicler, created 'a stir, because in those days a person from the backward community did not have a honourable place in society'.[9]

Just as the Poona orthodoxy were opening out towards him, Baloo chose to move with his family to Bombay. One reason for this was the plague of 1896, which was especially severe in Poona; another was the attractions of cricket at the centre. At first Baloo worked in Bombay with an army unit, and also played for the newly commissioned P.J. Hindu Gymkhana. This institution had been in two minds whether to admit him. The cricket captain, Kirtikar, naturally wanted to augment his bowling attack. All the same, he got his way only after 'pacifying a few Gujerati members as regards his [Baloo's] admission'.[10]

In this, the last decade of the nineteenth century, there were dozens of active cricket teams in Bombay. Where Parsi clubs were generally demarcated by locality, Hindu cricketers sorted themselves out on the lines of caste and region. Consider the names of some clubs established in the latter decades of the nineteenth century: Gowd Saraswat Cricket Club, Kshatriya Cricket Club, Gujarati Union Cricket Club, Maratha Cricket Club, Telugu Young Cricketers.

The smaller communities in this city of migrants also formed their clubs, such as the Mangalorian Catholic Cricket Club (for émigres from the southern port town of Mangalore), the Instituto Luso Cricket Club (for those coming to the city from Portuguese-ruled Goa), and the Bombay Jewish Cricket Club.[11]

A different category of clubs were those sponsored by companies and banks. Cricket teams were run by Thomas Cook, Forbes, Forbes and Campbell, the Bombay Gas Company, the Bank of Bombay, and the Army and Navy Stores. These were heterogeneous in their membership, with employees of various Hindu castes playing on the same side as Muslims and Christians, under the leadership of a senior manager, almost always an Englishman. One active club of this kind was run by the Bombay Berar and Central Indian Railway. It was this company that gave Palwankar Baloo a job, at the suggestion of its manager and cricket captain, a Mr Lucas.[12]

Baloo played for the B.B.C.I. Railway in inter-office matches, but for the Hindu Gymkhana otherwise. At this time, c. 1900, the most terrific excitement attended contests between the Hindu Gymkhana and leading Parsi teams such as the Baronet Cricket Club. There were large crowds ringing the ground, five or ten rows deep, with the overspill accommodated on the railway overbridge that linked the Gymkhana to the nearby Churnee Road station. The scene was made more vivid by the nearness of the sea. There was no Marine Drive then, and as a participant in those games recalled, 'the waves often used to beat over the rocks and enter the cricket ground'.[13]

The statistics of those matches are lost to history, but one may safely assume that Palwankar Baloo took plenty of wickets. From very early on he was regarded as the bulwark of the Hindu Gymkhana. One of his formidable opponents, Dr M.E. Pavri of the Baronet C.C., described him as

> one of the best native bowlers. A left-handed medium-pace bowler with an easy action. Has both breaks and a curl in the air and has a lot of spin on the ball. The most deadly bowler on a sticky wicket. May be called 'Rhodes' of India. A sound bat and an active field.[14]

Baloo's control was phenomenal, and his variations subtle. 'His pace was medium', recalled a Bombay journalist, 'but he could bowl from a very slow to a really fast one and send them by round to full over-arm action. He manipulated an amazing change of flight in the ball and set the batsman always guessing in each delivery, which was always different'.[15] From across India, a Calcutta cricketer who had observed Baloo at close quarters remarked that he was

> A fine left-hand bowler, who possesses marvellous stamina. Breaks from both sides. Has the easiest of deliveries. Seldom tires. Can bowl all day long. Keeps an excellent length. Never sends down a loose delivery. Understands the game thoroughly. Places the field to a nicety, catches come [to the fielders], they have not to go in for them. Decidedly a 'head' bowler.[16]

M.E. Pavri had called Baloo the '[Wilfred] Rhodes of India'. From this description he seems rather to have been a left-handed S.F. Barnes, to take another hallowed name from English cricket's Golden Age. From what I have read it seems clear that Palwankar Baloo was a spinner of great skill and subtlety, a worthy forerunner of such world-class Indian slow left-arm bowlers as Vinoo Mankad and Bishan Bedi.

By the early years of the twentieth century, Baloo's skills with the cricket ball were known as far afield as Calcutta. In that city lived a cricketing patron, the Maharajah of Natore, who had overwhelming ambition: to defeat the all-European Calcutta Cricket Club. One year he put together a side of top-class Hindus, including the wicket-keeper K. Seshachari from Madras, the fast bowler H.L. Sempre from Karachi, and Palwankar Baloo and his brother Shivram from Bombay. His side won, but the colonists, as ever, took their defeat without grace. After the match the captain of the Calcutta Cricket Club asked Natore how many 'gentlemen' there were in his side, insinuating there was no honour in Indian professionals defeating a side of English amateurs.[17]

Seven years younger than Baloo, Shivram was a hard-hitting batsman, a useful medium-pace bowler, and an outstanding field. Taller than his brother, and powerfully built, his trademark was a black belt that he wore around his waist. Understandably, we know far less of his early years in the game. But we do know that by 1906 he was regarded as one of the eleven best cricketers of his religion. For in February of that year, he was chosen with his brother to play for the Hindus against the Europeans of the Bombay Presidency.

The match inevitably carried nationalist overtones: for at this time, 1905–6, the Indian National Congress was renewing itself under two leaders from Western India, Gopalkrishna Gokhale and Bal Gangadhar Tilak. Across the country, in Bengal, the *swadeshi* movement has just been launched. Patriotic entrepreneurs had set up factories to compete with British capital. Radicals urged the boycott of foreign goods. Bonfires were being made of cloth made in the mills of Manchester.[18] In the last week of 1905, the Congress had met in the holy city of Benares, where the Bengali delegates urged a countrywide spread of their campaign. Tilak's paper, *Kesari*, agreed with the Bengalis. 'It is not so manly to resign onself to one's degraded position', it remarked, 'or to sit weeping in the house like women, but it is our duty to strive strenuously to remove the causes of our misfortune'.[19] Another Marathi paper asked for India to be granted Home Rule. Indians, it said, 'should fearlessly speak out their minds to their rulers without mincing words...'.[20]

The three-day match was played at the Bombay Gymkhana ground from 8th to 10th February, 1906. In its assessment of the two teams the *Bombay Gazette* praised Baloo, of course, and said of Shivram that 'he is Mr Baloo's brother and that is enough. He must keep up the reputation of the first bowler of India, his brother. Much is expected of his smartness in the field'.[21]

The Hindus batted first, and posted a decent score of 242, Baloo contributing 25 and his brother 24. 'Much to the disappointment of his admirers the "Little Man"' (Greig) was bowled by Erasha for 11. Erasha had figures of 6 wickets for 77 runs, Baloo had 3 for 41, and the Europeans were all out for 191. In their second knock the Hindus made 160 (Baloo 11, Shivram 16 not out). The rulers needed 212 to win. As they began their innings on the last day the play was 'marked with a deal of excitement and enthusiasm. Large throngs of people of every denomination—even larger than the previous two days—lined the ropes and greeted every stroke with loud ovation.'

The European challenge relied heavily on Greig. He began well, and had got to 27 when he was stumped by Seshachari off Erasha. The stumping was described in terms of justifiable pride by a newspaper from the wicket-keeper's home town, Madras. The batsman lunged, it said, 'and with a movement, meteoric in its quickness', Seshachari had stumped him. It was 'a superb piece of stumping worth going miles to see'; with it 'to all intents and purposes the match was won'. In the end the Europeans crumbled to 102 all out, with Baloo and Erasha each taking 5 wickets. In fact, the two bowlers bowled in tandem from the start of the innings to its end.[22]

The result of this cricket match was given an explicit nationalist interpretation by *The Tribune* of Lahore. This paper run by Punjabi Hindus had to wait three days before reports of the match were brought to it by the *Frontier Mail*. When the news came the paper had to range very far indeed in search for a suitable comparison. It finally settled upon another recent victory of Asia over Europe, that of Japan against Russia on the battlefield. The Hindu cricketers had apparently been as dignified in victory as their Japanese military counterparts. They had behaved 'with the noble self-restraint which characterized the Japanese over the fall of Port Arthur and all the subsequent victories which attended their arms, victories the like of which history has never recorded.. '. Through the three days of the match the Hindu cricketers 'did not play to the gallery; they were neither bumptious nor ostentatious; they did not think it necessary to appeal to the umpire every two minutes or to indulge in buffoonery.' But were the result to have been reversed, suggested the *Tribune*, then the English cricketers would have been vulgar and ostentatious in victory—mimicking 'the perfect pandemonium into which hoary England had been converted by modern Britons over the relief of Mafeking...' (this being a reference to the patriotic hysteria which overtook Britain during the Boer war).[23]

*The Tribune* interpreted the cricketing victory as a sign that a subdued and suppressed Asia was shaking off its shackles. Other papers welcomed it as a victory over caste prejudice. During the three days of the match the players of both sides dined together, the European with the Hindu, and the Brahmin with the Chamar. The way to this unprecedented intermingling had been previously cleared by the decision of the Hindu Gymkhana to allow Baloo and Shivram entry not only into its cricket field but into its café as well. Now, the course of the match and the contribution to the Hindu victory of the Baloo brothers provoked a long leading article in that respected voice of Hindu liberalism, *The Indian Social Reformer*. By 'openly interdining' with low-castes, it said, the Hindu Gymkhana would 'destroy for good' the 'silly barrier of pollution by touch'. The 'history of the admission of these Chamar brothers in the Hindu Gymkhana', continued the *Indian Social Reformer*, 'is a credit to all and has done far more to liberalize the minds of thousands of young Hindus than all other attempts in other spheres'. Indeed, the triumph of cricket over caste was

> a landmark in the nation's emancipation from the old disuniting and denationalizing customs. This is a conscious voluntary change, a manly moral regulated liberty, not, as in [the] railways [where members of different castes had willy-nilly to sit with each other], a compulsory change ... Hindu sportsmen of Poona and Bombay have shown in different degrees that, where national interest required, equal opportunity must be given to all of any caste, even though the offer of such opportunity involved the trampling of some old prejudices ... Let the lesson learnt in sport be repeated in political, social and educational walks of life. Let all disuniting and denationalizing customs in all high, low or lowest Hindus disappear and let India cease to be the laughing-stock of the whole world.[24]

In 1907, the Hindus, Parsis and Europeans began playing an annual cricket tournament known as the Triangular. In the five years that the tournament was held the Europeans won thrice, and the Parsis twice. The outstanding individual performer, however, was Palwankar Baloo. In the five matches he played between 1907 and 1911 he took 40 wickets at less than 10 runs apiece.[25]

Shivram also played for the Hindus in the Triangular, as, from 1910, did a third brother. This was Palwankar Vithal, born in 1886, and sent by Baloo to the cricket-minded Elphinstone High School. Vithal was a graceful right-hand batsman, with a penchant for the cover drive.

After leaving school Vithal accepted a job with the Greater Indian Peninsular Railway, where Shivram already worked. The youngster scored a sheaf of centuries in club cricket, and was chosen to play for the Hindus in the 1910 Triangular. The next year, an All India Team was due to tour England. From January 1911 trial matches were held in Bombay, for aspirants from all over the country. The selectors were seven in all—two Muslim, two Hindu, and two Parsi, with the venerable Jungly Greig in the chair. This ecumenism was reflected in the team finally chosen. They included six Parsis, three Muslims, and five Hindus. The captain, however, was a Sikh, the twenty-year-old Maharaja Bhupendra Singh of Patiala, just installed onto his *gaddi* by the Viceroy, Lord Minto.[26]

Despite the strong recommendation of the English coach supervising the trials, Palwankar Vithal was deemed too young to be sent to England. Baloo, of course, was chosen, and Shivram was nominated first reserve. The day before the ship was to leave a player from Kashmir dropped out, and Shivram had hurriedly to gather his gear and other effects. That same evening, the 4th of May 1911, a farewell was organized for the players at the Orient Club.

In England the Indian captain was not often to be found with his team. Patiala played a match at Lord's, and one or two more, but for the most part he was active on the London social circuit, partying and going to the races (There were many parties to attend that summer, for a new King had just ascended the throne). The captain's absence was a blow in purely cricketing terms, for this particular prince was a first-class batsman. And in social terms, for while he was away the side divided into Parsi and Hindu factions. Patiala also took with him, wherever he went, his five servants. This did not matter much, except that His Highness also insisted on having, close at hand, his secretary Keki Mistry, who at this time was perhaps the best of all Indian batsmen. Without Patiala and Mistry the tourists' batting was desperately ill-equipped to handle English wickets and English professional bowling. This showed in the results. Fourteen matches were played against the recognized English counties, of which two were won, ten lost and two drawn. Of the other matches, against such second-class teams as Ulster and the North of Scotland, the Indians won four and lost five.

The singular success, from the Indian point of view, was the bowling of Palwankar Baloo. He took 114 wickets at an average of 18.84 runs per wicket, and would easily have claimed 150 wickets had he more support in the field. The scorecards of the tour tell a tale that is truly uplifting. Three early matches were played against Oxford University at the Parks, the Marylebone Cricket Club at Lord's and Cambridge University at Fenner's. On these three great grounds, redolent with cricket history, trod this Untouchable who in terms of social background was as removed from the High Table as one could possibly be. But he could bowl. Against Oxford Baloo claimed 5 wickets for 87 runs, against the MCC he took 4 for 96, whereas at Cambridge he returned the superb figures of 8 for 103.

Baloo enjoyed success against all the top county sides. He claimed 7 for 83 against Lancashire, 4 for 127 against Yorkshire, 4 for 74 against Warwickshire, and 4 for 100 against Surrey. (In these matches the home team usually got to bat only once.) And when the Indians beat Leicestershire by 7 wickets, Baloo's figures were 5 for 92 and 6 for 93. He got a mere six victims in the only other victory, against Somerset, but made up somewhat with a strokeful 55 in his side's second innings. The real match-winner on this occasion was younger brother Shivram, who scored 113 not out as the visitors scraped home with one wicket standing. For the tour as a whole, Shivram stood third in the batting averages, scoring 930 runs at an average of over 27 per innings. He was, said one observer, 'the most promising of Hindu batsmen'.[27]

Back in 1904, the Parsi patron Sir Dorab J. Tata had begun negotiations on Baloo's behalf with the English county Surrey, who needed a left-arm bowler. That plan fell through, but when Baloo finally came to England he impressed more than one county. Indeed, he received several offers to stay back, and play in England as a professional. In the summer of 1911, he was already thirty-six, and a little past his best. He also suffered from synovitis, the swelling of the shoulder, an affliction brought on by being over-bowled. His performance was outstanding as it was. What might he have done without a sore shoulder and had he been five years younger? In an interview with the *Times of India*, Baloo 'modestly declared that he was not satisfied with the work he himself did with the ball and very rightly wished that the team had been sent six years ago when he was in his best form'. But his comrade Seshachari told *The Hindu* that Baloo 'is so good that he is good enough to play for any county'. The respected English critic E.H.D. Sewell commented likewise that Baloo 'is a bowler most of our counties would be very glad to have in their eleven'.[28] His performance was truly exceptional. In the ninety years since Baloo returned home, only one other Indian bowler, Vinoo Mankad in 1946, has claimed more than a hundred first-class wickets on a tour of England.

Overall, the Indian team of 1911 had performed much below expectations. In its retrospective of the tour a Bombay paper made the usual excuses: 'Climate, food, constant travelling, want of practice, a limited number of men to choose from in case of need—all these were unfavourable conditions against which the team had to fight'.[29] A long list of difficulties, not all of the writer's invention: yet one man, Palwankar Baloo, was able to rise above them.

According to one source, at the Orient Club's function to wish the team godspeed only Baloo and Shivram were not honoured with garlands.[30] But when the Indian cricket team returned to Bombay on 15 September by the steamship 'Salsette', there must have been garlands aplenty for its acknowledged hero. We know, for instance, of a function organized by the Depressed Classes of Bombay to felicitate Baloo. The community's pride was well-earned, for this erstwhile Untouchable had far exceeded the Brahmins and Muslims and Parsis and Princes who accompanied him to England. At this function, the *manpatra*, or welcome address, for Baloo was written and presented by Bhimrao Ambedkar. This, according to the *doyenne* of historians of Untouchability, Eleanor Zelliot, was the first public appearance of the man who was to become the greatest of all lower-caste politicians and reformers, and a figure of surpassing importance in modern Indian history.[31]

By virtue solely of his deeds on the cricket field, Baloo had become a hero and inspiration to countless Untouchables. And the young B.R. Ambedkar was one of them. By 1910 Baloo and Shivram were joined in the Hindu team by Vithal, an elegant right-hand batsman who had learnt the game at home and learnt his letters at the Elphinstone High School. Meanwhile, the youngest brother, Ganpat, was studying for a bachelor's degree at Elphinstone College, his fees paid by brother Baloo. But Ganpat would play cricket too. In January 1912 he was the undoubted star of the college cricket tour of Northern India. When the visitors defeated the famous Mohammedan College in Aligarh he topscored in both innings, with 58 and 40. And in a drawn match against the Maharaja of Patiala's XI, played at Rawalpindi, Ganpat claimed two wickets, effected two catches, and scored a brilliant hundred besides. Ganpat Palwankar played 'cricket of the highest class', remarked the college cricket historian: 'It was not the sum of his runs that was so much appreciated as the style in which they were obtained, for he employed a variety of strokes and his batting was perfect and true'.[32]

That same year, 1912, the Muslims were admitted into the annual Bombay tournament, which thus became a Quadrangular. The Quadrangular was generally referred to as the 'Bombay Cricket Carnival'. But there is also a reference to it as 'a sort of a Roman forum'.[33] In truth, it was a mixture of both. Sport was both spectacle and contest, an outing with friends and family but also a vehicle for suppressed social ambitions. The noise level at the Quadrangular was terrific, far higher than in an English or Australian ground. Shouts and screams were accentuated by drums and bugles. Spectators sang songs, shone mirrors, flew kites, and garlanded cricketers. Their enjoyment was huge anyway, but huger if their man hit a six or if their team happened to win.

Each team came to represent their community's pride, but there were individual match-ups that were keenly followed. One such was the battle between those two old stalwarts, Palwankar Baloo of the Hindus and J.G. Greig of the Europeans. At the time of the 1913 Quadrangular Baloo was already thirty-eight, but bowling as well as ever. Greig, three years older, was then serving as the Military Secretary to the Governor. He still took his cricket very seriously indeed. But when he came up against his old practice bowler he was quickly out to him, caught at slip by a ball that turned, the catch taken by the Poona youngster D.B. Deodhar.[34]

That year, 1913, Baloo was joined in the Hindu team by Shivram, Vithal, and Ganpat. The captain, however, was the batsman M.D. Pai. Pai was felicitated by his caste association, the Gowd Saraswat Brahmin Mitra Mandal, for achieving the 'highest honour to which a cricketer can aspire'. In his reply, Pai thanked his community for the reception they had hosted for him, but added that 'the honour of captainship should have been given to his friend Mr Balu, he being the senior and experienced player in the team'.[35]

Now Pai had been on that 1911 tour, struggling with the bat while Baloo shone with the ball. Nonetheless, his remarks bespoke of an extraordinary generosity. For in 1913 Mahatma Gandhi was still in South Africa, and the Hindu political élite was, by and large, still bound hand and foot to the Laws of Manu. A Untouchable cricketer of courage and skill could be chosen to play for the Hindus, but would he be made captain? Perish the thought. For the leader of a cricket team has to exercise his mind more often and more innovatively than a football or basketball captain. In this slow paced sport, it is the captain, and not the coach or manager, who decides the order of batsmen, the order of bowlers, and changes in the field. However, intelligence and foresight were commonly held to be the preserve of the high castes. Pai was a Brahmin, and Baloo was a Chamar. To appoint the spin bowler captain of the Hindus would symbolically upturn the hierarchy of caste. Admittedly, on grounds of talent and experience Baloo should long ago have been made the captain of the Hindus. Pai's speech to his caste-mates suggests that his team-mates would have found his elevation quite acceptable. But the merchants and lawyers who ran the Hindu Gymkhana did not.

In June 1914 the *Bombay Chronicle* commented, editorially, that 'the services rendered by Baloo to Hindu cricket are worth their weight in gold, and it speaks volumes for the wonderful vitality of the man that after the lapse of more than two decades he is still their foremost bowler'.[36] The next month the paper carried an angry letter by one 'C.S.T.' The previous year, said this disappointed fan, the Hindus had been robbed of a win by 'bad management and worse fielding'. 'There ought to be more permanent interest in Hindu cricket', said 'C.S.T.', 'in place of the spasmodic outbursts of frenzy which agitate the lovers of cricket'. The Selection Committee should make its choices early, and play the chosen players together in practice matches. 'The choice of a captain', he added, 'should be a free one and that onerous post should be in the hands of the best and most competent man on the field'. The letter writer was plainly hinting at Baloo, whom he elsewhere called a 'sure thing', the Hindus' 'crack bowler who can always do some work of outstanding merit.'[37]

In 1915 the Quadrangular was played at Poona, apparently on the insistence of the Europeans. They had lobbied hard for this, for, as one Indian critic sarcactically commented, in a Poona September 'the [social] season is in full swing with all its gaieties, the pitch is more like Home and the climate is less exhausting.'[38] The matches were played at the Poona Club, that old haunt of Baloo (and J.G. Greig). An early report suggested that all four Palwankar brothers were certainties. But when the side was chosen a week ahead of the Hindu–Parsi match Baloo was not in it. Apparently a selector had asked Baloo how he was, and the bowler, out of modesty, answered 'that he was not in his usual form but added that if he were selected he would gladly lend his services in the interests of Hindu cricket.' This diffidence was used as an excuse to drop him.

The *Bombay Chronicle* now received numerous angry letters of protest. These suggested that the Hindu selection committee had conspired to throw Baloo out. 'Now nobody will say that Baloo is quite the demon bowler he once was,' said one writer, 'but it cannot be denied that he is still a fine bowler, who is worth his place in any representative eleven'. The decision to dump him, remarked this correspondent

> has been received with great and justifiable surprise by the supporters of Hindu cricket. Baloo has been the mainstay of Hindu cricket for more than a decade and a half and his services in the cause of Hindu cricket have been invaluable. By every right of ability, of seniority, and of the services rendered to his side, he should long ago have been appointed captain of the team. He has not only been denied that right but now he has been excluded from the team itself.[39]

Intriguingly, the day after the appearance of this letter the *Chronicle* carried an explanatory letter from the Hindu captain, M.D. Pai. 'I was strongly in favour of Mr Baloo's inclusion', he wrote, 'but the hesitating reply of Mr Baloo showing his inability to keep up for three days forced the Committee to give him up'. The captain had urged that 'preference should be given to Mr Baloo, on whom I much rely as a bowler of sound and mature judgement.'[40] But his words were disregarded. That a captain should openly participate in a selection controversy was most unusual. Perhaps Pai deeply felt Baloo's omission, or perhaps he wished to forestall criticism in case his team performed poorly in the tournament.

What is notable about this controversy is the absence of any open allusion to Baloo's caste. Earlier that year Mohandas K. Gandhi had returned to India, but he had not yet found his political feet, and his views on Untouchability were not yet an object of public debate. The Hindu cricket fan who was also a social liberal had thus to express his suspicions by indirection.

Though caste was certainly the main reason why Baloo was not made captain of the Hindus, it did not help that he was his team's main bowler. Batsmen are cricket's aristocrats, who monopolize attention and awards. Back in the 1950s, the England batsman (and captain) Len Hutton was knighted. The half-a-dozen cricketing knights before him had all been batsmen too. The great Australian leg-spinner Arthur Mailey congratulated Hutton, then added: 'I hope next time it is a bowler. The last bowler to be knighted was Sir Francis Drake.'

Conventional wisdom holds that bowlers make poor captains. It is said that they are too absorbed in their own craft to pay proper attention to bowling changes or field placings. Batsmen, on the other hand, are free of personal responsibility when their own innings is over. The theory that batsmen make the best captains is an old one, and it is still widely accepted. The Hindu selectors who chose Pai over Baloo might very well have subscribed to it. One can imagine the progress of the discussion in the committee room: yes, he is wise and he is experienced; no, we do not really mind that he is a Chamar; however, we must not further burden our main bowler. Pai, the Brahmin and batsman, would thus always win out over Baloo, the Chamar and bowler.[41]

Between 1912 and 1919, there was, every year, a concerted campaign to have Palwankar Baloo made captain of the Hindu cricket team. Every year it met with failure. Then, in the months leading up to the 1920 Quadrangular, Mahatma Gandhi began speaking out against the practice of Untouchability. Now the pre-eminent leader of the Congress, he used his enlarged pulpit to return to a theme that had obsessed him since South Africa: the purification of Hinduism. Untouchability was 'a crime against God and humanity,' he remarked in May 1920: 'My conscience tells me that untouchability can never be a part of Hinduism. I do not think it too much to dedicate my whole life to removing the thick crust of sin with which Hindu society has covered itself for so long by stupidly regarding these people as untouchables.'[42] A little later, writing in his journal *Young India*, Gandhi suggested that divine retribution had made Indians the 'pariahs of Empire'. Their subjection to the British, he claimed, was a consequence of their own oppression of the Untouchables.

Non co-operation with the rulers, previously seen as a purely political act, was now being redefined as a 'movement of intensive self-purification'. Upper caste Hindus, thought Gandhi, 'must realize that if they wish to offer successful non co-operation against the Government, they must make common cause with the *Panchamas* [Untouchables], even as they have made common cause with the Mussulmans.'[43]

At this stage, Gandhi was a defender of *varnashramadharma*, the division of Hindu society into endogamous castes with their own hereditary specialisms. But the practice of Untouchability he thought contrary to *dharma*; it was, he wrote in October 1920, 'an instance of the evil of extremism in Hinduism.'[44] His attack on the institution was to become more radical later on, but even as it was, his criticisms were to attract wide attention. Other Hindus had questioned the practice in the past, but they lacked Gandhi's political standing. When he spoke millions listened, among them a growing number of Hindu cricket fans in Bombay.

This year, as usual, there was a slow and stately build-up to the Quandrangular. The club and office matches were finished off in August and September: now the Gymkhanas took over. In the third week of October the Hindu Gymkhana was playing a two day match against a visiting side from Rajputana. On the first day news came in of the death of Palwankar Ganpat, of consumption. He was only twenty seven. In his memory play was abandoned for the day.[45]

Ganpat's death hit his three brothers hard, but they gamely continued to do what they were best at: play cricket. The sporting public, Hindu or otherwise, saw in each Palwankar a distinctive combination of character and playing skill. Baloo was the patriarch, heavily-built, his hair greying, but at forty-five still a high class bowler. Shivram batted doggedly down the order and bowled usefully with the new ball: in the field, he was recognized by the thick sash around his waist. Vithal was by this time the premier Hindu batsman: perhaps he had specialized in that aspect of the game at the prodding of his brothers, who knew that batsmen were cricket's pampered aristocrats. With Baloo and Shivram ageing, it fell to Vithal to uphold the family's honour. He did it with style: as a Parsi journalist recalled, when he batted Vithal wore always a green tweed hat, known to the fan as 'sanssouci'.[46]

The 1920 tournament was scheduled for the first week of December. In mid November, the *Bombay Chronicle* ran a full page feature on the preparations of the different teams, their chances, and the likely response of the crowd. Speaking of the Hindus, the anonymous feature writer tastefully put the case for a long overdue elevation. 'It would not be out of place', he suggested

> to give expression to the very widespread desire that exists among the Hindu public that the captaincy of the team should at least for once be offered to

> P. Baloo... No Hindu bowler could claim such a distinguished and sustained record of achievement in first-class cricket extending over a large number of years as he ... [S]heer justice demands that his long and splendid cricket career should be crowned with the leadership of the Hindu representative team before he finally retires from first-class cricket. He is still a good bowler, but wonderful as his constitution is, age must tell sooner or later, and in a couple of years perhaps international cricket would have seen the last of him. The desire given expression to above is not the result of any doubt as to the capacity of M.D. Pai ... Pai has proved himself one of the best captains the Hindus ever had, and he could still be next year's captain. But it would be doing bare justice to the greatest bowler the Hindus ever had if Baloo were offered the captainship even once. One has not heard that Baloo cherishes the ambition of monopolising the position. He would, from what one hears, be quite content with holding the place for one year and would have no objection to playing under the leadership of anybody in future. In fact he has done this in the past and played under Pai, who in turn should not consider it *infra dig* to play under his great colleague.[47]

A week later the Hindu team was announced, with M.D. Pai as captain. Vithal and Shivram had been included in the eleven, but Baloo was dropped. Ten days still remained for the tournament to begin. In this waiting period Pai fell ill, and withdrew from the first match, which was against the Muslims. The Hindu selectors now appointed D.B. Deodhar as captain. Deodhar was a fine player but, as it happens, a Brahmin and a batsman. The Gymkhana's decision was a subject of furious controversy amongst its rank-and-file. There 'was much discontent prevailing among the members of the [Hindu] Gymkhana over the repeated exclusion of Mr Baloo,' reported one scribe: 'The trend of opinion among the bulk of the members who were present in the Gymkhana in the evening was that Mr Baloo should now be taken in the team and asked to captain it.'[48]

To the Palwankars, already bowed by Ganpat's death and Baloo's exclusion, Deodhar's appointment was a final, brutal blow. For both Vithal and Shivram were at least the equal in talent of the Poona cricketer and they had been playing for the Hindus for years before he had. As Vithal recalled in his memoirs, when Pai fell ill, 'amongst the players of the team myself and Shivram were the most senior and considering our ability and skill it was our rightful expectation that one of us should have been chosen captain. Many members of the Hindu Gymkhana also expected the same.'[49] In disgust, they decided to stand down from the Hindu team. Their explanation, published in the papers the day the Hindu-Muslim match began, still makes for compelling reading:

> It need hardly be said [wrote Vithal and Shivram] that the claims of one of us are superior to those of Mr Deodhar, and the [Hindu Selection] Committee's

> decision can only be characterised as unsportsmanlike in the extreme, inasmuch as they have apparently been influenced by the caste and social and educational status of their selection rather than his achievements or seniority in the field of cricket, and as such the Committee's decision can only be taken as partial with a bias in favour of caste. Social or educational status has no place in sport, when the claims of a cricketer of lesser social status are admittedly superior. In the decision the Committee arrived at, this vital principle of all sport appears to have been lightly passed over, with the result that the claims of one of us have been brushed aside as beneath contempt. This sort of shuffling of claims by the Hindu Selection Committee has compelled us to withdraw from the Hindu Representative Team this year, much against our desire to add our quota to the achievements of the Hindu Cricket Team. In arriving at this decision [not to play] be it remembered that we feel very strongly the covert or overt insult levelled at us as belonging to the so-called depressed class as it amounts to a nullification of our claims for recognition for all time. That such matters as caste should be the determining factor in Cricket is more than we can quietly bow down to, hence our decision to stand down from the Hindu Team this year. The impartial cricket-loving public, we feel sure, will at once understand our position and exonerate us from all blame for the step we have thus deliberately taken as it was on a question of principle and self-respect.[50]

The sentiments were unquestionably their own, although the statement itself might have been drafted by a better-educated member of the impartial cricket-loving public.[51] A small section of this public regarded the withdrawal as a 'revolt against authority', but numerous others approved of the action, believing that as 'self-respecting men [Vithal and Shivram] could not have done otherwise.' Among the strikers' supporters were those who approved of Gandhi's wider struggle against Untouchability. A movement was afoot to collect funds for a purse to be presented to Vithal and Shivram. Contributions were to be sent to 'Mr Govindji Vasanji, the National Confectioner, either at Chira Bazar, Girgaum, or at the Grant Road Terminus.' Five hundred rupees, then a considerable sum, was collected in the first twenty-hours itself.[52]

The Hindus won their match against the Muslims. The formidable Parsis were to be encountered next. Hectic parleys now commenced within the Hindu Gymkhana. Their outcome was summarized in a banner headline printed the day the final began: 'PAI CAPTAINING THE TEAM: BALOO BROTHERS PLAYING'. M.D. Pai, now fit, was to captain, and Vithal, Shivram and Baloo were all to play. The decision to reinstate the strikers and to call upon their brother, remarked one journalist, 'though belated, is a sensible one and is undoubtedly a concession to public opinion.' Baloo, wrote the scribe, was at first inclined to reject the call: it was 'on the urgent intervention of friends whose love of Hindu cricket surpasses their love for the Committee and its ways, that Mr Baloo consented to play in today's match.' In fact, the Hindu Selection Committee was suitably conciliatory, as in this letter written by its Secretary, S.A. Shethe:

> Dear Mr Baloo,
>
> I understand that you are hesitating to play though selected in the match against Parsis. I shall be obliged if you will kindly reconsider your decision and play. The interest of cricket will appeal to you as in the past.[53]

Honour was restored more fully when Baloo was appointed vice-captain. In what must certainly have been a pre-arranged move, Pai left the field while the Parsis were batting in the second innings. A sympathetic reporter commented on the 'excellent leadership' of Baloo, adding,'he displayed fine judgement in the management of his side's bowling.'[54] The match itself had a suitably dramatic *denouement*. The Hindus amassed a score of 428, with C.K. Nayudu scoring a century. They then dismissed the Parsis for 214, and asked them to follow on. Early in the Parsi second innings their captain, Dr H.D. Kanga, was injured and taken to hospital. The ninth Parsi wicket fell after lunch on the final day, and, assuming their side had won, the Hindu fans streamed into the ground with garlands. As they reached the pitch the umpire drew their attention to Dr Kanga, who was slowly emerging from the pavilion, a runner alongside him. The crowd reluctantly withdrew to the boundary's edge, where they stayed for the next two hours, as the last wicket pair of Kanga and Elavia played out time to draw the match.[55]

The struggle over the Hindu captaincy anticipated, by nearly forty years, the campaign to have a black man chosen as captain of the West Indies cricket team. The West Indies played its first Test matches in 1928; for the next three decades it was axiomatic that a white man, and a white man alone, could be the team's captain. Such remarkable cricketers as Learie Constantine and George Headley had to be content with being 'led' by fair-skinned sportsmen of demonstrably inferior skill. In his playing days Constanine had protested against this discrimination. He continued to speak out after he retired, joined by such men as the great historian and revolutionary C.L.R. James. It was James who was in the forefront of the campaign which, in 1960, resulted in Frank Worrell's appointment as the first black captain of the West Indies.[56]

The career of Palwankar Baloo also anticipated, by half-a-century and more, the much memorialized breakthrough into major league football of Jackie Robinson. Only in 1947 would the American public accept racially mixed teams in sport: but already, in 1896–97, the Hindus of Poona and Bombay were made to accept an Untouchable cricketer. Like Robinson after him, Baloo broke through a previously impenetrable social barrier as much by force of personality as by sporting skill alone.

In 1922, the Quadrangular was played in Palwankar Baloo's old home town, Poona. Three weeks before the matches began the *Bombay Chronicle* suggested that 'P. Baloo stands every chance of being the captain of the Hindoo team in view of his sound and thorough experience extending to many years of cricket tournaments.' Since Vithal and Shivram were also in fine form, the paper thought 'that the Hindoo team this year will be as strong as any participating in the Quadrangular.'[57]

The captain and players were to be chosen by the local sponsors, the Poona Hindu Gymkhana. The city was a conservative one, and its Hindus, by and large, never had time for Gandhi. Unlike the members of the P.J. Hindu Gymkhana the Brahmins of Poona were not convinced that Untouchability was altogether a bad thing. The Poona Hindus chose S.M. Dalvi as captain, and Vithal and Shivram went on strike again. The Hindus won their first match, narrowly, and had now to play the Parsis in the final. A compromise was attempted, whereby M.D. Pai would be appointed captain and Vithal and Shivram would agree to return. But Pai refused to play ball, and the brothers stuck to their stand. A complete nonentity, Dr Prabhakar, was asked to lead the Hindus. The Parsis, by contrast, were at full strength. Expectedly they won by a handsome margin.[58]

The press comment on the Hindu defeat was curious. Before the final the *Chronicle* said that the 'Hindu team will hardly be representative without a trio [the Baloo brothers] whom everybody will miss ...' Afterwards it suggested that if the defeat 'will only serve to shed more light on this *faux pas*, real or imaginary, the moral which distills out of this year's tournament will have been sufficiently emphasised.'[59] The *Mahratta* of Puné appears to have drawn a different moral from disunity and defeat. 'We do not know what exactly was the apple of discord', it remarked

> but it is more than probable that it must have been the captainship ... [We] do not mean to put one caste against one another, but our idea is that the healthy spirit of rivalry kindled by such inter-communal games must be maintained at a high level. We congratulate the Parsis on their deserved success and wish that the Hindus will make up their deficiency and will not allow their private grudges to hamper their efficiency.[60]

This, to me, reads like a back-handed criticism of Vithal and Shivram. The *Mahratta* wanted them to suppress their 'private' grudges in the interests of the community. Someone who saw the Hindu failure in a different light was the radical playwright B.V. ('Mama') Varerkar. The sidelining of Vithal and Shivram in the 1922 Quadrangular inspired him to write a remarkable play on the bloody intersection where the politics of cricket met the politics of caste.

Entitled *Turungachya Darat* (At the Gate of a Prison), the play was written in the weeks following the Quadrangular, and first peformed at the New Imperial Theatre in Bombay on the 1st of February 1923.

The play is structured around two central oppositions: the reform-minded Hindus versus the reactionary ones, and the catholic, open-minded city of Bombay versus the prison that was Poona. Its climax comes when a Brahmin owner of a bank moves his operations from Poona to Bombay, and decides to make an Untouchable his manager. As he puts it, 'Yesterday we made the very serious mistake of leaving out Vithal and Shivram Chambhar and lost in the Quadrangular cricket tournament. I do not want to lose in the battleground of life by leaving you out.'[61]

Varerkar was inspired by the cricket field to make a more general statement on behalf of social reform. I do not know how his play was received, but it might very well have played a part in what was to follow. For at the next Annual General Meeting of the Hindu Gymkhana, a vote of censure was passed against the selectors of the previous year's team. When the tournament came back to Bombay, in 1923, they set against the claims of tradition the call of the Mahatma, and the fact that in both 1921 and 1922 their team had lost heavily. Now the management of Hindu cricket in Bombay was dominated by *banias*, or merchants, who were perhaps more pragmatic and certainly less ideological than the Poona Brahmins. Crucially, for the case at hand, Gandhi was himself a bania. The concerns of the members reached the selectors, who appointed P. Vithal as captain.[62]

A ten year campaign on behalf of the Chamar cricketers had finally succeeded. How would the new captain do? In the early matches the Hindus defeated the Muslims by an innings, while the Europeans prevailed over the Parsis. The rulers this year did not have Rhodes and Hirst, but were pretty strong all the same. They batted first, and sent the Hindus on a leather hunt. 'It was a marvel to many,' wrote one reporter, 'that the Presidency were able to pile up runs like apples against the bowling which played such a great havoc on the Mahommedan only last week.' The Hindu team were irritable, and showed it. Their main bowler, S.M. Joshi, complained that he was being unfairly no-balled by the Muslim umpire. A friendly critic concurred: this umpire, he said, 'seemed to have left his glasses at home and gave himself up to absurd rulings.'[63]

The Europeans posted an impressive total of 481. The Hindu reply was built around a composed and assured hundred by captain Vithal. With Deodhar and Nayudu also scoring half-centuries they reached 475 all out. Three full days of cricket had passed, watched by a large and appreciative crowd. 'Every inch of space was occupied and the crowd at the tree end was at least ten deep. Every pavilion was full and hundreds were watching the game from house-tops, while some were perched on trees.' During the partnership between Vithal and

Nayudu, wrote one reporter, the crowd clapped so much that the sound 'was similar to the sound of sea-waves dashing to the floor.' The captain's century brought forth a surge of 'maddening joy.'[64]

At the conclusion of the Hindu first innings only one day's play remained. The European captain, Travers, now suggested that since a result was impossible they might as well call it a draw. Vithal answered that since twenty thousand fans had come to watch the match they must play it out. The Europeans went in again, and this time found S.M. Joshi in his best form. As he handed him the ball Vithal told Joshi, in Marathi, that it was time to 'start Bhairavi'. The bowler was a fine classical singer, and Bhairavi is the last *raga* sung or played in a concert. Thus inspired, Joshi took 7 for 39 as the Europeans crumbled to 153 all out.[65]

After S.M. Joshi's magnificent spell of bowling the Hindus required 162 runs to win. Two hours of play remained. Now Vithal played another master stroke. Instead of the wicket-keeper-batsman J.G. Navle, a careful and orthodox player, he sent in the big-hitting C.K. Nayudu to open with K.G. Pardeshi. Nayudu smashed the bowling all over the park, and outside it. One six landed on the Bombay Gymkhana pavilion, another on the Waudby Road. Pardeshi also scored at a brisk pace. When Nayudu was dismissed twenty runs were left to get. The captain promoted himself, and hit three slashing boundaries as the Hindus won in a canter.[66]

In his memoirs, Vithal wrote that he would 'never forget the moment' when he hit the winning run. As the ball crossed the boundary,

> groups of spectators one after another jumped up from the tents and ran towards the wicket. A few among them carried both of us (Pardeshi and myself) on their shoulders to the pavilion, shouting joyously. On reaching the pavilion everyone rushed to shake hands with me. Many European ladies congratulated me saying 'O Vithal, well played, congratulations Vithal'. The reason for these congratulations (as I came to know afterwards) was that they had taken a bet on the result of the match and had won against their own menfolk.[67]

This description is confirmed by the *Bombay Chronicle* report, which speaks of how 'at the end of the game a seething mass of humanity invaded the pavilion and expended their enthusiasm and exuberance of hilarity near the players.' Three thousand rupees were immediately subscribed for a Prize Fund. The donors, in these last days of the Khilafat movement, included Hindus as well as Muslims.

In an editorial on the tournament, the *Chronicle* noted that 'the success of the Hindu team was largely due to the confidence which its captain inspired. The heartiest congratulations of all lovers of cricket are due to him and to his team and no less to the Hindu Selection Committee which did not allow a pernicious caste prejudice to come in the way of selecting the right man to lead the team.' The same issue contained the same sentiments expressed more evocatively by a letter writer. 'The Hindus' brilliant victory,' said Vijayashram, 'was due more to the judicious and bold step of the Hindu Gymkhana in appointing Mr Vithal, brother of Mr Baloo—premier bowler of India—who is a member of the Untouchable Class to captain the Hindu team. The moral that can be safely drawn from the Hindus' magnificent victory is that removal of Untouchability would lead to Swaraj—which is the prophecy of the Mahatma.'[68]

Vijayashram's letter carried the heading 'Hindus' Brilliant Victory and its Moral.' Three days later the paper printed a letter by P.R. Lele titled 'Vithal's Victory'. The Quadrangular final, said Lele, while exciting and surprising in itself, also had 'a special interest attached to it from the Indian National point of view'. For Swaraj would not come until the curse of Untouchability remained. The sporting sphere had been heavily tainted by prejudice, wrote Lele: 'The untouchable communities have supplied the best cricketers during the last eighteen years but not one year was an untouchable raised to the dignity of captainship of the Hindu team....' This year, at last, the prejudice was challenged, and the Untouchable captain responded by leading from the front. Vithal's victory, suggested the letter writer, was moral and political rather than purely cricketing. 'The happiest event,' he said, 'the most agreeable upshot of the set of matches was the carrying of Captain Vithal on the shoulders of Hindus belonging to the so-called higher castes. Hurrah! Captain Vithal! Hurrah! Hindus who forget caste prejudice! Mahatma Gandhi Maharaj ki jai!'[69]

Was Gandhi following all this? The *Bombay Chronicle* reached him every day, for the British jailors in Yeravada were, as jailors go, generous and decent people. Did he read the sports pages? Not normally, but in this case one of his cricket-minded followers might have alerted him to Vithal's victory. The *Collected Works of Mahatma Gandhi*, alas, are silent on this score. More than the Mahatma's views one wishes one knew how the other Palwankars felt. Shivram, in fact, also played in the match, this his last Quadrangular appearance. Baloo would have watched his brothers play and, at the end, soaked in the sweet smells of a victory that he had so long struggled for. Vithal's team lost to the Muslims in 1924 but won the Quadrangular again in 1925. The next year the Quadrangular was played in Poona in September. The weeks before the Quadrangular were marked by rising tension between Brahmins and Non-Brahmins in and around Poona. But Vithal's recent successes meant that even the most hide-bound Brahmin had to accept him as captain of the Hindus. As in 1923 and 1925, the Hindus met the Europeans in the final. The key Hindu bowler S.M. Joshi was not playing, owing to a knee injury. In his place came L. Ramji, a fearsome fast bowler from Ranjitsinhji's hometown of Jamnagar, who bowled with a large vermilion *tilak* painted on his forehead. Played on a rain-affected wicket, the match was a low scoring thriller. The Hindus conceded a first innings lead of 62, and eventually the Europeans were set a meagre 117 to win. Vithal made astute bowling changes, and despite the low target had a close-set field throughout. Ramji and Chandarana took early wickets while the European captain, A.L. Hosie, batted resolutely at one end. With less than twenty runs to get Hosie cut a ball hard, but D.B. Deodhar took a brilliant catch in the gully. This was the turning point, for the Europeans then crumbled to 105 all out. At the end the losing captain had tears in his eyes.[70]

In four years Palwankar Vithal had led the Hindus to three victories. This last win might have given him the most pleasure, for it was a desperately close-fought match, a match played in reactionary Poona and at the ground where his beloved elder brother had slaved and bowled. Baloo was never allowed to enter the pavilion of the Poona Club, but it was in that pavilion that Vithal received the Quadrangular trophy. At the ground and afterwards, he received tributes aplenty. He and his men were féted with 'at homes' and '*pan suparis*', and even congratulated by the now conservative *Mahratta* for coming out 'with flying colours against the Europeans in a game native to them.'[71] Vithal was constrained to insert a collective acknowledgement in the newspapers: 'I have received a number of telegrams and letters congratulating the Hindu Team for their victory in the Quadrangular Tournament. It is not possible for me to write to each of them separately. I, therefore, hereby thank them for all their kindness and sympathy, and hope they will kindly accept it.'[72]

Vithal always underlined his debt to the eldest of the Palwankars. 'I must mention with respect and gratitude my brother Shri P. Baloo,' he once wrote: 'His advice and instruction were very useful and his deep knowledge about the game was always helpful to me.'[73] But he was a real hero in his own right. His skill with the bat and his artful captaincy had won him a wide circle of admirers. In his memoirs, Vithal writes of the affection he received from the Bombay public, and elsewhere too. He had certainly 'tasted the sweetness of popularity.' Once, when he was playing in Rajkot for a team sponsored by the Jam Saheb of Nawanagar, a crowd gathered round the players' tent asking: 'Where is Vithal? What does he look like?' At this Ranji himself asked him to stand on a table, and announced to the assembled fans: 'See! This is Vithal!' And in Calcutta the rush of fans screaming 'esho', 'esho' (come! come!) so unnerved him that he had to escape through the back door of his host Gymkhana.[74]

An impartial witness to Palwankar Vithal's terrific popularity was Vijay Merchant, who was himself destined to lead the Hindus and to become India's leading batsman. A Bombay boy born to privilege, Merchant was in his early teens when Vithal was in his pomp. Years later, he recalled the impression the great Hindu stalwart had made on him:

> 'Vithal': a slim, alert, elegant personality with that well-known green tweed hat on his head and a gracefully held bat in his hand that would swing easily when he reached the wicket. ... From thousands of cricket lovers there would come the spontaneous cry: 'there comes Vithal'.
>
> 'Vithal': the moment one heard the name... spectators would visualize all the grace and charm of Indian batsmanship.... With supple wrists, keen vision, perfect judgement of flight and agile footwork, Vithal had mastered the art of [batting]. He used to play his strokes with ease whether in front of the wicket or behind it. But one superb stroke of his that I cannot forget is the cover drive. Nowadays lot of effort and power goes into this stroke because of the off-side cordon. But due to his timing Vithal used to score more runs on this side of the wicket, effortlessly, through perfect co-ordination of wrist and leg movements... He used to score fast because of his art of placing the ball in the gaps.[75]

The years of Vithal's greatest triumphs, 1923 to 1926, coincided with the arrival on the political stage of Dr B.R. Ambedkar. Ambedkar had returned to India in 1923, with a doctoral degree from London and another from Columbia University in New York. He had previously qualified for the bar from Grays' Inn. While Vithal was leading the Hindu cricket team, Ambedkar was making a name at the Bombay Bar and, when the court was in recess, in politics. He travelled through the villages of the Deccan, seeking to build a base among the depressed classes. In his speeches Ambedkar would recall his own association with the first and greatest of Palwankars. As a student and teacher in Bombay, he had 'looked at the solid fame of the Untouchable bowler with pride.' As a little-known lecturer in Sydenham College, he had organized meetings to felicitate the bowler and worked for his elevation to the city's Municipal Corporation. Now, as he sought to establish his credentials with the Untouchables of Western India, Ambedkar would tell his audiences of his early attempts at promoting the proper recognition of Baloo's achievements.[76]

In 1929 the youngest of the Palwankar brotherhood retired from first-class cricket. But the patriach had other work ahead of him. For Baloo went on to play a role in one of the most celebrated episodes of modern Indian history. This was the fast unto death undertaken by Mahatma Gandhi while in Poona's Yerawada Jail in September 1932. Gandhi was protesting the decision to award separate electorates to the Untouchables, a move he thought would take them away from the Hindu fold. But B.R. Ambedkar believed otherwise; he saw a future for his people only outside the stifling social structure of Hinduism. With both men adamant, Gandhi's fast extended over several weeks, ending only after a pact was forged between the two principal disputants, which gave Untouchables more seats in the legislatures in exchange for the abandonment of their claim for separate electorates. The two key intermediaries in this pact were the South Indian social worker M.C. Rajah and Palwankar Baloo.[77]

Five years after the Poona Pact, however, Ambedkar and Baloo found themselves on opposite sides. The Poona Pact had broken down, with the lawyer setting up his own party in explicit opposition to the Congress. In the elections of 1937, the first with an extended franchise, Baloo was persuaded by the Congress to stand from a Bombay constituency. To his dismay, he found that he was pitted against Dr Ambedkar, who was by now certainly the most eminent Untouchable leader in the region, having (in a manner of speaking) supplanted the cricketer himself.

This contest between Baloo and Ambedkar was the final twist in a long, complex relationship. Once, the cricketer had been the young student's hero. Later, in 1920s, after Ambedkar had returned from England, they would meet to discuss the fate and future of the Depressed Castes. When the lawyer began cultivating a mass constituency he would invoke his association with Baloo. When Ambedkar disagreed with Gandhi on separate electorates the cricketer helped bring about a compromise. The Poona Pact had broken down, and now Ambedkar sought to change his religion. Baloo, on the other hand, still put his faith in the well-intentioned Hindu. Thus, a quarter-of-a-century after the young Ambedkar had presented the welcome address to Baloo after his epic 1911 tour of England, the two men came to fight an electoral battle in the city of Bombay.

The candidates for Bombay were all vetted by the Congress strongman, Sardar Vallabhbhai Patel. Almost twenty years later, a Bombay journalist was still puzzled at the candidate's selection: 'Baloo was a Harijan, but there were plenty of other aspirants. He was a popular cricketer, but unknown to politics. The selection caused much surprise because few had suspected that Sardar was a cricket lover.'[78]

It was not so much love of cricket as knowledge of politics that prompted Patel's decision. Baloo was chosen as a sporting hero, who had once been a hero of his opponent as well. More to the point, he was a Chamar, and Patel knew from the Census of India that these city wards had a fair contingent from that particular caste. The canny Sardar must also have hoped that the choice would pin Ambedkar down to his constituency, stopping him from making extensive speaking tours in support of his other candidates.

The Congress High Command sent out its stars to bat for Baloo. Consider the report of a packed election meeting held at Matunga on Saturday, 9th January 1937. The Congress candidate was introduced by Patel's own right-hand man, K.M. Munshi, shortly to become Home Minister in the Bombay Government. Baloo, said Munshi, 'had been a great cricketer in his younger days and had once scored [off] many an opponent. Hence let the opponents take heed that they had to face a first-class bowler'. 'A vote for Baloo', continued Munshi

> is a vote for the Poona Pact. That seat for the 'E' and 'F' Ward should be fought for tooth and nail. It is a seat which is of an all-India importance. Dr B.R. Ambedkar, who went to the Round Table Conference, entered into the historical Poona Pact, and even before the ink was dry on the paper, he tried to secede from the Hindu faith. Every vote for Mr Baloo was a vote for the Poona Pact. If Baloo falls, the Poona Pact falls, and with it all of us fall.[79]

After Munshi came Baloo. The cricketer told the voters that

> he personally was not interested in contesting the elections. Though he had not taken [a] very prominent part in politics, he had always come forward to help and take part when necessity demanded. Otherwise, he preferred to remain in the background. The call of the Congress came. At the last moment he agreed to stand on behalf of the Congress, and he did not even know from what constituency he would be asked to contest the seat in the assembly.
>
> After the nominations were filed, he came to know that he was contesting the same seat as Dr B.R. Ambedkar was contesting. It was providential coincidence. As he said before he did not want to go to the Legislature, but what were they to do when seats were reserved for them in the House. They had to be occupied. He was sure the voters would cast their vote for him, the Congress candidate as against Ambedkar.[80]

Other reports suggest that Ambedkar had filed his nomination before Baloo. It is clear nonetheless that the cricketer was diffident and deeply unsure about challenging the rising star of the low castes. Although they had recently had political disagreements they had once been friends. Baloo's son and nephew both told me that he was very reluctant to fight Ambedkar in the elections of 1937.[81]

The Marathi-language Congress paper, *Navakal*, forcefully campaigned on Baloo's behalf. It reminded its readers of how Ambedkar 'had himself accepted Baloo's greatness many times.' The lawyer had often expressed his 'great respect and regard' for the cricketer. It offered, in illustration, the story of how Ambedkar was once felicitated at the hands of Baloo at a function organized by the Cobblers Union. This, in truth, actually showed the remarkable emergence of Ambedkar as an Untouchable leader. For once, as in 1911, Ambedkar had felicitated Baloo; now it was the other way around. The paper seems to have recognized this, for immediately after recounting the incident it asked its readers 'to vote for Baloo and not be hypnotized by Ambedkar's personality.'[82]

On polling day, it was reported that Ambedkar's supporters came to vote in trucks, the Congressmen in cars. But many would have walked to the booths or taken a train. In the end, Ambedkar got 13, 245 votes, while Baloo received 11,

225. It had been a close-run thing. Later, the *Bombay Chronicle* suggested that Baloo's defeat was due to a 'spoiler', the labour leader Joglekar who had stood as an independent and garnered 10,000 votes. If the Congress had prevailed upon Joglekar to resign, complained the paper, then 'Dr Ambedkar would have been positively swamped.'[83]

The cricket historian will note the interesting fact that Baloo's decision to fight an election was a 'world-first' for a professional cricketer, anticipating the much later moves in the same direction of Guyana's Roy Fredericks and Pakistan's Imran Khan. But politically correct radicals, writing from the vantage point of time, will at once vest the Baloo-Ambedkar battle of 1937 with a deeper meaning. Baloo, they will say, was a forerunner of the collaborationist low-caste politicians of today, who wait for a few crumbs to fall from the table of those dominantly high-caste parties, the Congress and the B.J.P. By the same token, they will see Ambedkar as the precursor of politicians with a greater sense of dignity and self-respect, those who insist that only Dalits, 'the dispossesed', can represent other Dalits.[84]

As ever, the radicals will be partly right but mostly wrong. For one thing, in their integrity of purpose both cricketer and constitutional expert stand apart from all kinds of Dalit politicians today. For another, at a time when the Dalits of western India were starved of heroes it was Baloo who showed them, by his feats on the field and by his great personal dignity off it, that they were no less than the caste Hindus. Over the years, with a sharper awareness and consolidation of their rights, Dalits came to regard scholars and lawyers as more likely leaders than sportsmen. In this sense Baloo prepared the way for Ambedkar, much as (in the context of Indian nationalism) moderates like Gopalkrishna Gokhale prepared the way for Mahatma Gandhi.

Let me leave the last word to a now forgotten newspaper columnist. In 1929, Vithal was dropped from the Hindu team, to make way for rising young talent. With his dropping the 'last of the Baloo family after years of meritorious service has been unceremoniously driven from first class cricket.' Thus wrote one 'R.V.M.', in a moving tribute to the brothers, a tribute marked by deep knowledge of the game of cricket and a subtle understanding of its sometimes brutal social context. The Hindu team's announcement, he remarked,

> abruptly ends a thirty years' unbroken connection of the Baloo brothers with Hindu cricket. Nowhere else does the history of cricket supply such a glorious page. Thirty years and a single family. One brother after another raising the Hindu cricket edifice higher and yet higher, spreading its brilliance, along with their own, all over India and beyond.

The individual brothers were recalled, one by one. First the patriarch:

> And what a proud record to contemplate! It was Baloo who began Hindu bowling as such. With what wonderful wiles did he accomplish single-handed the herculean task of putting the Parsi and European veterans out, only those knew who intelligently watched him doing it. Bowlers on the other side might come and go but Baloo plodded on for ever..

Then, the younger siblings:

> Baloo brought Shivram into the field and the best fieldsman he became, with considerable bowling and batting powers in addition. Then came Vithal ... He made his first appearance at the Marine Lines Parade Ground, when the Parsi Parekh had a hat-trick and Warden a century against the Hindus. Vithal, however, was not one of the 'tricked' ones. He played with the sweeping forward style that alone could withstand the fast swerving left-handers of the Parsis. He wielded this weapon with considerable effect and gradually stayed the rot year after year, with centuries against the Mahomedans and the Europeans. To his help then came Gunpat with his pretty style and quick movements. There was thus a time when the Hindu team included all the four brothers at one and the same time, and people fondly called the Hindu side as 'Baloo brothers plus 7'.

'R.V.M.' now showed how sporting skill could vanquish social prejudice:

> Did ever a family establish such a record? Could a Hindu lover of cricket having the least culture within him ever dream of breathing against such pillars of Hindu cricket any ignoble reference to their caste? Could a Hindu cricketer think of them with anything but respect? The late Pandharinath Telang, the Hindu Jessop, noble-minded as he was, could never think of Baloo as other than a dear comrade. Sir Chunilal [Mehta] never entertained any ugly thought of the Baloo brothers 'depressed' class.

But society, it seems, sometimes moved more slowly than the cricketers. The final steps to the summit were the hardest:

> Baloo though senior was deprived of the captainship. He soon retired and the matter was hushed up. Shivram retired before such a question could crop up in his case. Then it came to the turn of Vithal. But time and again he was put down. His juniors were thrust over his head. No wonder the Hindus failed—miserably failed—yet the die-hards would not listen to justice and reason. But the force of circumstances was too great and after a lot of higgling, at long last, they 'liberalized' themselves enough to throw the captainship at Vithal.[85]

The history of cricket does in fact have pages filled with the deeds of brothers: the Graces of England, the Pollocks of South Africa, the Chappells and the Waughs of Australia, the Hadlees and Crowes of New Zealand, the Wettimunys of Sri Lanka, the Flowers of Zimbabwe, above all, the Mohammeds of Pakistan. In cricketing skill and achievement the Palwankars of India were comfortably the equal of them all. These other families, moreover, had to fight their demons on the field alone: whereas the Palwankars were sinned against most grievously by the society into which they were born. Why then are they so wholly forgotten? One reason is that they played before India became an 'official' Test playing nation. Another is the unconscionable ahistoricism of the Indians, their disregard for documents, records, remembrances and past heroes. While the Palwankars lived and played it was all too different. Men like 'R.V.M.' knew what they were worth. Men like Dr B.R. Ambedkar knew it too. It is past time that they were restored to their rightful place in the history of Indian cricket, indeed in the history of Indian social emancipation.

## Notes and References

1. Geo W. Briggs, *The Chamars* (Calcutta: Association Press, 1920), pp. 20, 58, 228, 241.

2. The versions, respectively, of Baloo's nephew K.V. Palwankar (in an interview with me), and of an obituary in the *Times of India*, clipping in K.V. Gopalaratnam Collection, Sports Authority of India, New Delhi.

3. P. Vithal, *Maze Crida-Jivan* (Bombay: Bharati Publishers, 1948), pp. 11–12; Bal J. Pandit, *Khara Kheladu* (Poona: Vora and Company, 1959) p. 11; interview with K.V. Palwankar, Bombay, November 1996.

4. Pandit, *Khara Kheladu*, pp. 11–12.

5. Benny Green, compiler, *The Wisden Book of Cricketers' Lives* (London: Queen Anne Press, 1986), p. 354; Vasant Raiji, *India's Hambledon Men* (Bombay: Tyeby Press, 1986), p. 61.

6. Interview with Y.B. Palwankar, Poona, July 1999.

7. Vithal, *Maze Crida-Jivan*, pp. 10–13; interview with Bal J. Pandit, Pune, July 1999.

8. Pandit, *Khara Kheladu*, pp. 16–17; Vithal, *Maze Crida-Jivan* p. 14; interview with K.V. Palwankar, Bombay, December 1996.

9. Pandit, *Khara Kheladu*, p. 17.

10. Anon., 'Hindu Cricket', *Indian Social Reformer*, Volume 16, Number 25, 18 February 1906.

11. The information in this and the previous paragraph comes from contemporary newspaper accounts.

12. Interview with K.V. Palwankar, Bombay, December 1896.

13. Sir Chunilal V. Mehta, 'Beginnings of Hindu Cricket', in *Diamond Jubilee*

*Souvenir of Parmanandas Jivandas Hindu Gymkhana, 1894–1954* (Bombay: published by the Gymkhana, 1954).

14. M.E. Pavri, *Parsi Cricket* (Bombay: J.B. Marzban and Co., 1901), p. 164.

15. J.C. Maitra, writing in *The Sportsman*, Special Quadrangular Number, 30 November 1929.

16. H.C. Muckerjee, *The Indian Cricketers' Tour of 1911* (Calcutta: published by the author, 1911), p. 20.

17. N.N. Langrana, 'I Gaze into the Fire', in *Cricket Association of Bengal Silver Jubilee Souvenir* (Calcutta: CAB, 1956).

18. Sumit Sarkar, *The Swadeshi Movement in Bengal, 1903–1908* (Delhi: People's Publishing House, 1973).

19. *Kesari*, 2 February 1906, in *Report on Native Newspapers for the Bombay Presidency* in Oriental and India Office Collections, Britsh Library, London (hereafter *RNNBP*).

20. *Bhala*, 1 January 1906, in *RNNBP*.

21. *Bombay Gazette*, 8 February 1906.

22. *Bombay Gazette*, 10 and 12 February 1906; *The Madras Mail*, 15 February 1906.

23. *The Tribune*, 23 February 1906.

24. Anon., 'Hindu Cricket', *Indian Social Reformer*, Volume 16, Number 25, 18 February 1906.

25. Calculated from A.A. Fyzee, H.N. Contractor, D.P. Thanawala and Vijay Merchant, compilers, *Fifty Years of Bombay Cricket* (Bombay: Thacker and Co., 1946).

26. P.N. Polishwalla, *Representative Matches in India from 1892 to 1919* (Bombay: published by the author, 1919), pp. 64–67.

27. These figures are taken from S.K. Roy, compiler, *India-England Cricket Visits, 1911–1946* (Calcutta: Illustrated News, 1946).

28. Muckerjee, *The Indian Cricketers' Tour of 1911*, pp. 153–54, 159, 109.

29. *The Indian Spectator*, 23 September 1911.

30. Vithal, *Maze Crida-Jivan*, pp. 17–18.

31. Eleanor Mae Zelliot, 'Dr Ambedkar and the Mahar Movement.' unpublished Ph D dissertation, University of Philadelphia, 1969, pp. 133, 252. Also interview with Professor Zelliot, Berkeley, March 1998.

32. Jamshed Dinshaw Antia, *Elphinstone College Tours* (Bombay: published by the author, 1913), pp. 194ff. There was actually a fifth brother, Krishna, who died very young. In deference to his memory P. Vithal titled a chapter of his memoirs 'Panch Palwalkar', a reference to the greatest of all Hindu brotherhoods, the five Pandavas, or 'Panch Pandeshwar.'

33. 'The Bombay Cricket Carnival', *Bombay Chronicle* (hereafter BC), 5 September 1913.

34. D.B. Deodhar, *I Look Back: An Autobiography* (Madras: Sport and Pastime, 1966), p. 69.

35. *BC*, 1 October 1913.

36. *BC*, 2 June 1914.

37. *BC*, 7 July 1914.

38. See *BC*, 29 May 1913.

39. *BC*, 3 September 1915.

40. *BC*, 4 September 1915.

41. There have been some successful bowler-captains in the history of cricket: such as Australia's Richie Benaud and Pakistan's Imran Khan. Yet the bias persists: bowlers who, like Baloo, have outstanding tactical minds are denied the captaincy simply because they are bowlers. One such case is that of the current Indian spin bowler Anil Kumble, a cricketer of maturity and intelligence who has never been asked to lead his country.

42. *Collected Works of Mahatma Gandhi* (hereafter *CWMG*), Volume 17, pp. 471, 534.

43. *CWMG*, Volume 18, p. 377.

44. *CWMG*, Volume 19, p. 8

45. *BC* (Weekly Edition), 24 October 1920.

46. A.F.S. Talyarkhan, 'Before Memory Slams the Door', in *Official Souvenir of the Silver Jubilee of the Bombay Cricket Association*, 1930–1954 (Bombay: BCA, 1954).

47. *BC*, 15 November 1920.

48. *BC*, 3 December 1920.

49. Vithal, *Maze Crida-Jivan*, p. 88.

50. See *BC*, 4 December 1920.

51. The statement was probably drafted by L.R. Tairsee, the reform-minded Congressman and industrialist who was to later become the President of the P.J. Hindu Gymkhana.

52. *BC*, 4 December 1920. Govindji Vassanji used to regularly advertise in Gandhi's own journal, *Young India*.

53. *BC*, 7 December 1920.

54. *BC*, 9 December 1920.

55. Deodhar, *I Look Back*, p. 33.

56. C.L.R. James, *Beyond a Boundary* (London: Hutchinson, 1963).

57. *BC*, 24 August 1922.

58. D.B. Deodhar, *I Look Back*, p. 41; S.K. Roy, editor, *Bombay Pentangular* (Calcutta: Illustrated News, 1945), p. 100.

59. *BC*, 10 and 21 September 1922.

60. *Mahratta*, 24 September 1922.

61. Bhargavram Vithal Varerkar, *Turungacha Darat* (Bombay: Lalitkaladarsha Natak Mandali, 1923).

62. As recalled by J.C. Maitra in *BC*, Sunday Edition, 17 October 1937.

63. *BC*, 11 December 1920.

64. *BC*, 13 December 1923; *Navakal* (Bombay), 13 December 1923.

65. Vithal, *Maze Crida-Jivan*, pp. 90–98.

66. C.K. Nayudu, 'Lessons from a Long Innings', *MysIndia*, 25 October 1953.

67. Vithal, *Maze Crida-Jivan*, pp. 98–99.

68. *BC*, 15 December 1923.

69. *BC*, 18 December 1923.

70. Vithal, *Maze Crida-Jivan*, pp. 3–4, 61–62, 119; 'Cricket Then and Now: An Interview with Prof. D.B. Deodhar', *Frontline*, 17 January 1992.

71. *Mahratta*, 26 September 1926. Notably, the *Mahratta* did not mention the Hindu captain by name or caste.

72. *BC*, 4 December 1926.

73. Vithal, *Maze Crida-Jivan*, p. 156.

74. Ibid., p. 162.

75. Vijay Merchant, foreword, in Vithal, *Maze Crida-Jivan*.

76. Dhananjay Keer, *Dr Ambedkar: Life and Mission* (third edition: Bombay: Popular Prakashan, 1971), pp. 39–40, 86.

77. C.F. Pyarelal, *The Epic Fast* (Ahmedabad: Navjivan, 1932).

78. *BC*, 7 July 1955.

79. *BC*, Weekly Edition, 10 January 1937.

80. Ibid.

81. Interviews with K.V. Palwankar, Mumbai, November 1996, and with Y.B. Palwankar, Pune, July 1999.

82. *Navakal* (Bombay), 11 January through 17 February 1937.

83. *BC*, Weekly Edition, 28 February 1937.

84. The Untouchables were once known as the 'Depressed Classes', later as the 'Scheduled Castes' or as 'Harijans', but now choose to be known increasingly as 'Dalits'.

85. 'R.V.M.', 'Hindu Cricket and Baloo Brothers', *BC*, 30 November 1929.

# 2.

# A Book of Her Own, A Life of Her Own
## The Autobiography of a Nineteenth-Century Woman

Tanika Sarkar

(On getting married) 'I went straight into my mother's arms, crying, "Mother, why did you give me away to a stranger?"'

(After marriage) 'My day would begin at dawn and I worked till two at night ... I was fourteen years old ... I longed to read books ... But I was unlucky, those days women were not allowed to read.'

(Learning to read at twenty-five) 'It was as if the Great Lord himself taught me how to read. If I didn't know even that much, I would have had to depend on others ...'

(Looking back on her youth) 'In the meantime the Great Lord had decked my body out just the way a boat is fitted out... How strange it was: So many things came out of my body, yet I knew nothing of their causes.'[1]

These are some important words and themes from *Amar Jiban*, the first autobiography written by a Bengali woman, and very probably the first full-scale autobiography in the Bengali language. Her writing and her life stand in a peculiarly significant relationship to each other, since the author, Rashsundari Debi, a housewife from an upper-caste landed family in East Bengal, seemed to possess none of the things that presumably make a woman's life noteworthy.

It was an uneventful, unremarkable life. Rashsundari was born around 1809 in Potajiya village in Pabna district, in a landowning family. When she was twelve, she was married off to Sitanath Ray, a prosperous landlord from Ramdiya village at Faidpur. From the age of fourteen, she looked after the entire household and brought up twelve children. When she was twenty-five, however, Rashsundari made a daring departure. She secretly taught herself to read and studied all the religious texts that her home possessed. Later, she also learnt to write. At fifty-nine she became a widow, and her autobiography

Excerpted from Tanika Sarkar, *Hindu Wife, Hindu Nation: Community, Religion and Cultural Nationalism*, Permanent Black, Delhi, 2001.

was finished in the same year, in 1868. She revised and enlarged it when she was eighty-eight.

Only one event of an exceptional kind had interrupted the even, quiet rhythms of a pious housewifely existence. Orthodox Hindus of those times believed that a literate woman was destined to be a widow. In Rashsundari's own family there was so much talk against women's education that she would not even look at a piece of paper lest she was suspected of reading.[2] The first tentative experiments among liberal Indian reformers and Christian missionaries to educate women from reform-minded families had produced a sort of orthodox backlash and had hardened Hindu opinion against it. The meek and submissive housewife had no doubt at all that she was going against the grain of familial and social expectations. This one act of disobedience, then, partially deconstructs the 'good wife' role she played all her life.

Why did she, on her own, and in great trepidation, make this deeply transgressive departure? And what bearing does this desire and this achievement have on the fact that Rashsundari was the first Bengali person to write out her own life, to recreate, even invent it through autobiographical act, and thereby gather it closer to herself and possess it more fully? What were the resources available to her that could have produced this desire and what are the new possibilities that we can read into women's lives and women's writing from the presence of this desire?

In the book Rashsundari explains that it was an irrepressible urge to read a particular sacred text that made her struggle to read.[3] The book was *Chaitanya Bhagavat* [*CB*], the first Bengali biography of Chaitanya, the Krishna-maddened saint of medieval Bengal who had promised salvation to the poor, the low-caste, the woman—categories excluded by the Brahmanical orthodoxy from higher spiritual learning.[4] She went on to read other lives of Chaitanya and of Krishna.[5] Her reading, then, had a lot to do with lives divine and saintly. With a covert design that hid behind a seeming unintentionality, Rashsundari was audaciously structuring her mundane life story on that sacred pattern. Each detail of a thoroughly commonplace and homebound life was arranged to exemplify a godly intervention, the crowning proof of which was her apparently miraculous access to the written word. Her life was meant to be read as if it was enclosed within a divine purpose, as almost an extension of God's own life. It was as if the two lives—God's and the devotee's—were intertwined within a single narrative frame, interanimating each other. In fact, the last sections of the autobiography describe, without any apparent sense of incongruity, not events from her own life, but from the various lives (incarnations) of Vishnu himself.[6]

Rashsundari read from a fairly wide spectrum of late medieval devotional (bhakti) texts and her reflections drew largely upon terms that have long and multiple lineages within Hindu religious discourses. Unless we refer often and in some detail to this thick web of intertextuality, *Amar Jiban* will make only a limited and emasculated sense—as a mere string of random effusion and exhortation held together by a few sparse facts from a commonplace life.

Again, even though the history of her own times and place seems remarkably absent within the text itself, the book, as a material product created by a woman and printed for a nineteenth-century readership with an assured interest in a woman's writing, belonged crucially to her century. We need to explore the insertion of historical processes into the life as well as into the text, even though Rashsundari herself showed no overt preoccupation with them.

Vaishnav bhakti in Bengal (devotional discourses and practices that established a direct emotional connection between Vishnu in his incarnation as Krishna,[7] and the devotee), seemed to grant an unprecedentedly large and free space to the woman. The great body of bhakti lyrics glorified the illicit love between Krishna and the cowherd maidens (*gopinis*) of Vrindaban, of whom Radha was of paramount importance. A popular trope within devotional expression was to borrow the woman's voice and emotions. Esoteric cults loosely affiliated to Vaishnavism placed a powerful emphasis on the practice of sexual rites between a man and a woman who were not married to each other. Though all these traditions seemed to privilege the woman's experience and emotions in multiple and prominent ways, they delineated, at the same time, a fundamentally problematic space for her by largely containing the libertarian impulse and possibilities within devotional meditation and sexo-yogic practices. Ultimately, their combined effect was to heighten the sheer instrumentality of the woman's body and emotions within devotion itself. Again, even though post-Chaitanya bhakti had generated an immense body of religious writing in Bengali, and had stimulated reading habits among sections of Vaishnav women and low-caste rural households, Vaishnavism had tense and paradoxical perspectives on the matter of scriptural and textual knowledge. Rashsundari's devotion and writing as a woman, therefore, related in complex ways to traditions which were partly enabling but partly so constricting that she needed to make crucial departures and breaks of her own within bhakti.

Rashsundari made a major innovation in religious as well as in literary conventions by articulating a devotional statement through the autobiographical mode. There were at least two distinct Bengali language resources available to her for writing about divine intervention in human lives, although none was autobiographical. One was the genre of medieval and late medieval *mangalkavyas* or verse narratives about the exploits of a deity who establishes his/her worship on earth by working through a human agency.[8] These would generally be sung or recited by professional expounders of sacred texts (*kathaks*) with explanations and commentaries. Shorter versions would be orally transmitted by women during women's rites.

Initially these cults had low-caste, folk origins and were shunned by the Brahmanical orthodoxy. Several centuries of rule by Muslim dynasties in Bengal, however, saw a decline in the socio-political hegemony of Brahmins. They sought to retrieve it by appropriating some of these deities within the mainstream Hindu pantheon. A number of upper-caste poets composed *kavyas* or long sacred ballads about them and Brahmin kathaks read them out to village gatherings. This partially—though only very partially—closed the cultural gap between upper and lower castes and gave Brahmins a larger entry and control within what used to be autonomous subaltern beliefs and practices.

As an upper-caste Vaishnav woman in an orthodox family, Rashsundari would have listened to readings and practised rites connected with these cults and texts. She, however, never mentioned them. It seems that in her remembered and self-constructed life, Rashsundari chose to opt out of the world of women's culture, piety and collective rites with their songs, ritual, colour and bustle. The choice has wider connotations which we shall explore later.

The other tradition available to her and one which did inspire her devotion, was that of Vaishnav hagiography. She herself had read at least two of them—*Chaitanya Bhagavat* [*CB*], and *Chaitanya Charitamrita* [*CC*]. *CB*, written by a disciple of a close acolyte of Chaitanya, and within fifteen years of Chaitanya's death, has a captivating narrative flow and combines quotidian, intimate details with an effusive, hyperbolic mode of devotional expression.[9] *CC* was composed later by Krishnadas Kaviraj under the inspiration of a theologian who belonged to a group of scholars whom Chaitanya had sent to Vrindaban to prepare a Vaishnavite canon for Bengal. These theologians (Goswamis), had worked out a consensus in the mid sixteenth century with the various Vaishnav sects in Bengal which gave their texts canonical status among Bengali Vaishnavs. The *CC*, unlike the Sanskrit Goswami texts, was written in Bengali.[10] It could, therefore, have a far wider reach and popularise the theological concepts of the Goswamis among non-learned *bhakts*. It also provided a model for the theological discussion in the vernacular that was built around the unfolding of a life-story.

Rashsundari drew much from both texts. She divided her writing into small sections, dealing with specific themes, and organized the sections into broad parts, covering whole phases of her life. She also had access to a chaste, literary vocabulary, and a fast-flowing, vivid style. Yet these hagiographies would not adequately serve her purposes. She needed a sustained, autobiographical mode to deal with the life events of an ordinary woman devotee, not holy chronicles about the wives and mothers of saints. She, therefore, needed to improvise.

There was yet a third alternative available to her, an oral model for recording the popular miracle lore connected with the lives and activities of ascetics and holy men and women. Their sacred status was confirmed through tales of ecstatic trances and of miraculous manifestations. Rashsundari, however, was secure in her status as a successful housewife. She had neither renounced her mundane life nor aspired for extraordinary powers and competencies. Her closeness to God could only be proved by her own writing. It was at once a miracle in its scope of achievement as well as a record of God's intervention in her life. Yet, it was a miracle that she alone had witnessed and her self-written life alone could testify to it. Unlike all these other modes of recording divine intervention in human lives, the autobiographical mode was indispensable for her. Her religion, her life, and her writing thus connected with one another to form an unbroken circuit.

By making her autobiography and her piety dependent on each other, Rashsundari tried to make two statements. The very act of writing established that her relations with God were more nuanced and more intimate than those that exist between most human beings and divinity. She also needed to problematize her own relationship to her household or *sansar*, since, on the surface, this sansar seemed to exhaust the entirety of her lived experiences. We need to explore the different meanings of this term in Hindu discourses and locate the forms of excesses beyond it that had been worked out in devotional and philosophical traditions. We would then find the ways in which *Amar Jiban* drew upon as well as departed from them.

Sansar is the domain of the householder, the stage of *garhasthya*, a vital phase within the prescribed four-stage life-cycle of a pious Hindu. Only an ascetic may renounce this realm of worldly responsibilities. The observance of prescribed ritual, caste and gender norms that had been spelt out by the Vedas and subsequent sacred law-codes would constitute the essence of a pious life or dharma. The woman enters sansar through the sacrament of marriage, the only sacrament that is available to her. For her, sansar is the unending flow of domestic work and responsibilities, primarily connected with cooking, serving, and child-rearing. Ideally, the woman should have no other religious activity, except for some prescribed ritual observances.

In a broader, theological sense, sansar, as governed by the scriptural prescriptions and injunctions (*vidhi nishedha*), is sustained by the rule of karma. This is the conviction that actions performed in one life bear results through successive rebirths and that only a strict obedience to the prescribed rules of sansar would eventually wear out the fruits of past action and deliver a human being from the karmic order of rebirth which is fundamentally painful.

Sansar is thus the site of dharma as well as a site of trials. Some of the later philosophical schools sought to make out a domain which would confirm yet also transcend the rule of sansar.[11] For our purposes, we may, perhaps, rather schematically identify three such sites.

Parts of the Upanishads had postulated an ultimate and fundamental identity between Brahman or Absolute Reality and Atman or the individual self also among individual selves.[12] According to Shankaracharya, a 'beginningless ignorance', stemming from Brahman's illusion-bearing power of maya, makes the individual self erroneously identify itself with a particular and finite body-mind, in a state of separation from and opposition to other selves. Only a few seers can, in this life, realize the deeper reality and achieve liberation from the bonds of karma. The rest are trapped within maya and are condemned to a strict observance of *vidhi nishedha* or prescriptions-injunctions.[13] It is interesting that while the source of human sorrow is located indirectly in a stratified and self-divided human order, a transcendence is sought within metaphysical knowledge alone. At the same time, the more the hierarchical order of the empirical world is left intact, the more intense is the emphasis on the essential oneness of all selves. While Shankar's monistic philosophy belongs to the realm of erudite speculation, the dichotomy between an apparent reality and a deeper truth obscured by maya became a part of universally accessible religious common-sense. We shall find resonances of this in *Amar Jiban*.

A second form of excess was constituted by body-centred philosophies. Certain lower-caste, esoteric, popular religious sects, some of which were loosely affiliated to Vaishnavism, aspired to trap divine energies, even divinity itself, within the human body through ritualized violations of purity-pollution taboos and secret sexual rites. They proclaimed a body-centred philosophy, stressing the primacy of bodily sense-perceptions over scriptural knowledge. Propagated largely through songs that encoded their rites and theories, their philosophy of *dehavad* had become familiar to nineteenth-century villagers, even though upper-castes, on the whole, considered them deviant and contemptible. *Amar Jiban* uses fragments from dehavad but the influence is limited. Even though the body-centred philosophy with its defiance of caste and pollution taboos seems an attractive and liberating form of excess over sansar, a lot of the texts reveal that the female body and emotions were supposed to be used in an instrumental capacity, for filling the male body with extraordinary powers which would eventually liberate it from all desire for the woman. Nor were they unmarked by the deep-seated conviction in the innate depravity of the woman which characterised upper-caste codes.[14]

For Rashsundari herself, it was the tradition of Krishna-centred devotion (which, in Bengal, also included Chaitanya as an object of adoration) that was of paramount importance. From the thirteenth century onwards, Bengali Vaishnavism had developed a rich stream of devotional literature, both in Sanskrit and in the vernacular.[15] The core of it dwelt on Krishna's early sport (*leela*) in the holy land of Vrindaban. An aesthetic code, derived originally from classical literature, provided the pattern for devotion. The devotee vicariously entered the leela by identifying himself/herself with one or other of Krishna's associates at Vrindaban. While most devotees were supposed to internalize the mood of the lesser companions, the love between Krishna and his most cherished lover Radha was the supreme object of contemplation for all Bengali Vaishnavas.

The *Bhagavat Puran*, a medieval devotional text on Krishna's erotic leela, was acknowledged as the primary source of religious knowledge within Bengali Vaishnavism. The leela acquires a distinctive configuration here. Krishna sports with thousands of cowherd boys and girls (gopas and gopinis) of humble caste who are dearer to him than the arrogant higher castes.[16] He asks married gopinis to seek pleasure with him and fills all of them with infinite bliss. It is a pastoral idyll of endless love and ecstatic pleasure, of eternal music and fragrant flowers, where sansar and its unbending vidhi-nishedhas stand suspended. The devotee, through mere contemplation of such bliss, finds access to a image of surfeit. Yet the laws of sansar are not entirely inverted or cancelled out. What the image of surfeit promises is, rather, a dream of the values of sansar, taken to the limits of their possibilities.

The Krishna of *BP* is a male figure who fills thousands of gopinis with equal bliss. Radha, as a separate figure, has not yet made an appearance in this text. We have a god who brings nothing but pleasure to his many devotees in equal measure, a king who plays with shepherds. Here power dreams of an absolute condition of hegemony where it may translate itself as love and fulfillment for the powerful—the human devotee, the low-caste, the woman.

Religious imagination, however, could not indefinitely sustain this state of infinite bliss. Inexorable existential and social problems of pain and inequality re-enter the narrative and fracture it at different points. A polygamous patriarchy had imagined itself as capable of satisfying endless women equally. Later devotional texts introduced the figure of Radha who breaks up the undifferentiated mass of loving womanhood. She loves Krishna with an angry, resentful love, straining against the basic asymmetry within the relationship, since Krishna must love others and must eventually leave her to eternal *viraha* (pain of separation). Her resentment forms a language through which the devotee articulates the arbitrariness of God's power over the world and a human condition marked by inequality. A Sanskrit couplet, ascribed to Chaitanya, expresses a passionate yet resentful longing for Krishna in a language of unusual violence: 'Let that immoral faithless one come and ravish me.'[17]

The Vrindavan of *BP* had been a condition of uninhibited, unbounded fulfillment. In other Vaishnav works, problems of a patriarchal order clash with the articulation of devotion in an erotic mode. If an endless love-play becomes the ideal repository for the most perfect relationship with the most desired being—that is, with God—then to be adequately demanding and challenging, to be worthy of a lifetime of yearning, that desire cannot be confined to conjugal boundaries where the love object is already attained. Most of post-Chaitanya devotion agreed on the illicit nature (*parakiya*) of Radha-Krishna love.

Here sansar acquires yet another meaning. It is the ensemble of licit relationships that bars Radha's way to Krishna. A paradox is set up: the world of patriarchal injunctions, insisting on the woman's unconditional monogamy, is her dharma, yet desire for Krishna is a call coming from God himself. The erotic situation corresponds to a spiritual problem. Karma enjoins submission to the rules of sansar, yet sansar, with its unending demands and rigid prescriptions, is an obstacle that thwarts a complete surrender to God. God calls out to the devotee and goes back empty-handed. Sansar is divinely-ordained and also an impediment. The paradox makes both God and the devotee weep.

There was, then, within bhakti, a problem of reconciling faith with a painful world order. When they reflected on Hinduism, Christian missionaries were traumatized over the absence in it of a Manichaean division of the world between God and the Devil, by the ascription of an obviously skewed earthly scheme to a divine and not a diabolical agency.[18] For the Vaishnav, faith begins with an acceptance of God's work while arguing about its disorders. This was often conveyed through yet another devotional trope that shocked missionaries; abuse of God.[19] Since submission to divine will is founded on an already-given (and, hence, already-transcended) critique of the world order, faith involves a critique of the way faith must be.

To these ways of negotiating with God and sansar, Chaitanya had added another possibility—a congregation of devotees who could be assured of equal access to salvation by the existence of a new scheme of devotional activity that was available to all: not caste status or scriptural learning but simple faith expressed through ecstatic singing and chanting of God's name. Salvation was to be easier for the socially dispossessed since their hearts had not been hardened by pride. The promise of spiritual equality empowered Chaitanya (himself a Brahmin) and his largely upper-caste acolytes to undertake a massive proselytization campaign among low-caste yet socially and politically significant groups—artisans, traders, manufacturers, tribal chieftains.[20] Possibly, the success of Islamic proselytization was judged to lie in its congregational practice and its conviction in an unstratified spiritual order. Even though some post-Chaitanya sects and groups did violate Brahmanical injunctions about caste and gender, on the whole Chaitanya's bhakti was not meant to transform broader social relations. Rashsundari's Brahmin family was devoutly Vaishnav, but deeply orthodox.

These, then, very crudely, are the shapes of sansar, and the ways in which an excess is created beyond them. How much of this would have been available to an unlearned housewife like Rashsundari? Although Vaishnavism had generated reading habits and sacred vernacular texts in abundance for subordinate groups, and although women in the mendicant orders were often literate,[21] all the women in Rashsundari's family were insulated from literacy.[22] Even in the freer atmosphere of her mother's home, where the village school was taught, and where Rashsundari as a child was told to spend her days since her friends were unkind to her, she was not expected to learn anything. She did pick up the letters from the work that the boys were doing, but she told nobody about it.[23] Not only did Brahmanical custom continue to reign in upper-caste homes, Vaishnavism itself was ambiguous on the matter of scriptural learning, counterposing simple faith to the path of knowledge. Since the unlearned was privileged over the arrogant Brahmin scholar, by the same token learning would remain restricted.[24]

Yet much of Vaishnav doctrines could be orally transmitted at a fairly high level of conceptualization. Ritual occasions within households or local congregations organized recitations and commentaries (*katha* and *path*) as well as devotional music (*kirtan*) which was interspersed with an expounding of texts. Texts were, therefore, quite ubiquitous, penetrating into even oral performances. The *BP*, for instance, would be read out over a month at a time. Morning sessions would be devoted to recitations from the Sanskrit original and, in the evening sessions, their meaning would be expounded in Bengali.[25] This way, an unlearned listener gained what has been termed phonetic competence—that is, an overall understanding over whole blocs of Sanskrit terms. At the same time, she would also acquire 'linguistic competence' over each word that was read out and explained from the Bengali texts.[26] I would suggest that this notion of dual competence may be extended from the realm of words to that of concepts. The simultaneous exposure to recitations from the erudite Sanskrit, as well as from the more accessible Bengali texts, created a 'phonetic' grasp over complex conceptual problems in Sanskrit works and a literal, 'linguistic' competence over each idea in vernacular theological expositions. Popular religious songs and literature move with effortless ease into knotted theological problems.

Yet the notion of a shared culture cannot be pressed too far. Ordinary labouring people and women were excluded from a systematic cultivation of interest and understanding by a lack of leisure and by rules of seclusion. Women's religious life was confined to routinized and elaborate worship of the family idol and a range of women's rites. Rashsundari wrote that she and her kinswomen were excluded from these recitations which were held in the outer male quarters.[27]

There was, then, a ubiquity of sacred texts which established a visible, powerful bond between reading and piety. Snatches of recitations would penetrate into women' quarters. At the same time, women interested in a more complete and autonomous understanding were simultaneously stimulated and frustrated by imperfect access. The fact that Vaishnav mendicant women read fluently would aggravate their sense of deprivation. The nineteenth-century premium on women's education and orthodoxy's criticism of reformism added a new twist to the situation. Vociferous abuse of women's education would frighten the woman aching to read. It would also make her realise that very close to her women like herself were being helped to read.

Excited by such fears and such desires, Rashsundari worked out a double-edged position *vis-à-vis* her sansar. She underlined her obedient surrender and unqualified success here. At the same time she took care to indicate that a deeper truth lay veiled behind this apparent reality, this partial truth, this maya that was her sansar.

By evoking this contrast, Rashsundari reserved an interior space for herself which was her faith. She praised open both sansar and faith to accommodate a new figure: the serious yet domesticated woman bhakti who has created her own autonomous and individual life of devotion within the household. The striking thing about her faith was the way she insulted it from all that sansar had to offer to her piety: temples, religious festivals, domestic rites and rituals, the family idol, initiation by the family guru or religious preceptor. Even though she would have participated in all of this, she simply did not write about it. Her autobiography, therefore, resisted her lived life more than it reflected it.

Rashsundari chose to ground her faith in something that her sansar withheld from her—reading and writing about sacred matters. By refusing the resources that prescribed religion gave her as a woman, Rashsundari, in effect, laid claim to an ungendered religious activity, to spiritual equality with men. Within her writing, she chose to withdraw from all collected and shared acts of devotion into an entirely interior activity. In pre-print days, reading, especially of sacred texts, used to be loud or at least mumbled. Since her reading, for a long time, was a deep secret, Rashsundari had to engage in the unusual mode of silent reading. The enforced silence underlined the privacy of the act. This was a space, a room of her own in a household where she had brought nothing of her own, not even her own name: 'The name that I had brought from my father's home has been lost. Here I am just the mother.'[28]

The claim to a non-feminine, individualistic religious practice went against the grain of orthodox prescriptions. It also went beyond nineteenth-century reformism. Reformers did not see women's education as a self-absorbed, self-centred activity. It was meant to be the basis of a companionate marriage, it was to train the woman into a family-oriented piety.[29]

Yet the boldness of Rashsundari's claim went largely unnoticed, in her own world, as well as among later readers. Jyotirindranath Tagore, a leading avant-garde literary figure, wrote an admiring preface to her book. He found her sound housewifely qualities wholly admirable and a fitting rebutttal of orthodox fears about educating the woman.[30] Later on, the nationalist scholar Dinesh Chandra Sen saw in her the self-effacing image of feminine nurture, an icon cast in the image of the Motherland herself.[31]

Partha Chatterjee uses her writing as an example of the appropriation of a woman by a male rationalist enterprise, shaped, in its turn, by Western power-knowledge.[32] Each of these readings unproblematically annexed a complex, highly individual endeavour by a woman to a different agenda and narrative, and considered her story as concluded, exhausted of any other possibility after that. I would suggest that these linear readings could only be enabled by missing out on the various writing devices with which Rashsundari complicated her agenda.

There are difficulties in reading the text since Rashsundari simultaneously occupied two very different sites: that of a conformist housewife in an orthodox family and of an early woman author engaged in the highly public, audacious act of writing about her life. The two compulsions could be fitted together only by devising a novel mix of rhetorical modes that would mask a public unveiling of her life and recast it as an expression of prescribed Vaishnavite self-abnegation and humility as well as of proper womanly modesty and obedience. What emerged out of such constraints was a sustained, skilful and delicate double-speak, enabling her to announce her problems and her triumphs without letting go of her Vaishnav humility or her feminine modesty. It also insidiously portrayed her own gender-marked experiences as highly problematic ones, without using the mode of overt critique.

A multi-intentioned, polysemic content lay blandly enfolded within seemingly innocent statements. In the very first colophon, she described herself as 'lowly, ignorant that I am, and a woman, moreover.'[33] While colophons are conventionally self-deprecating, Rashsundari stretched hers to evoke other possibilities. She bracketed herself within the same categories that Chaitanya had promised to save—the low-caste, the ignorant, the woman. By using near-identical terms she obliquely involved the promised inversion of status, the assurance that lowliness is a condition of salvation. In the same sentence she also subtly reminded us about the remarkable feat that a person as deprived as herself has accomplished by writing the book. And she did all of that without recourse to open self-praise or self-aggrandisement.

She let us know how pretty she was by simply repeating what others had said about her. In fact, she even composed a little verse about her looks: 'Everyone called me a little golden doll.' Her neighbours used to comment on her attractiveness: 'Whoever marries her will be truly blessed.' She would not say that she was a domestic success. She simply said that all her in-laws were extremely kind and no one ever had a word of criticism about her all these years.[34] Indirect statement or reported speech could convey what she could not directly say about herself.

Rashsundari attained a level of sheer mastery in signifying something very different from what she was saying overtly. She did it by a careful framing of her direct statements. She would conclude an episode with pious sentiments, resigning herself to divine will. At the same time, she surrounded it with vivid details that described very painful consequences flowing from her obedience. As a result, the surface message got scrambled and confused so that she appeared compliant, and, also, a victim-figure precisely as a result of that compliance. She had been extremely eager to please others as a child. She began to help out an old and infirm relative with domestic chores without letting others know about it. When her family learnt about it, they praised her so much that she volunteered to do all the housework. All good, womanly instincts, that pleased her family and, later, her readers. She, however, concluded the episode with a surprise sequel that can wrench our thinking on to very different tracks. 'That was the end of my days of playing. Now I worked all the time.'[35] She made only a factual statement about herself, but the words are packed with resonances. Popular folk verses have often repeated the same problem: 'Let us have a last quick game together, for the son of a stranger (i.e., the husband) is coming to take me away and I shall never play again.'[36]

The strategy was deployed with meticulous long-term planning, spread over three chapters, in the course of which she gradually introduced the theme of her secret reading. She prefaced the event with long, vivid and richly-detailed accounts of the gruelling household labour that she regularly performed. There is a moving description of how she had found no time for a single meal for two whole days. She saved the narration from the taint of self-pity or resentment by frequently inserting phrases like: 'Why should I talk of such matters? ... It is shameful to even think of these things.' She finished up with: 'Thinking over the ways of the Lord, I began to laugh. I never mentioned it to anyone.'[37] She had it both ways. She proclaimed her predicament to the whole world through print and she reserved the image of the self-effacing Hindu wife who suffers her deprivations with smiling forbearance.

She conveyed powerfully how a little girl was brutally uprooted from her home and grafted abruptly on an unknown family. It seemed to her that God had given her a life-sentence. 'I have been incarcerated within the prison-house of this sansar. There will be no release for me till the end of my days.' She immediately followed it up with a song of praise. 'The mind is overwhelmed when I ponder over your mercy. You have been kind to your subjected daughter.'[38] Mercy here referred to the fact that her healthy body stood up to this strain. Yet, obviously it was the strength of a slave that God had blessed her with. Again, her use of the somewhat strange word 'subjected' robs God's mercy of some of its content even though her intention had been to indicate that the painful experience bore happy results. Words, intentions, and effects are conjoined in a curious syntax to produce multiple meanings, all at odds with one another. The long-range effect was to build a strong sympathy base for her act of disobedience, her reading. The final impression is one of insidious, delicate, masked expressions of pain that complicate gestures of compliance but that also always stop short of criticism.

At only one place does the dialectic between the submissive devotee and the self-aware victim figure break down, or, rather, Rashsundari chose to snap out of the endless transaction between the two. Towards the end of the third chapter she expanded the prison-house metaphor quite meticulously. Her new home would not relieve her from work to visit her natal home. The few occasions that she did get permission, she was let out for a few days like a prisoner out on parole. Servants would surround her like so many prison-guards. Even when her mother was dying, she was not allowed to pay her last visit. She ended her chapter with a reproach, a cry: 'Dear God, why did you ever make me a part of humanity!'[39] This is one chapter, one statement that ends without a single recuperating word of praise.

Wherever she referred to the social order, she referred to it as a part of God's design.[40] God, thereby, is held responsible for patriarchal oppression, for her own searing experiences. She had an alternative which she chose not to use—that of describing her oppression as a violation of God's will. Her choice indicates something about her relationship with her God. The more smilingly and patiently she offered her devotion the more she underlined the tyranny of his rule. The devotee's surrender accentuates divine despotism rather than absolves it.

Rashsundari's devotion, then, had a more complex design than either willed surrender or critique. That ambiguity and tension inform her manipulation of the *yatra* or folk-theatre metaphor. These theatres, with their travelling companies, their elaborate stage props and musical accompaniment, had acquired tremendous popularity in nineteenth-century villages.[41] The director-cum-manager was called *adhikari*. Rashsundari described God as the adhikari of a play unrolled before her eyes. The play is presumably about her own life, but she is alternately an actor and a spectator while God has scripted and directed it: and he is watching it too, since the whole purpose of the play is to amuse him. The subject of the play has no clue at all as to the direction of the script, nor does she have any control over it. She allows herself to be blindly manipulated.[42]

Interestingly, the only role that she seems to be playing is as the mother of a son.[43] Probably this was so because it is the only empowering role a woman could play. At the end of the act God comes and takes the son away. She copes with the pain by telling herself that it had been only a play, his leela.

God also enacts his many lives (incarnations) before her eyes. There is a crucial difference between her life as theatre and God's lives as yatra. She is helpless before her own life while God scripts his own. He changes roles—as Ram, as Krishna, as Chaitanya—and begins a new play the moment the old one begins to weary him.[44] The metaphor ties up with philosophical speculations on the origins of creation: that creation itself is maya, an illusion conjured up by God to amuse himself. It has personal resonances as well. It expresses not just the spiritual helplessness of the devotee but also the specific social helplessness of the woman whose passivity and fatalism are deeply scored with gender inequalities. A woman's life is lived out in a permanent condition of homelessness—in a literal sense.

A feeling of marginalization had probably accompanied the spread of this immensely popular art form in the nineteenth century, making out within the spectacle the boundaries between the director/author and the actors: between the play on stage and the passive spectators. A mid-twentieth-century novel tried to describe the first destructive impact of this new art form upon a local community. It completely disrupted the older, more collective performances of devotional music where everybody sang about their own bhakti. This gave way to a spectacle, alienated and distant, which could only be passively consumed.[45]

Rashsundari's self-alienated life was a thing of endless surprise, wonder and marvel. The devotee gains a purchase on the divine spectacle of leela at the cost of learning not to identify with her own life.

A possibly exaggerated account of childhood fears creates the space to let God into the narrative. The problems could have been overemphasized since, in a number of ways, Rashsundari was luckier than most girls of her time. Even though she was fatherless, her relatives loved her, and she was brought up by a wise, serene and adoring mother. Since the family was affluent, and the girl pretty, fixing a match was not a problem. In fact, she was kept at home well beyond the usual age of marriage since her mother would not let her go. Even in her new home, the in-laws loved the bride. Her first experiences contrast sharply with the more typical feelings of another girl-bride: 'Every time my mother-in-law looked at me a pint of blood would dry up in my body.'[46]

These facts emerged only incidentally while Rashsundari dwelt on her many fears and anxieties. More childish and sheltered than her companions, she was a butt of their teasing. She also had a morbid fear of kidnappers. In a world filled with troubled apprehensions, the first words about God came from her mother, who tried to remove her fears. This, incidentally, also marks the first appearance of the mother in the narrative, bearing the words of God. It is the only purpose she serves in the autobiography. She tells Rashsundari: 'Why should you fear anything, we have Dayamadhav [the name of the family idol] at home.'[47] It was as if the mother gave birth to the idea of God.

She continued to nurture and develop the idea and to remove other fears. Rashsundari had another bout of terror when she first discovered that she was the daughter of a dead man. 'All these years I had thought that I was just my mother's child.' She wept at the new discovery because the notion of a dead father aroused the dread of ghosts. Her mother consoled her again with the name of Dayamadhav.[48]

The third time that God's name was invoked, and developed at some length, was when a fire broke out at home and the frightened children ran away and lost their way. Their cries of distress brought out some villagers who took them home. Rashsundari thought that Dayamadhav had heard her cries and come to her rescue. The mother then explained the different grades within divinity which were interconnected as sedimented layers within one single truth. Human agency had been used by Dayamadhav to rescue children who had appealed to him. Yet, while Dayamadhav was the specific name and shape in which God was contained within their particular family, the Great Lord who rule over the whole world was Parameshwara. 'He belongs to everybody. He has created everything in this world, he loves everyone, he is the Lord God of us all.'[49]

Although the first mention of God was as a family idol which seemed to affirm a polytheistic divinity, eventually a monotheistic God is established. From the third section till nearly the end of the book God is called Parameshwara. The designation is curious since this is an appellation rarely attached to Krishna. On the other hand, Christian missionaries and monotheistic religious reformers like the Brahmos called their God by this name. Rashsundari seems to have extrapolated a non-Vaishnav designation to her God. He is also, for much of the book, a curiously faceless, abstract figure without any of the lush and vivid mythological attributes of Krishna. The family idol, a central figure within a devout Vaishnav household, is never once described in the book.

When Rashsundari came to know about God, 'on that very day my mind sprouted the first seeds of intelligence.'[50] Her way to God was thus through thought. It was the cerebral way, not the pietistic, emotive, ecstatic or ritualistic ways that are commonly associated with women's devotion. This way would be along an intellectual trajectory of reading and writing.

God came to Rashsundari not as an icon nor as myth and ritual, but as words spoken by the mother. The mother came into the text only to bear the words of God. The two were linked within a single structure to remove a nervous child's constant fears. The structure broke down when, at twelve, Rashsundari heard that she was about to be married off. Terrified, she rushed to her mother to ask: 'Mother, will you give me away to a stranger?' Her mother tried to rise to the occasion with a denial. But this time her words rang false and she was crying.[51]

Rashsundari's world—held together by her mother's reassurances—crashed around her as she realised that her mother was lying and that her mother was, after all, as helpless and vulnerable as Rashsundari herself. She was a woman. In utter terror, her words choking her, Rashsundari tried to retrieve something of the early structure of reassurance. 'Would Parameshwara come with me?' Her mother replied that he would go with her wherever she went. Bereft of the precious, living, human mediation of the mother, a male God was left to Rashsundari as the memory of her mother's speech, as the promise of reassurance. He was, therefore, both a residue and an extension of her mother. A male divinity had to be imagined who was free from the limits and vulnerabilities of a mother. At the same time he was entirely a creation of that mother.

When the terrible, unbelievable ordeal of parting arrived, and the little girl lost her home, her birthplace, her mother and every face she had known all her life, Parameshwara was the only bit of her old identity that she carried with her from her old life. In a new place, filled with total strangers, where even the spoken dialect would be different, she went over his name again and again within her terrified heart: 'I admit it was only out of fear that I called out to you.'[52] She made clear what location and function she had allotted to God in her life—deliverance from fear and pain. What she is silent about, yet what comes through from her subsequent experiences, is how inadequate God was to the task. By the end of the book the early expectation had gone. God was now a powerful, whimsical figure who played with her life. She could only hope that he would show pity for her. 'Even if you are cruel to me, I shall call you the Merciful One.'[53]

Her mother had been, above all, her teacher, her guru. Rashsundari took great care to establish that she had none other. Even though in Vaishnav households the family guru is a powerful figure who ritually purifies the body and the mind, Rashsundari did not mention hers. Nor did she refer to her other prescribed religious activities. She made the narrative bare of all influences that would have gone into the making of her religious life. Both Pabna and Faridpur had old and strong Vaishnav associations,[54] but *Amar Jiban* is silent about them. What is most striking is that she did not discuss what the sacred texts, the ones she had mastered against such odds, had to teach her.

By making her mother bear the entire weight of a complete religious instruction that must have actually been acquired piecemeal through her entire life, Rashsundari endowed her mother with a specifically nineteenth-century role. In Vaishnav hagiographies, the mother is a source of nurture but not of instruction. For the nineteenth-century Hindu revivalist-nationalist, on the other hand, the Hindu woman, being untainted by Western pedagogy and values, being ruled by Hindu scriptures alone, had escaped colonization—in contrast to the Hindu man. As the sole bearer of a lost freedom and as the site of a new nation, she was the purest influence and source of instruction within the Hindu home.[55] Liberal reformers, on the other hand, believed in the modern pedagogical principle that an enlightened mother was the best early guide for eduction as well as for morals. In fact, they based their arguments for educating women on this conviction.[56]

Obliquely, this move of Rashsundari made a larger point. The mother's teaching, however, potent, had ceased in her life from the age of twelve. From a very early age, then, Rashsundari's spiritual growth would have been self-made. As we shall see, *Amar Jiban* is a jealously individualistic narrative, shaping the material of her life around the lonely efforts of a heroic individual. In this sense, too, it is a typically nineteenth-century product, with something of the *bildungsroman* about it. Debendranath Tagore's *Atmacharit* was an autobiography similarly patterned on a lonely spiritual quest where he gathered the ingredients of his religion all by himself. The difference lies in the organizational, mobilizational, institutionalizing imperatives that structure the later part of his book.[57] Rashsundari's gender-constrained religious activism, in contrast, had to be confined to reading and writing.

Rashsundari wrote out her life as a series of trials that she survived with God's grace. We have referred to her childhood fears. The real ordeal, however, was married life. Marriage began with a forced parting from everything she loved. The event was synonymous with great grief, with copious weeping. Bengali girls were generally married off very early, for ritual compulsions demanded that they should be in their husband's home when puberty set in. The loss of the natal home at childhood has been described in all nineteenth-century women's writings as a traumatic experience, uprooting a child from the security of her own home and exiling her forever to the mercy and control of total strangers.[58] Other women recorded excruciating memories—how a mother went blind with continuous tears after losing her daughter this way.[59] A genre of devotional songs described the annual three-day visit of the Goddess Durga to her parent's home. They were immensely popular all over Bengal in the eighteenth and nineteenth centuries—at a time of growing affluence among some upwardly mobile agricultural and commercial castes and the spread of Brahmanical patriarchal customs among them.[60] Already, sixteenth-century law codes had hardened Brahmanical gender injunctions—including the propagation of infant marriage for girls—to shore up the declining socio-political hegemony of Brahmins after centuries of Muslim rule in Bengal, large-scale conversions to Islam, and the spread of syncretic practices.[61] The powerful estate of Krishnagore had in the eighteenth century reinforced Brahmanical orthodoxy.[62] The *agamani* songs about Durga's mother and her searing pain as the time of parting draws near, would, then, have a double resonance for Bengali women. Women, by their late twenties, could well be daughters aching for their mothers as well as young mothers pining for their married daughters.[63]

Rashsundari described the ways which regulated her movements as a new bride as the rules of old times or *sekal*. Hers was a pious, deeply orthodox Hindu family, governed by Brahmanical injunctions and untouched by Westernized, reformist values. This was precisely the authentic Hindu space that militant Hindu revivalist-nationalists of the nineteenth century valorized as the domain of residual freedom, an abode of happiness that constrasted with the deprivations and humiliations of colonial rule. An icon was constructed of the true patriotic subject, the good Hindu woman with her simple dress, her ritually pure conchshell bangles and red vermillion mark, her happy surrender and self-immersion in the sansar, and her endless bounty and nurture expressed by cooking and feeding. She was charged with an immense aesthetic, cultural and religious load in nationalist writings, as Annapurna, the goddess of food, as the bounteous Motherland.

Apart from reformist contestations of this image of Hindu female virtue, women's own writing from the 1860s seriously interrogated its foundations.[64] These shared two major planks of criticism—the withholding of education from women, and the trauma of early patrilocality and forced planting of little girls in new families. Rashsundari, who was a pious Hindu housewife herself, occupying the concrete social space marked out by the icon, and who otherwise was careful to surround her statements with sentiments of obedience, was nevertheless quite outspoken in her assessment of the system. 'I am filled with loathing when I look back on all that ... the coarse clothes, the heavy cumbrous jewellery, the conchshell bangles, the vermilion mark ...' She used images of blindness, of dumbness and of paralysis, of the blind-folded bullock moving mindlessly round the oil-press, to describe the gamut of injunctions that governed the bride.[65] She was condemned to strict silence, to limited, awkward movements, to the absence of all contact with most older and male relatives. Since the boundaries of permitted movement varied in each family, no bride was quite sure of the exact scope of restrictions. As a much older wife with several children of her own, Rashsundari had thought it might be forbidden for her to appear before her husband's horse. Throughout her text she enviously compared her fate with that of 'modern' girls who were blessed with education 'these days.' In her day, everyone believed that 'women were fit for nothing except domestic drudgery.'[66]

She herself was obedient and her in-laws affectionate. Yet, grafting remained a pain-filled process. Incarceration was the recurrent image for this stage. 'I was caged for life, in this life there will be no escape for me ... I was snatched away from my own people ... and given a life sentence ... I would shed tears in secret but since I had to spend my life with these people, I eventually became a tamed bird ...'[67] The love she gave her in-laws was not spontaneous affection but the result of training and necessity, the habit of the caged bird.

At fourteen Rashsundari was looking after the entire household without any help. Her world was the kitchen, and her 'cage' had distinct spatial connotations. She was in charge of the many ritual requirements of the family idol, she nursed her mother-in-law, looked after a stream of unexpected guests and cooked two meals every day for at least twenty-five people.[68] Her account of her daily work deconstructed the iconic figure of the contented female in two crucial ways: she listed her service to the family idol as work and not as the emotional release and aesthetic gratification that it is meant to be for women. She also went into a very full account of the gruelling work-schedule, although all the time thanking God for her strong body which could take the strain. She thus rid the image of womanly nurture of its association with emotional fulfillment and remade it in the image of a slave. She made a similar reconstruction with the image of mothering. The hard, unassisted, continuous work involved in nursing a series of twelve babies in quick succession was conventionally read as the cherished devotional or patriotic icon of happy, self-effacing motherhood. Rashsundari restored the feel of slog to the image. All night a stream of children would keep her up. 'One would say, Mother, I want to piddle, another would say, Mother, I am hungry, the other one would say, Mother, take me in your arms.'[69]

She extended the same idea with brilliant success to the theme of food—on cooking, feeding, eating and fasting. She literally spent her entire youth cooking and feeding others. In the prosperous East Bengal countryside, among affluent families, the preparation of excellent meals of immense variety and skill was a constant preoccupation. Women were graded, and family memory organized, according to the meals that had been brilliantly prepared and lovingly served by women. On the other hand, ritual fasting and even starving as a matter of preference among women was valorized in a whole range of prescriptive texts and literature.[70] Her eating was a peculiarly non-structured, uncertain activity. Nineteenth-century behavioural manuals that taught women proper deportment in their new homes confessed their helplessness on the matter. 'My child, I can give you no good advice on this. If you serve yourself, you will be called shameless. If you wait for others to serve you, you may have to go without food.'[71] Even in far more 'modern' families, women faced the same problem.[72] In fact, femininity was crucially tied up with a professed indifference to food, to the habitual neglect of eating. Interestingly, the same prescriptive authorities that had relegated women to a lifetime of not-eating in the middle of endless feeding, and had fixed this role in the image of Annapurna, the goddess of food, had also imagined the terrifying counter-image of Kali, the primal female force that devours Creation itself. Female saints would often exercise their saintly privilege with bouts of voracious eating and with demands of being physically fed.[73]

Rashsundari described her acts of cooking and feeding as hard work. She made no reference to the possibility of excitement in cooking, the gratification of feeding loved ones, the aroma and taste of memorable dishes that she would have prepared as a successful housewife. She frankly and humorously talked about her senile greed for good food in old age, as if age had somehow defeminised her and released her from prescribed inhibitions.[74] She emptied out the act of cooking from associations of creativity and filled it with hard labour, with deprivation. She refused the iconic privilege of Annapurna.

She was quite clear about the deprivational aspect. 'Forget about being cared for in other ways, most days I did not even get to eat two proper meals.'[75] She once went without a meal for two days since guests arrived without notice and the high standards of family hospitality had to be maintained by the wife, who offered up her own meals. At night, her children would get up and interrupt her meals and she had to stop eating to tend them since their bawling disturbed her husband's sleep.[76] It was not possible to share the problem with him. Rashsundari chose to refer to Krishna as a father, although in sacred myths Krishna played a number of familial roles, but never that of the father. She refused the more conventional feminine approaches to him—as his mother or his lover. As a Bengali woman, both those roles would have involved her in the act of providing nurture. She was tired of being the source of nurture. In the realm of religious imagination, she needed to create a source of stable nurture for herself.

If the kitchen was a cage, so was the sexual body of the young woman. Rashsundari's first child was born when she was eighteen. Till the age of forty-one, she gave birth, as roughly two-yearly intervals, to eleven more children. Lying-in rooms were notoriously insanitary and childbirth was surrounded with a range of extremely exacting rituals.[77] Vaishnav households had somewhat more lenient ritual expectations, and that, along with the mild and healthy climate of her birthplace, probably accounts for her unimpaired good health.[78] Childbirth would still have been a dangerous moment in her life. Census figures show that in the nineteenth century the highest incidence of mortality among Bengali women occurred in their most fertile years.

Rashsundari summed up these years in her life in a few terse words: 'The Lord only knows what I went through all these years.'[79] We find little about her husband in *Amar Jiban*. We are told that he would be impatient when babies cried at night, that, bound as he was by strong ties of custom, he was of no help to her in her desire to read. He cried when she was seriously ill and given up for dead, but he also said stoically: 'Is she gone? So let it be then.'[80] There are no memories in the book about the time when they were young together. His own death was described as a social catastrophe, making her ritually inauspicious. She said that she had lost her 'crown of gold', not that she had lost a limb—which would have signified the loss of something far greater than social status. She followed it up with an extraordinarily strange statement: 'I do not regret what God had willed.'[81] If convention demanded that she did not speak openly about her sexual relations with him, it certainly would not recommend such fatalistic stoicism in reporting her husband's death. Other widows had left long, loving accounts of their husband's last moments.[82] She also departed from the norms of a widow's speech in a small but significant way: whereas widows are expected to see their prolonged life as a curse, Rashsundari thanked God for her long life.[83] There was no effort at preserving the memory of her sexually active years, except as a bind. The husband, as a partner in that life, is equally absent. Was that entirely the effect of inhibition?

The Hindu marriage system, which revivalist-nationalists valorized as a domain of affect, compensating for a miserable colonized existence in the public sphere—a domain which they were committed to save from all colonial intervention—initiated the conjugal relationship with a traumatic separation from the childhood home and an abrupt termination of childhood. Cohabitation was ritually obligatory from the onset of puberty, often when the girl's body was not mature enough to sustain sexual penetration.[84] There was no question of choice, of consent, of cancelling the tie and shifting to another partner, however incompatible the marriage or whatever the problems with the husband. The husband's polygamy or even his death would not dissolve the marriage bond. The sexually most active years in a woman's life would coincide with the years of most exacting labour. It would also lead to dangerous and draining childbirths. In this situation it is, perhaps, necessary to read her silence about her sexual experiences not as inhibition, as repressed speech, but as a turning away from her own sexuality which would appear as little more than a trap for her.

Rashsundari was forty when her first son was married. She did not conceive after that.[85] It was customary for parents to terminate regular sexual relations at that point, and we may assume that this was what happened to her, since forty-one was too early for an onset of the infertile phase. Rashsundari described her middle age, which was presumably free from sexual activity, with affection and nostalgia. It was a time of relative power and privilege, a point where she emerged as a figure of considerable authority within the household. She was the mother of grown-up sons, a mother-in-law. For the first time, she used the words, 'My sansar.'[86] It was a time of integration.

The new experiences of her life coincided with a new view of religion. At the very end of the book she gave conventional and familiar names, forms and myths to God. For the first time, too, she addressed him by the name of the family idol. A self-created God, wrested and saved from her mother's home, was merged into a shared, collective devotional knowledge. She ascribed to herself the usual range of religious practices permitted to a Vaishnav woman of means: endowing the family idol, providing for an annual congregational feast. Her religion now expressed a family of property and status, and no longer the lonely struggles of the bhakti. Yet something new remained in her endeavour. The money she endowed came not out of family inheritance but from the proceeds of her own publication.[87]

In Vaishnavite hagiographies, closeness to divinity is established through trances or through miracle-making abilities. Rashsundari had no claims to extraordinary powers since they were incompatible with her secure housewife status. Yet her own signs had to be in some ways within the realm of the marvellous, the unusual, to establish the seriousness of her bhakti. She formulated a series of what we may call tamed, domesticated, everyday miracles, non-supernatural in manifestation, yet sufficiently wondrous to be ascribed to divine inspiration. They were located in changes within her own body, in her ability to dream strange dreams, and, finally, in her ability to read.

Certain normal, expected bodily changes were interpreted as signs of a wonderful and persistent care with which God had altered her body for the different stages of life. Her youthful body had been healthy, pretty and fertile. In middle age the strength remained but fecundity dried up, as befitted the respected seniormost woman in a large household. As the house filled up with a younger generation, and her responsibilities dwindled, her strong body began to age and decay, shedding its old capabilities. She now awaited her last journey across life with a lightened load. With this account Rashsundari defamiliarized a normal female life-cycle by imparting a sense of wonder at the perfect fit between the body and its changing functions. The familiar body was made strange, exotic and holy, the sign and site of God's handiwork. 'Plain eyes can see it quite clearly.'[88]

The supremacy of sense-perceptions as the primary source of religious knowledge, and of the human body as the object of this knowledge, tie up with strands within body-centred popular esoteric cults. Yet, unlike them, Rashsundari did not seek to manipulate and stretch the limits of the ordinary body. To her, the normal changes themselves were infinitely wondrous. The cultic practices involved a relationship with a male body and the object was to impart great powers to that. In a way, then, it was a replication of the patriarchal order on a different register. Rashsundari's religious project, however, was autonomous and self-centred.

Her dreams were occasionally anticipations of events that were about to happen. She dreamed, for instance, that she was reading the *CB* before she had learned to read. The next day, accidentally, she managed to identify the book. It had, therefore, been a message from God. Similarly, she had a vision of a shower of golden flowers, symbolizing the birth of a male grandchild. She also dreamt of things that had happened without her conscious knowledge—for instance, the death of a son. She even saw a ghost once.[89] These experiences were close to abilities that a whole range of otherwise ordinary women might possess, powers of a rather low grade that singled them out as curiosities rather than as people touched by the divine. Rashsundari, however, linked them up with a superior spiritual competence by pointing out the parallel with dreams seen by fathers of Ram or Chaitanya.[90] Dreams, therefore, became a privileged access to a superior reality.

The unexpected retrieval of a long-lost object in an unchanged, unblemished condition, was interpreted as yet another sign from God.[91] Some essence of herself had remained in his safe custody, retaining its old lustre even though her mortal body had gone into decay. The retrieval of lost objects, we must remember, was also an essential part of miracle tales.

Her reading was the fourth and most important miracle in Rashsundari's life. She first read a sacred book in manuscript form.

Vaishnav manuscripts were profusely produced from the seventeenth century onwards, and manuscripts remained much in use till the mid-nineteenth century. These were, however, awkward to handle since the stained paper was too fragile to be sewn together. Leaves were pressed between illumined wooden covers. Each page had to be detached while being read.[92] Reading was, therefore, a delicate, time-consuming process, involving careful movement. It acquired the aura of an act of worship. Books were also extremely expensive.

Rashsundari's family possessed quite a few, indicating an unusual degree of investment in reading.

Rashsundari had longed to read since she was fourteen. When she was twenty-five, she dreamt that she was reading the *CB*. The very next day, her husband told a son in her presence to replace it among other manuscripts. She identified the manuscript by its illumination, and later she detached a page and hid it. She also surreptitiously acquired a palm-leaf on which her son was practising letters. Then, over a very long time, and in deepest secrecy, she matched the letters on the leaf with those on the page. With great efforts of memory she also recalled the letters that she had learnt as a little girl and identified them. Eventually, she became *jitakshara*, master of the word, a magnificent term which she coined herself.[93] Much later, she learned to write and read printed books with support from her grown-up sons who had received the new education. 'I discovered that printed letters are the best.'[94]

For a long time, her reading ability remained unsuspected. Only a few maidservants were later trusted with the secret. Much later, her widowed sisters-in-law were told, and, contrary to her apprehensions, they were delighted and eager to learn from her.[95] But for quite some time reading was a forbidden pleasure. It was not an act of rebellion since it was a secret and she did not let it interfere with her other duties and obligations. On the surface, nothing had changed. In reality, a miracle had taken place.

It was a transgression of the deepest kind. She was now a woman with a double-life. As a Vaishnav, Rashsundari used the pattern of transgression that was most familiar to her to describe her condition. She structured it on the mode of the illicit love of Radha for Krishna, the conflict between the woman's religion within sansar and a higher religious urge turning her against it. She used expressions very familiar to the literature of divine illicit love. Her household was against her desire, there was no one to help her, she had no time for it. It split up her very self, yet she acknowledged its divine inspiration. It had taken hold of her entire being. 'I was forever yearning.'[96] It is interesting that orthodox critics of women's education were convinced of an equation between the woman's intellectual desires and her sexual immorality. One kind of transgression was conflated with another kind. When girls' schools were first started in Calcutta, the editor of a Bengali newspaper sarcastically offered his services to teach girls at night.[97] The reformist leader Sibnath Shastri's mother was an educated woman. When his schoolteacher discovered this, he immediately sent her a letter through the little boy, asking her for a secret assignation. If a woman was educated, she must be immoral.[98]

If this was the kind of attitude that Rashsundari expected from her milieu, what were the resources that could have given her hope? Rashsundari said that in her youth she would hear her elders fret about the new-fangled interest in women's education. 'Now, of course, we are ruled by a female sovereign. ... This is the age of Kali.'[99] Victoria's rule was coupled with Kaliyug, the last and most degenerate period within the Hindu time-cycle of four ages. For Rashsundari, the terms would carry very different resonances. If Victoria's rule heralded a modernity that promised education for woman, then it was a resource and not a burden for her. Possibly, a Vaishnav notion of time reinforced her choice. Post-Chaitanya bhakti had welcomed Kaliyug, when the saviour Chaitanya had been born. In this age, women, low-castes, and the ignorant were blessed with a larger possibility for salvation. If this was an age of decline, it was also a time for more generous hopes. Interestingly, this trope within Vaishnav piety found a resonance among the liberal rationalists of the nineteenth century who hoped for a deliverance from social malaise through reform and education. Rashsundari knitted the two kinds of hope together: Kaliyug was a time of love and salvation for all, it was a time when girls were taught to read. 'Blessed, blessed be this Kaliyug.'[100] A Vaishnavite and a gendered construction of time met to contest a dark perspective on modernity that was shared by a traditional Brahmanical orthodoxy and the Hindu revivalist/nationalist alike.[101]

By claiming that God had taught her to read, Rashsundari took her place within the new domain of the great secular miracle-tales of nineteenth-century Bengal. For colonized Bengalis, excluded from most of the exalted public stations of life where their transformative abilities would have registered themselves, a mastery over the new education was the only way of proving individual greatness. A new realm of secular miracle literature had shaped itself around marvellous accounts of such mastery. Rashsundari's book was read as a sign of traditional womanly virtues. Yet its very production places it within the new genre. The appropriation of a radical departure as a traditional virtue was something more than a misreading. It was a process that enabled an absorption of the new into commonsense.

I was interested in *Amar Jiban* not only because it initiates the autobiographical genre in Bengali and because it is one of the earliest examples of women's writing in the language. Nor was it entirely because *Amar Jiban* is a rare and early example of an individual woman's devotional quest, articulated in her own words. My interest was sharpened as I came to realize how different the text had turned out to be from what I had expected of a woman's autobiography, a woman's writing, a woman's bhakti.

The erotic mode had been singularly privileged within Vaishnavism and among popular, esoteric cults. For a lot of women, bounded by an unbending patriarchy, it carried access to an imagined erotic relationship of immense richness. Krishna could also be appropriated as one's child, framing the absorbing female experience of mothering within a more perfect world of meanings. Rashsundari's Parameshwara, however, was a very different God. He had an ambiguous and problematic role in her life.

There were other departures as well. It would be simple-minded to posit a straight connection between female subjectivity and female writing, to assume that the latter reflects the former in a direct, unmediated way. In fact, for the writing woman, the act of writing itself reconstitutes her subjectivity in radically new ways. Yet, a woman's writing is far too easily related to the cultural world it came out of. In *Amar Jiban*, on the other hand, there is very little by way of the direct speech of women, or speech-effects specifically associated with the woman's world—no proverbs, riddles, tales, pungent and earthy idioms. Her prose is far removed from everyday, colloquial forms. The language is definitely not gender-marked.

In sharp contrast to expectations from women's writings, the book is astonishingly bare of visual or sensuous content. There are no descriptions of exterior landscapes, nor of domestic scenes. There is no impression of taste, sound or smell. The objects she handled, the spaces she passed through, the faces she saw bear no features in her narrative. The great rivers and waterways of Pabna and Faridpur—Padma, Brahmaputra, Ariyal Khan—are condensed into the single image of a boat-journey through the rivers of life. They also shape a dream-sequence where her dead son comes to meet her on a tiny boat, across the great, melancholy expanses of a river. Events that took place around her are similarly condensed. There is a brief poem on an epidemic fever at her Faridpur village.[102] But there is very little about anything else. At the time the book was being revised, her birthplace Pabna had became the seat of a highly-organized peasant agitation against the arbitrary cesses and rent-enhancements that a group of landlords had imposed on tenants. Around the same time, Untouchable cultivator castes of Faridpur had gone on strike to improve their low ritual status, and had refused to work for the upper-caste gentry.[103] Rashsundari was a landlord's daughter and a landlord's wife. She, however, made no mention of these events even though they must have made a considerable stir in her milieu.

*Amar Jiban* is a curiously self-absorbed narrative. Other people appear simply to make a very specific point about her and then they disappear. They do not have an independent life of their own within her text, nor do they live out relationships with one another. It is uncompromisingly non-dialogic. The husband, who had been given a few perfunctory references in the main body of the text, was granted a separate, brief section towards the end of the first part of the book because, she felt, people would want to know about him. A curiously impersonal obituary was therefore appended, for narrative requirements, not because she wanted to talk about him.[104]

She turned the narrative focus intensely and exclusively upon herself, first of all by abstracting herself from her concrete world. 'I came to Bharatvarsha (India), and spent a long time here. This body of mine, this mind, this life itself have taken different forms.'[105] She lived out her life in two villages. They are, however, absent, except as mere names. Nor are there more intimate, familiar locales—the sub-division, the district or even the province. Her time-scale is oddly precise, very different from *CB*, *CC*. She departed from popular, rural ways of patterning time and memory: pinning down a human event by referring to a natural one like a flood or a famine, or by referring to an event of local importance. There is no local time, village time, family time. She gives herself nothing less than a whole sub-continent and almost an entire century to live in.

In their larger historical–geographical dimensions these landmarks were remote to her lived life. Yet, evidently, they were meaningful to the design of her self-created, narrated life. At the time she was writing, a united Indian empire had emerged, renewed and revamped after a sub-continental uprising.[106] Bharatvarsha, then, was an effect of a new political reality. The name also occurs in the *CB*.[107] The Vaishnavite pilgrimage circuit, spreading from Nabadwip in Bengal to the Puri temple in Orissa (which was a gateway to South Indian temples), to Mathura-Vrindavan in North India and Dwarka in Western India, gave Vaishnavas a vivid sense of a large, sacred geography. Again, when the book was being written, the nineteenth century had already self-consciously separated itself out from an undifferentiated mass of time, a recurrent replay of identical historical cycles. It had come to see itself as the site of a new and unique history, which gave time a direction, a teleology.[108]

Rashsundari needed this large context to abstract herself from her actual lived life. She transcended its narrow limits and its inability to intersect with grand historical narratives by giving herself the largest possible temporal and spatial frames that she could relate to. Her life could now become an adequate site for the play of a grand divine purpose.

Autobiography, as a genre, most obviously confuses the boundaries between the word and the world, deluding us that it is a life we are reading and not a text. I found that *Amar Jiban* thwarted these expectations persistently. In very many ways, its textuality is underlined by the distance it sets up between Rashsundari's lived experiences and her narrative preoccupations. It was through writing a book that the life she wanted to express could live.

In its textuality and conditions of being, *Amar Jiban* was a nineteenth-century production, although Rashsundari seldom reflected upon her times.[109] They gave her a publisher, a printer, a market for her writing. They created a modern readership that would want to read about an ordinary woman. They also gave her a language that she could write in—a vernacular prose which was accessible to a neo-literate person with no training in the classical languages or in English. It was a prose that could express the life-events of a housewife as well as the devotional exhortations of a devotee.[110]

If nineteenth-century processes had enabled the writing of *Amar Jiban*, they remained incomplete, even botched-up. And here I have a personal debt to recount. A hundred years after Rashsundari, in the early decades of this century, a grand-aunt of mine was seized with the desire to read. Her affluent, educated, upper-caste family was uncooperative and she had to keep her desire a secret. The only reading matter that would come her way were paper packets carrying groceries from shops into her kitchen. The paper came out of torn pages from schoolboys' exercise books, scored over with sums and spelling lessons. While cooking the evening meal, she would pore over them in the flickering light from her hearth-fire.

Rashsundari's life and writing stood at the confluence of two orders of patriarchy, and of women's desires. On the one hand, there was her relationship with the bhakti tradition. It allowed the woman, seeking an excess beyond a homebound existence, a certain ambiguous space. On the other hand, there were her own times, when a new system of liberal pedagogy came to include women as its target. This, however, was riven with doubts about its own agenda. If a liberal pedagogy was a weapon of the colonizer, it asked itself, would the education of the woman not indicate a possible surrender to colonization? In any case, liberal reformism operated within severely narrow margins, even inside its middle-class boundaries.[111] For other women, seized with the hunger for the written word, it had little to offer beyond stray pages torn out of school exercise books.

## Notes and References

1. Rashsundari Debi, *Amar Jiban* [*AJ*], pp. 18, 22, 31, 44. Reprint of 1897 edition in *Atmakatha*, *Ananya* publications (Calcutta, 1981). *AJ* was first published in 1876. A second, enlarged version came out in 1897, a third one in 1906, and a fourth edition appeared in 1956.

2. *AJ*, p. 23.

3. Ibid., p. 21.

4. Vrindaban Das, *Sri Chaitanyacharitamrita* (ed.), Kanchan Basu (Calcutta, 1986), p. 143. Vishnu is the preserver of Creation who has taken on different incarnations

in different ages to save and protect the world. From early medieval times, major devotional traditions developed around the incarnation of Krishna who spent his youth among the low-caste cowherds of Vrindaban, which devotees associate with the important pilgrimage centre located at modern Uttar Pradesh. Later, he became the king of Dwarka and played a major role in the battles which the epic *Mahabharata* narrates. Chaitanya, who founded a massive, popular devotional movement in Bengal, was born in 1486 in a Brahmin Vaishnav family at Nabadwip, the major centre of Brahmanical scholarship in medieval Bengal. A noted scholar himself, he later became an ascetic, and preached an extremely emotional form of bhakti that was accessible to all castes and which required public congregational singing and dancing in Krishna's name. His acolytes started a vast proselytization campaign in all parts of Bengal. A group of disciples went to Vrindaban and prepared a theological canon for Bengali Vaishnavas. Chaitanya was deified in his lifetime and became a central figure of adoration. He died around 1533. *CB* was composed about fifteen years after his death. Interestingly, the Chatianya movement generated the first (and a very rich) corpus of biographical literature in the Bengali language. Studies of the Vaishnav movement in Bengal are vast and highly interesting. I have particularly used S.K. De, *Early History of the Vaisnava Faith and Movement in Bengal* (Calcutta, 1961); Ramakanta Chakrabarti, *Vaisnavism in Bengal, 1486–1900* (Calcutta, 1985); Hitesranjan Sanyal, *Bangla Kirtaner Itihas* (Calcutta, 1989).

5. *AJ*, p. 41.

6. Ibid., part II.

7. Ramakanta Chakrabarti, chapters 4 and 5.

8. Sukumar Sen, *Bangla Sahityer Itihas* (Calcutta, 1965).

9. It was particularly detailed about Chaitanya's early years. Although its accessibility made it immensely popular its scholarship was not very highly thought of.

10. Sukumar Sen, Introduction to Krishnadas Kaviraj, *Chaitanyacharitamrita* (New Delhi, 1963).

11. Accounts of holy women in June McDaniel, *Madness of the Saints: Ecstatic Religion in Bengal* (Chicago, 1989), Swami Gambhiranand, *Shri Ramakrishna Bhaktamalika* (Calcutta, 1952).

12. R.C. Zaehner, *Hindus Scriptures* (Calcutta, 1992).

13. Satish Chandra Chatterjee, 'Hindu Religious Thought', in K.W. Morgan (ed.), *The Religion of the Hindus* (Delhi, 1987); U. Bhattacharyya, *Bharatdarshanshar* (Calcutta, 1949).

14. Sudhir Chakrabarti, *Sahebdhani Sampradaya O Tader Gan* (Calcutta, 1985); Manindra Mohan Bose, *The Post Chaitanya Sahajiya Cults of Bengal* (nd, Calcutta reprint, 1986).

15. S.K. De, *Early History.*

16. Thomas J. Hopkins, *The Social Teaching of Bhagavat Purana*; J.A.B. van Buitenen,

'On The Archaism of the Bhagavat Purana', in Milton Singer (ed.), *Krishna: Myths, Rites and Attitudes* (University of Hawaii, 1966).

17. Kaviraj, *Chaitanyacharitamrita*, p. 616.

18. W. Ward. *A View of the History, Literature and Religion of the Hindoos*, vol. 2 Serampore, 1815).

19. Ibid.

20. Ramakanta Chakravarti, *Vaisnavism in Bengal*. Also Hitesranjan Sanyal, *Bangla Kirtaner Itihas* (Calcutta, 1989).

21. Hitesranjan Sanyal, *Bangla Kirtaner Itihas*; ibid.; Asit Kumar Bandopadhyaya, *Bangla Sahityer Itibritta*, vol. 5 (Calcutta, 1985).

22. *Amar Jiban*.

23. Ibid., p. 8.

24. See Vrindabandass, *Chaitanya Bhagavat*, for a forceful attack on the empty arrogance of Brahmin scholars.

25. W.J. Wilkins, *Modern Hinduism: Being an Account of the Religion and Life of the Hindoos in North India* [1887] (New Delhi, 1987).

26. Paul Singer, 'Book Of The Hours And The Reading Habits Of The Later Middle Ages', in Roger Chartier (ed.), *The Culture Of Print—Power and the Uses of Print in Early Modern Europe* (Cambridge, 1989).

27. *Amar Jiban*, p. 37.

28. Ibid., p. 56.

29. Ghulam Murshid, *Reluctant Debutante: Responses of Bengali Women to Modernisation* (Rajshahi, 1983). Also *Bamabodhini Patrika* (Calcutta, 1863).

30. Preface to *Amar Jiban*, 1897 edition.

31. Preface to *Amar Jiban*, 1957 edition.

32. Partha Chatterjee, *The Nation and Its Fragments*, *op. cit.*, chs. 6 and 7.

33. *Amar Jiban*, p. 2.

34. Ibid., p. 19, p. 7.

35. Ibid., p. 14.

36. Bhabataran Datta, *Bangladesher Chhara* (Calcutta, n.d.).

37. *Amar Jiban*, p. 26.

38. Ibid., p. 17.

39. Ibid., p. 27.

40. Ibid., p. 26.

41. Subir Raychoudhury (ed.), *Bilati Yatra Theke Swadeshi Theatre* [translation required] (Jadavpur University, 1971).

42. *Amar Jiban*, p. 70.

43. Ibid., p. 71.

44. Ibid., pp. 73–75.

45. Advaita Mallabarman, *Titash Ekti Nadir Nam* [translation required] (Calcutta, 1956).

46. Saradasundari Debi, *Atmakatha,* first published Dacca, 1913. Reprinted in *Atmakatha* (Calcutta, 1981), p. 7.

47. *Amar Jiban*, p. 8.

48. Ibid., p. 9.

49. Ibid., p. 12.

50. Ibid.

51. Ibid., p. 14.

52. Ibid., p. 18.

53. Ibid., p. 72.

54. Ramakanta Chakravarti, *Vaisnavism in Bengal.*

55. See Tanika Sarkar, 'Hindu Wife, Hindu Nation: Domesticity and Nationalism in Nineteenth-century Bengal,' in Tanika Sarkar, '*Hindu Wife, Hindu Nation: Community, Religion and Cultural Nationalism*' (New Delhi, 2001).

56. Ghulam Murshid, *Reluctant Debutante.*

57. Debendranath Tagore, *Atmacharit* (Calcutta, 1898). Reprinted in *Atmakatha.*

58. Kailashbashini Debi, *Hindu Mahilaganer Durabashta* (Calcutta, 1863), would be a particularly good example.

59. Gnanadanandini Debi, 'Smritikatha,' in Indira Debi (ed.), *Puratani* (Calcutta, 1957).

60. Tanika Sarkar, 'Hindu Wife, Hindu Nation.'

61. S.K. De, *Vaisnava Faith and Movement in Bengal.*

62. *Diwan Kartikeyachandra Rayer Atmajibancharit* (Calcutta reprint, 1956).

63. Tanika Sarkar, 'Hindu Wife, Hindu Nation.'

64. Kailashbhashini Debi, *Narishiksha* (Calcutta, 1884).

65. *Amar Jiban*, p. 21 and p. 31.

66. Ibid., p. 33.

67. Ibid., p. 19.

68. Ibid., p. 24.

69. Ibid., p. 29.

70. Nandalal Seal, *Vratakatha* (Calcutta reprint, 1930). A whole host of behavioural manual for women, written in the late nineteenth century, advised a cultivated disregard for food.

71. Saudamini Gupta, *Kanyar Prati Upadesh* (Dacca, third edition, 1918).

72. Even in the highly enlightened Tagore family, married women faced a disconcerting uncertainty in relation to a regular flow of meals. See Gnanadanandini Debi, 'Smritikatha.'

73. See lives of Lakshmididi and Gopaler Ma in Swami Gambhirananda, *Shri Ratmakrishna Bhaktamalika* (Calcutta, 1952). Also June McDaniel, *Madness of the Saints.*

74. *Amar Jiban*, p. 70.

75. Ibid., p. 24.

76. Ibid., p. 25.

77. W.J. Wilkins, *Modern Hinduism*, p. 9.

78. Ibid., p. 10.

79. *Amar Jiban*, p. 24.

80. Ibid., p. 55.

81. Ibid., p. 45.

82. See Saradasundari Debi, *Atmakatha*. Also Kailashbashini Debi, '*Atmakatha*', in *Atmakatha*, vol. 2 (Calcutta, 1982).

83. *Amar Jiban*, p. 78.

84. There was a detailed discussion of the brutal, even fatal effect of sexual penetration into immature female organs during the Age of Consent debates in 1890–91. Prior to 1891, there was no legal bar to cohabiting with wives above the age of ten. See Bengal Government Judicial, FNJ C/17.1, Proceedings 104–117, June 1893.

85. *Amar Jiban*, p. 36.

86. Ibid., p. 32.

87. Ibid., p. 80.

88. Ibid., p. 44.

89. Ibid., pp. 50–51, p. 56, p. 60.

90. Ibid., p. 50.

91. Ibid., pp. 63–64.

92. J.C. Ghosh, *Bengali Literature* (1848), p. 20.

93. *Amar Jiban*, p. 21.

94. Ibid., p. 42.

95. Ibid., p. 38.

96. Ibid., p. 23, p. 28.

97. *Samachar Chandrika* (1831), in Brajendra Nath Bandopadhyaya (ed.), *Sambadpatre Sekaler Katha*, vol. 2 (Calcutta, 1941).

98. Shibnath Shastri, *Atmacharit* (Calcutta, 1952), p. 22.

99. *Amar Jiban*, p. 28.

100. Ibid., p. 77.

101. On the representation of Kaliyug in the nineteenth century, see Sumit Sarkar, 'Kaliyuga, Chakri and Bhakti: Ramakrishna and His Times', in *Economic and Political Weekly*, 18 July 1922.

102. *Amar Jiban*, p. 60. On Pabna and Faridpur, see W.W. Hunter, *The Imperial Gazetteer Of India*, vol. 7, 1883.

103. Ibid.

104. *Amar Jiban*, p. 57.

105. Ibid., p. 2.

106. An earlier reference to *Meyerajar rajatwa* (rule of a female monarch) by the village people shows that Victoria's rule was a widely-known political fact. *Amar Jiban*, p. 23.

107. Vrindabandass, *Chaitanya Bhagavat*.

108. See Sumit Sarkar, 'Kaliyuga, Chakri and Bhakti.'

109. Apart from a reference to Victoria's rule, there is no other mention of any political event of her times. About social developments, she approvingly referred to the growth of women's education and to the spread of print culture.

110. Bengali prose had existed from at least the sixteenth century, but a prose literature came into its own from the early nineteenth century, along with the spread of print.

111. Schools for girls remained largely restricted to Calcutta in the nineteenth century and their numbers were extremely limited. Despite Rashsundari's enthusiastic anticipations, only women from families influenced by liberal reform would enjoy access to education. See Usha Chakrabarti, *Condition of Bengali Women Around the Second Half of the Nineteenth Century* (Calcutta, 1963). The tradition of employing Vaishnav medicant women to educate upper-caste Hindu women remained largely restricted to families with considerable property rights, possibly because of the necessity to train them in property management, if the need arose. See B.C. Pal, *Memories of My Life and Times, vol. 1* (Calcutta, 1932).

# 3.

# The Past in the Present

RUSTOM BHARUCHA

We begin with memory, and more specifically, with the mnemonic devices and learning processes that are nurtured in childhood. Nostalgia, I should emphasize, is not Komalda's* concern here, but as I urge him to reflect on the intricate links between memory, folklore and oral history, he begins of his own accord to draw on very specific games that he played as a child. As I listen to him, I realize how casually he prepares the ground for the insights that follow on the transmission of fairy-tales; orality and literacy; and larger speculations on time, genealogy, and 'cultural memory', in which the identities of specific communities are grounded.

This chapter begins very much at home, within the cultural moorings of Komalda's own Oswal Jain family, but it ends with oral genealogies of tribal communities in Rajasthan. As always the span of Komalada's connections is wide and socially differentiated, even as the contexts of individual cultures are respected and held within the shifting contours of his memory.

## Memory

LOOKING BACK ON MY CHILDHOOD, I REMEMBER A 'MEMORY GAME' THAT I USED to play when I was around five or six years old. By this time I had already begun to write. Someone in the family would place a lot of things on a table—all kinds of household items, like matchboxes, playing cards, utensils, and so on. After we had looked at these objects for a few minutes, they would be concealed under a bed sheet, and then as many of the objects as we could remember had to be written down. The one who remembered the largest number of objects would win. As I recall this game today, I realize that we

Excerpted from Rustom Bharucha, *Rajasthan, An Oral History: Conversations with Komal Kothari*, Penguin Books, New Delhi, 2003.

*Komal Kothari (1929–2004) Indian folklorist who lived and worked in Rajasthan. Made contributions to the study of musical instruments, oral traditions and puppetry. Patron of Manganiyar and Langa music; founded the Rupayan Sansthan for furthering study of Rajasthan's traditions. Editor.

would remember the objects best by placing them in different categories. So, for instance, the *chimta* (tongs), the *katori* (bowl), and the *thali* (plate) would be identified with 'the kitchen'. Even today, when you think of all the intricate memory games that continue to be played all over India, during rituals and festivals, you will find that they are invariably built around the principle of categorizing objects in specific ways.

We used to play this memory game while I was still living in the village of Kapasan, before my family moved to Jodhpur. Here in Kapasan I also remember playing *gulli danda*—one of the most popular children's games in India, which is played with any number of variations in different regions. At the heart of *gulli danda*, I would say, are very intricate calculations which are made on the basis of how far you can throw a stick—the calculations are so minute that at times you have to measure distances in fractions. As a matter of fact, I was very good at fractions and all kinds of problems in arithmetic, as a student at the Sumer School in Jodhpur in my early years.

I still remember Parashuramji, our arithmetic teacher, who would come into class and promptly start writing questions on the blackboard very quickly and in beautiful handwriting. As students we had to work out the answers in our heads and write them down, before Parashuramji would wipe the questions off the board. And then, he would begin his interrogation. While I and my nephew Swatantra, who was the same age as me, invariably scored full marks, many of our classmates would be in trouble. The problem was that Parashuramji had a peculiar way of punishing them. If, for instance, a boy had only got twenty sums correct out of forty, he would expect Swatantra and myself to actually slap the boy twenty times, once for each wrong answer. Naturally, we felt awkward and also a bit scared, because some of the boys were a lot bigger than us, and they could easily fix us after class. So we decided to slap them very lightly. But Parashuramji would have none of this and would then proceed to demonstrate how they should be slapped by slapping us!

Numbers played a very important role in my childhood education, and when I look back on it I realize that we learnt our tables by chanting them in unison on a single note. Mind you, we didn't study tables, as is the normal custom today, from two times two up to twelve. We knew our tables all the way to hundred—and not just the prime numbers, but fractions as well. So we could calculate tables on the basis of one and one fourth, two and a half, one and three quarters, and so on. All these tables had to be recited. Invariably, they were conducted by one guruji, who would sit in the classroom of our *poshal* (elementary school) and make us learn these tables by heart. As the tables got more intricate, we used to explore different pitches; the brighter the student, and the more he wanted to impress the teacher, the higher the pitch he would use and the more accelerated the pace of his rendition. But the basic principle that I would like to stress here is that if you have to learn anything by rote, then you have to *chant* your text. Then only will it enter your deeper memory register.

Each culture has different ways of calculating numbers—for example, we can calculate in fours, using the thumb to count the divisions on the insides of our four fingers in consecutive order—one two three four/five six seven eight/... all the way to sixteen. Sometimes we calculate on the basis of three—one two three/four five six/seven eight nine, and this kind of counting invariably ends on fifteen. Of course, we also count in the 'western' way in which each number is an independent unit—one, two, three, four ... all the way to ten. That's the cut-off point. The intricacy of calculation depends to a large extent on the basic unit of calculations—is it three or four or five? Earlier, when there were sixteen annas to a rupee, for instance, most calculations were based on the unit of four. Sometimes, while working with nomadic communities, like the Kalbelia, for instance, we found that the basic unit of their calculations is eight—never nine or ten. And the amazing thing is that they can calculate up to thousands on the basis of the numeral eight.

It's strange how we remember certain things from our childhood, and at the same time, we forget so much. For instance, while I can still chant some of the tables that I learned in school, I have a hard time remembering nursery rhymes. In fact, I cannot recite *dohas* (couplets) that I knew by heart when I was around twelve years old. My friend Vijay Dan [Detha], on the other hand, can actually talk through poetry. At one time I could have recited for hours and hours on end *chhand alankar* in Hindi, the rules of prosody and rhetorical embellishments—I could have differentiated between different *chhand* like *savaiya*, *muktadam*, *harigitika*, and so on. Today, with difficulty, I might be able to recite one or two dohas, but otherwise, my memory has failed me. Even folk songs I am not able to sing freely. Of course, as soon as a song is sung, I can recognize it; I know how it will proceed melodically, rhythmically, and so on. What I have discovered is that memory operates in different ways, and these differences are linked to specific genres.

## Remembering Stories

Let us turn to stories in this regard. I remember one particular story that my maternal aunt used to tell me as a child. There must have been around five to six children around me at that time, including my younger brother Keshav, who is just sixteen months younger than I am. We would all demand that our aunt tell us the story of Chida-Chidi.[1] And what was the story? It had something to do with a pair of birds who would swing on a string suspended on a well's pulley. One day, this string broke, and the birds fell into the well. I remember what a strong impression this story made on me as a child—but, though it was deeply imprinted somewhere in my memory, for the longest time I couldn't remember it at all. When I started to work on folk stories, then I tried with great difficulty to recall this story and, suddenly, it came alive vividly. At that very moment, I realized that when Chida-Chidi fell into the well, they didn't die as I had imagined earlier; rather, they flew out of the well into the sky. What a relief that moment was for me, because I realized that the birds were alive.

The question, however, that needs to be asked is why my aunt, who must have told us that story over and over again, never told us that the birds flew away. As I understand it today, I would say that we, as listeners, have to realize that the birds flew away. The teller of the tale, in this case my aunt, is not meant to give us the meaning of the story. This I would regard as a very important clue. When we started collecting children's stories, particularly those told to under seven-year-olds, we discovered that in no folk story whatsoever is anything like a moral or a maxim added to the story itself. Folk stories were never meant as teaching aids, which is how they are being used these days. Basically, I would say they were taken to be some sort of realization—but you must be prepared to 'realize' your answers, not necessarily when you hear the story for the first time but at any point in your life.

Nowadays we find that children are taught the moral of a particular tale. This was not the case in the earlier practice of story telling, as I experienced it. In contemporary situations, children are told stories, and are then expected to tell the stories back to the adults in their family during breakfast or whenever. They are quizzed—what did the lion do? What did the rabbit do? And what happened at the end of the story? As the child rattles off the answers, we feel pleased that something has been learned. Story-telling today has a function, which was not the customary practice in earlier times.

One reason for this is that the stories we heard in our childhood were not necessarily shared with anybody else. So, while I remember hearing Chida-Chidi from my aunt, I don't have any recollection myself of telling this story to any of my friends. In other words, I didn't become the carrier of this particular story—it lay deep in my memory for many years, but it was never shared as I am sharing it with you now, or as I have reminisced about it in recent years with many people in different forums. Now, as I have become the carrier of the tale, I realize that there is a certain 'format' in the telling of children's stories. Invariably, they are told by an adult to a child, never by a child to another child. This is one reason why we, as children, never felt the need to tell stories beyond listening to them.

## Modalities of Remembering

The origins of stories are mysterious, but not unknown. When we started collecting folk stories in Borunda, we would begin by asking people if they remembered any story from their childhood. And, almost unfailingly, the answer would be an emphatic 'no'. But when we would persist, sometimes for as long as a month, 'When you were put to sleep, surely someone must have told you a story?', most people would remember being threatened with a slap: 'Go to sleep, or else ...' But then, gradually, the stories would begin to emerge.

Take my elder brother, for example, who came to visit me in Jodhpur shortly before he died at seventy-three. I remember asking him if he remembered anyone telling him a story when he was a child. At first he said, 'Nobody used to tell stories in the family.' So, for the next three to four days, whenever I saw him at breakfast or dinner or tea, I would repeat my question. Finally, one morning he told me that he did remember something, but it was only one line from a story he otherwise no longer remembered. Then I asked him: 'Can you remember who told you the story?' Very vaguely he recalled the name of Heera Bai, who worked as a maidservant in our family; he thought she had told him the story. I asked him further: 'Can you remember who else in the family was around you at that time?' He recalled the company of my two older sisters, Deep Kunwar and Tej Kunwar—Heera Bai would tell the story to these three children, when they would be snuggling under their *rajais* (quilts) on winter nights. 'Can you remember,' I asked, 'where our family was living at that time?' 'Parbatsar,' he recalled. And sure enough, as my mother confirmed for me, my brother must have been around five years old when our family was in Parbatsar, and Deep Kunwar and Tej Kunwar were already born at that time. My mother also recalled Heera Bai, a widow from the Sadh community who must have been around thirty-five to forty years old.

Now, if we take into account all these facts, it is not difficult to confirm the age of the story in question. If a seventy-three-year-old man is recalling a story that was told to him when he was five years old, and the woman telling him the story was around thirty-five to forty years, then, historically, this tale must go back at least one hundred years. I, too, heard this story during my own childhood, and it continues to be heard in any number of versions, in practically every part of Rajasthan, from Alwar to Udaipur to Banswara. The story lives on.

If you had to ask me to tell you the story right now, I wouldn't be able to give you anything more than the bare facts. There is this child who wants to see his *nani* (maternal grandmother). On the way to her house, he meets a lion, a wolf, and a dog, who want to eat him. Each time the boy says, 'I'm very lean and thin. Let me go to my nani's house, where I'll fatten myself up by eating a lot, and then when I come back, there will be more of me to eat.' When he does come back, however, he gets inside a drum, which rolls him safely all the way back home. *Chal meri dholki dhamak-a-dham*—that's the central line of the story that my elder brother had remembered from the forgotten story told to him as a child by Heera Bai.

Now, it's strange how, even as you ask me to tell you the story right now, this line acts as a kind of memory cue—the details of the story I cannot give you, but the substance I remember. What we have discovered from our research on stories is not only that people *do* remember at least one story, even after claiming that they don't remember any; we have also found that most of the stories told to children at a very early age are animal tales. The religious and mythical stories from the Ramayana and the Mahabharata follow somewhat later.

If, as I mentioned earlier, children are not the carriers of tales, then how do these stories get around? In almost any given context in Rajasthani society, we have found in our research that it is not necessarily the mother who tells stories to her children; even the grandmother is not the carrier of tales, as is often believed, especially if her husband is still alive. Most of the time we have found that it is widows living and working in families as domestic helpers who are the key story-tellers. It is these widows who bathe the children, send them to school and attend to all the odd jobs at home; it is they who clean the kitchen, wash the utensils, and tell children stories when they go to bed. Once we were able to identify the widow as the carrier of tales, our methodology for collecting stories was greatly facilitated. We only had to identify the widows in any particular village to acquire stories to add to our collection.

I would not underestimate the role of memory in the telling—and re-telling—of any story. At one level, if I happen to be a good speaker and have a certain command of the language and the form of the story that I am narrating, I might be able to remember a story more effectively. As I told you earlier, I don't have this capacity to remember. But this also makes me think about how important it is to forget. If you do not have the capacity to forget, your life could become very complex. Indeed there are a lot of things related to the family, all kinds of social tensions, which have to be forgotten. Else this cluster of problems would make it very difficult for us to live. So, in any given society we need to ask what things are retained in one's memory, and which ones get released. What are the processes of remembering and forgetting? Here the reality is that I am talking to you about memory, by using my memory, and my memory is fading.

* * *

Listening to Komalda acknowledge his failing memory, even while witnessing it come alive, is a leitmotif that runs through this book. Whether one is dealing with a children's story like 'Chida-Chidi' or an oral epic like 'Pabuji',*

*Pabuji ki phad-traditional art of story telling in Rajasthan; meaning The Screen of Pabuji or, O, Read of Pabuji. Pabuji is a 14th century hero and the performance consists of the singer pointing out each scene on a 30 ft long sheet with a stick. His wife holds a lantern. The Bhopas are the performing community. Editor.

memory lies at the core of any narrative. However, there are different modalities, structures and forms of remembering, which will become only too evident when we deal with women's songs. Here we will note how a song can never be sung the same way twice even by the same women. More mysteriously, the same song can be sung collectively by all the women, even by those who may never have heard it before. How is this possible? How does one remember a song that is not consciously part of one's memory? These are some of the enigmas of folklore.

I would like to return now to one little clue that Komalda acknowledges while recalling the 'memory game' he used to play as a child in Kapasan: the fact that he could write by this time. How is memory affected by the act of writing? This brings us to the time-tested, yet unresolved problem of relating orality to literacy. Listen now to Komalda tease out the contradictions of this relationship through one direct encounter with traditional musicians.

## Orality and Literacy

In the 1950s, I used to transcribe songs dictated by a few Langa musicians living and working in the Jodhpur area. All of them were illiterate. Later we thought that if they could join adult education classes they would be able to read and write, and this would make it easier for us to collect songs written by them. But this is not how it turned out. We found that when Lakha, one of our chief musicians, learned how to read and write, he needed to consult his diary before he could begin to sing any song. To this day he continues to do this, but the rest of the singers, who are illiterate, don't have to touch a book and they will be able to render hundreds of songs.

So literacy raises a lot of complex questions relating to memory. On the one hand, you can fall back on the written word when your memory fails, but in those contexts where the written word is not available, then the brain itself develops a capacity to memorize—there is simply no other option. What we find is that, when folk musicians, become literate, the text of their songs diminishes—it gets squeezed and squeezed in relation to its early size. Or else, through frequent performances of the same song, there is a new learning by rote. On the other hand, the nomadic Kalbelia women who are illiterate can sing songs with thirty or forty or fifty lines with no memory lapses whatsoever, even though the order of the lines in the song remains totally fluid.

The larger problem we are talking about is the difference between the oral word and the written script. Even today, in some rural areas, writing is often regarded as some kind of magic. After all, how does one account for the fact that twenty people looking at some black scribbles on a page can read the same thing? Ironically, even when we try to involve villagers in adult education movements, we continue to play on their fears—'if you don't know how to read, someone can cheat you of your land or your property, you should know what you're signing', and so on. Isn't this how we promote literacy campaigns? Today, even the very act of signing anything continues to be a source of fear for most neo-literate villagers.

How has this condition existed for so long? The truth is that low-caste people have been prevented from becoming literate in our society. Traditionally, there have been two sectors in Indian society that have pursued literacy—the Brahman communities, with all their religious and astrological practices, the reading of almanacs, and so on; and the trading communities, whose priorities are more utilitarian, connected with the day-to-day activities of buying and selling, the calculation of grains and transportation costs. Unlike the literary and learned Sanskrit traditions, both oral and written, monopolized by Brahmans, the Bania tradition, which is known as Katantra, is predominantly spoken and functional and has nothing to do with Sanskrit learning.

There's a popular story in Rajasthan that highlights the material priorities of literacy in the trading communities. A peasant goes to a Bania merchant from whom he has taken a loan. The pen wedged on top of one of the Bania's ears falls down—this is where they normally keep their pens. The peasant picks up the pen and returns it to the Bania saying, 'Here, take your *chhuri* (knife).' 'Why *chhuri*?' asks the Bania, 'it's only a pen.' Then the peasant says, '*Ap ki chhuri hi mere gale pe phiri thi*' ('Your knife has cut my neck').

To get back to memory, I would say that with the rise of literacy, new support systems have emerged to facilitate the memory of oral traditions in folklore. There are a lot of things that we may not be able to remember, but all we have to do is to consult a book or a reference library, and more recently, a website. In this regard, I think it's important to keep in mind that folklore is always contemporary, even when it deals with cultures and communities who continue to live outside of modernity. If the past continues to have any meaning in society, it survives; otherwise, it disappears, not unlike a ripple on the surface of a lake, which breaks sooner or later.

> Obviously there's a lot more to be said about orality and literacy than this fragment suggests. A.K. Ramanujan, for instance, in his classic essay on 'Who needs folklore?' (1999) calls our attention to the 'interpenetration' of orality and literacy, and not just their 'opposition'.[2] Emphasizing that the 'classical, the written and the fixed' are not necessarily yoked together, Ramanujan provides numerous examples to subvert stock associations that the 'folk' tradition is necessarily oral and fluid. The Vedas, for instance, are fixed, but were not written down until two hundred years ago, following centuries of

oral transmission—a transmission that testifies to the phenomenon of 'oral literacy', as Narayana Rao has termed it.[3]

On the other hand, folktales transmitted orally with numerous variations may have fixed motifs embedded in their structures, not unlike refrains in folksongs, which never change. These fixed motifs in turn may be linked to written versions of the tale, which may have precipitated their oral renditions in the first place. So it is deceptive to assume that an oral tradition necessarily precedes a written one, because their relationship is a lot more volatile and multivalent. Indeed, 'different genres', according to Ramanujan, contain 'different proportions' of what remains 'fixed' in any oral rendition—the order of words and phrases in a proverb, for instance, is set and repeated verbatim. In a joke, however, almost everything can be improvised apart from the punchline.[4]

.... For the most part, however, Komalda does not specifically address any written text in the course of his reflections on orality in order to problematize its vagaries. Instead of texts, Komalda addresses larger contexts of time and genealogy without which specific utterances of memory would be meaningless.

* * *

## Time

In the rural areas of Rajasthan, when you ask someone, 'What is your age?' you are not likely to get a clear answer. But it is more likely that you will be told that in such-and-such *kal*, or more precisely, drought year, I was three years old, ten years old, and so on. *Chhapanna, Chhabbisa, Behtara*: these are very well-known time-markers of particular famines. So people will talk about their age only from the point of view of these acute famines. This is their way of measuring the past.

In everyday life, we find that most people can go back to three generations in their families: father, grandfather, great-grandfather. Beyond that, a person generally does not know anything about his past. Of course, if he makes the attempt, there are always sources that can verify the past beyond three generations. What happens is that while a person may know his father's activities intimately and his grandfather's slightly less so, a few things from his great grandfather's life as well will somehow reach his ears.

Let me tell you a story in this regard about my own family, which I heard from my grandmother when I was a child. My great-grandfather was the Diwan of Ratlam state. In this state, there was a king who was old and had two sons—the older son who was his rightful heir and a younger one. My great-grandfather conspired with the younger son to get his brother sent away to a distant place, during which time the younger son poisoned his father, captured the fort of Ratlam, and declared himself king. Now this was the British period when it was not possible to say, 'The king is dead, long live the king.' Rather, the king is dead, and now the kingdom will have to revert to the emperor, who in turn will appoint a political agent to look after the kingdom. Such was the case with all princely states like Ratlam. Here too the younger son could not be recognized immediately as king; it was not an automatic process. To facilitate his appointment, my great-grandfather played a critical role, and somehow or the other, perhaps by bribing the British officers, he managed to get the younger son declared king. By this time the older brother had taken shelter in Jaipur, where another branch of the family developed, while my great-grandfather became the Diwan of the new king in Ratlam.

Today, I can view this episode from the past only in the larger context of a conspiracy. But for my grandmother, it was no conspiracy. On the contrary, she had deep regard for the intelligence of my great-grandfather and the details by which he managed the coup so effectively. I still remember one detail—a locked door, which would have prevented the old king from being killed, had my great-grandfather not arranged for an elephant to break the door down. Many such sensational details were part of the story that I heard from my grandmother. Later, it appears, after becoming the Diwan of the new king, my great-grandfather was accused of embezzlement. This must have been around the 1880s. He was put in jail for eighteen years, during which time his case was taken up by the Privy Council in London. He won the case and received an enormous monetary compensation, Rs 1 lakh for each year of imprisonment, which was a fortune at that time. So this is how the story has come down to me from three generations ago.

Let us examine a different story now, involving a low-caste community. This story comes from a low-caste Bhambhi boy in the village of Borunda, who looks back three generations to his great-grandfather, who worked as a *kasid* (postman) in that same village. Everyday this man would go to Jaitaran, which is almost twenty-one miles away from Borunda. He would get up early in the morning, walk those twenty-one miles, collect the *dak* (post), and come back in the evening to Borunda. He did this for twenty years with no payment whatsoever. All Bhambhi families were expected to provide at least one person to serve the *jagirdar* (feudal lord) of the village, thereby enabling the other family members to be free to earn their living. So in this way the Bhambhi great-grandfather's services had been indentured to the jagirdar. Naturally, we were sympathetic when we heard this story—twenty years of work, and no payment. Those were hard times. But on hearing us talk this way, the boy got angry: 'What are you talking about? Why don't you see that my great-grandfather was capable of walking forty-two miles every day? Don't you see what strength he possessed? Why are you talking about money?'

On hearing this response, it struck me afresh that there is more than one way of looking at things. How do you put elements of the past together, and where do you put them? In what frame of reference? Whose frame of reference?

## Genealogy

Now these are merely individual recollections of the past. What happens when you deal with larger groups and their modes of remembering the past? Take the genealogists from musician groups like the Langas, Manganiyars, and the scheduled castes. These genealogists can easily go back fourteen to eighteen generations. And they can recall all kinds of details—for instance, so-and-so's great-great-great-grandfather had four sons; from the older son, this family emerged, from the younger son, another branch of the family grew, and so on. Most people think that Langas and Manganiyars survive only as singers of folk songs, but they don't know that these traditional musicians also earn their living by maintaining the genealogy of their patrons (*jajmans*).

Indeed, the genealogical record of the Langas and Manganiyars, which is entirely oral, is often regarded as definitive. In controversial decisions regarding whether or not a marriage can take place across two sub-castes, it is their sources that are ultimately relied upon. Yet another way by which the Manganiyars preserve the genealogy of their patrons is in the form of a panegyric called the *shubhraj*, in which the well-being of the jajman family is ensured by poetic references to all the people in its ancestry. This is yet another way of remembering family histories across generations....

Apart from the traditional musicians, there is another kind of genealogist—the *Bhat*—who keeps a record of all the births in the male line of individual families. Actually there are two kinds of *bhat*—the *Mukhbancha Bhat*, who relies entirely on his memory for his oral recitation, and the *Pothibancha Bhat*, who has meticulous written records to fall back on. Both these *bhats* visit homes on an average of once every three years, generally on occasions like marriage, childbirth, or any festival. By contrast, the *panda* (priest), who also keeps records of all the deaths in individual families, both in the male and female lines, is generally consulted in holy places like Hardwar, where people go for death ceremonies, the immersion of the ashes, and other related rituals. At such places, the two essential questions that are asked of any *yatri* (pilgrim) are: *Kis gaon ke ho? Apka jat kya hai*? (Where are you from? And to which caste do you belong?) What is amazing about this genealogical system is its quick retrieval of information. This has yet to be studied adequately. While the written records of the pandas in Devanagari script go back more than twenty generations, the Pothibancha Bhats are also literate, but they use an invented script for their records that is impossible for others to read.

Now, how does genealogy affect the ways in which people are addressed in specific families? My great-grandfather was Jawahar Chand. He had one son called Khuman Singh. Khuman Singh had two sons—Dulah Singh and Berisal Singh. Dulah Singh had four sons, and Berisal Singh had eight sons. Now all male members in the family are identified by the suffix '*ot*', which means 'son of'. So I am Berisalot, but since my father Berisal was the son of Khuman, we (I and my seven brothers) can also be identified as Khumanot. My cousin on the other hand, Daulat Singh, was the son of Dulah Singh, so he can be called Daulat Singh Dulahot, but since Dulah Singh was also the son of Khuman Singh, he too can be addressed as Khumanot, like myself and my brothers. So, you see how at some levels the genealogical names separate, only to meet up again.

Another vital aspect of genealogy concerns the husband-wife relationship. I am an Oswal—this can be regarded as my jat (caste)—but my sub-caste (*sakh*) is Dugar. Kothari is only a title—originally it referred to people who looked after the army stores (*kothar*). Now, the point is that I can only marry within the Oswal caste, but I cannot marry another Dugar. Likewise, since my wife's sub-caste is Bordia, my children can marry neither into the Dugar nor into the Bordia sub-caste groups. Likewise, since my mother was a Kankaria Bhandari, none of my children can be married into the group. I can even go so far back as my great-grandmother who was from the Mohnot Mehta sub-caste group. So even to this day no one from my family can marry into this group.

Now, all these rules are there for a very simple reason, and that is to define the areas of incest, so that they can be avoided. In different groups we encounter different incest rules. Once you know the rules that apply to your family, then it becomes possible to determine into which families you can be married, and with which families marriage is prohibited. In this way, entire genealogies of families have been determined over the years.

## The Story of Puniā

There are oral genealogists from low-caste and tribal communities as well. But their recitation of the past draws primarily on mythical references. For instance, they will talk about how the sun and moon were born, how the sea emerged, how agriculture came into existence, and so on. The recitation of the Bhil and Garasia genealogists, for instance, is very like the Puranas.

In the Puranas, there are primarily five divisions—*sarg, pratisarg, kalpa, manvantara, and pralaya.*[5] It is only with *manvantara* that human beings come into existence; it is from this point in time that genealogy begins. The earlier parts of the life-cycle deal with the evolution of nature.

Significantly, most of the low-caste genealogists, who also function as Mukhbancha Bhats, are from the acrobat communities, such as the Nat, the Rajnat, and the Badi. These acrobats recite the genealogies of low-caste communities like the Meghwals, who are associated with leather-related occupations and weaving. While the Badis operate in the western desert zone, the Nats function in other parts of the state, rather like the itinerant *kathputli* (puppetry) groups, who are known as Balaion ke Nat, in the area of Nagaur from which they originate. However, this is not how the puppeteers identify themselves in other parts of Rajasthan and the rest of India, where they present themselves as Bhats....

What is important to stress is that the upholding of genealogy is perhaps stronger in the low-caste groups than in the upper castes. For example, if a Bhat had to enter the home of an Untouchable, say, a Bhambhi's home, then if there is one cot in this home, then the Bhat will sleep on that; if there is one *roti* available in this home, then it will be eaten by the Bhat. The Bhats charge the lower castes large sums of money to maintain their genealogy, and their poor patrons have no other option but to pay through their noses. The irony, of course, is that the Bhats themselves are from the lower caste. But, as is well known even among the lower castes, there is a hierarchy.

So, for example, between handling the carcass of an animal, skinning it, tanning it, and making a shoe out of the leather, there are levels of respectability. The *mochi* (cobbler) would be of a higher status than the *rangai*, who is responsible for the tanning of the leather, and so on. At times there are contradictions within the caste hierarchy. From an upper-caste perspective, the *dhobi* (washerman), for instance, is not considered Untouchable, but for the untouchables themselves, he is Untouchable. Likewise, there are hierarchies among the lower castes as to who provides the genealogies for whom.

When you listen to these genealogies, you are forced to confront the fact that low-caste people in India have been denied basic human rights for centuries. If we compare their situation to what we see in the great Hindu myths of the country, can we expect low-caste people to survive on them—on the myths of the *savarna*, the upper castes? We know that no society can survive without its myths. Indeed, I would go to the extent of saying that no caste can be fully acknowledged without a genealogy. So what are the myths of the low-caste communities? Where can we find these myths? I would say that it is in the genealogical records of the Mukhbancha Bhats that we come across the stories of their origins, which enable us to understand how they have survived as groups and from where they have derived their strength.

Let me at this point share a story with you that will give you a more concrete idea of the oral genealogy of low-caste groups.[6] Many years ago, on one of my field-trips, I and my colleagues were passing through Pipalia village near Chhoti Sadari in Mewar. I think we must have arrived around 8.30 in the morning in this village where we saw 400–500 people sitting in one place listening to two genealogists, Mukhbancha Bhats, who were reciting a story with intricate rhythms patterns beaten on the *dhol* (drum) with sticks, on both sides. We noticed that these Bhats had arranged a lot of things around them for an acrobatic performance—ropes and bamboo structures and poles. But now they were reciting the genealogy of a particular community called the Raut, as we came to know from listening to the narrative. The acrobatic stunts would follow after the genealogical record was complete.

During this narrative, there were a number of stories told relating to the ancestry of the Raut community. One story was particularly interesting. It concerned a man called Punia. Before his time, it appears that no agriculture was practised. Of his own accord, Punia decided to grow some *makka* (maize). From where he learned to do this, one doesn't know, but he sowed the field and the makka grew well. Finally, when the crop was ready and he was preparing for the harvest, the Sun and the Moon arrived. Both these gods told Punia, 'without us, could you have grown your crop?' He said, 'No, it would have been impossible. It's because of the rays of the sun that I got light, and because of the moon that my crops could sleep in the cool of the night. So without your help, I could have done nothing.' Then the gods said, 'Why don't you give us our share?' So he said, 'Certainly, not just my share, but whatever I've got, you can take it.' Promptly the Sun and the Moon moved into the fields, but they had never seen such plants growing in their lives. Now, makka grows on the stem of the plant, on the top of which are some flowery tendrils, which look very beautiful. So the Sun and the Moon decided to take the top part of the plant and leave the rest for Punia. Inevitably, the top part amounted to nothing, while the stem of the plant on which the makka grows yielded a rich harvest.

Next year, Punia decided to grow another crop. And this time he decided to grow *jawar* (sorghum). So he ploughed the field, planted the seeds, and again, the crop was wonderful. Once again, when it was time for the harvest, the Sun and Moon arrived, and repeated what they had said earlier: 'Without us, would you have been able to grow your crop?' And he said, 'No, not without you.' 'Our share?' said the gods. And Punia said, 'Take whatever you want.' Since the last time they had taken the upper part of the plant which had resulted in nothing, this time the gods decided to take the lower part. Punia agreed.

Since jawar grows on top, Punia was lucky once again, because he got a rich harvest, while the gods were left with nothing but straw.

Now, after this story was told, one of the Mukhbancha Bhats raised an open question to the hundreds of people sitting in front of him: 'You've all heard the story, what do you think about it? Can you identify the Sun and the Moon?' And four to five hundred people, almost in one voice, shouted in unison: 'Chandravanshi, Suryavanshi.' Now, these are the names of the feudal lords from the Rajput community.[7] From this response it became very clear to me how genealogical records contain information not only about how a particular community sees itself, but how it sees other communities, particularly from the dominant section of society. This particular genealogical account is not merely a record; it is also a satirical comment on the exploitation of the upper castes, who are ignorant of the most basic realities of life. And yet, they continue to deny people their means of livelihood.

Another story narrated by the Bhats involved the building of a temple for the mother goddess by the Raut community. The temple was built, everything was fine, it was beautifully constructed, but there was one slight problem. In every temple there is a *kalash* (rounded pinnacle) that is placed on top of the *shikhar* (tower, dome). Now, the kalash of his particular temple was made out of gold, and it was very heavy. Many men tried to lift it, but failed to do so. Finally, the elders in the Raut community decided that only a virgin girl would be able to lift the kalash. So, any number of girls tried to lift the kalash, from the Brahman, Rajput, and Bania communities, but it didn't budge. Finally, a girl from the Raut community came and touched it, and the kalash was easily lifted and put on top of the temple. Once again it is obvious that this story comments on other groups, in this particular case the alleged purity of upper-caste women. It reveals what the Raut have to say not only about their own genealogical record, but about those groups which are more privileged than their own.

> Listening to Kamalda tell these stories makes me realize the many ways in which 'history' is shaped and remembered. Not history in the formal sense of 'itihasa', but more in the Puranic sense of an old story—'bahut purani bat hai'—in which people's values and beliefs are vividly set forth. We have here an instance of how history can be performed—not just through oral narration, whose specific resonances Komalda doesn't spell out but which he suggests through the rhythmic beats of the drum and the cries of a very interactive audience. Let us also not forget that this 'history' is followed by acrobatic stunts of which, sadly, we don't have a description. So we have to imagine the 'gulach khana' (somersaults), 'rasi pe chadhna' (tightrope walking), 'gol gol ghumna' (whirling on a pole suspended in the

air), demonstrated by the 'Mukhbandha Bhats'. These recorders of the past are also the entertainers of the community. Oral genealogy and gymnastics share the same ground.

While the stories of the Raut community are legendary, the response to the story of Punia—a collective vocal one, as Komalda affirms—makes it clear that it has been comprehended not just dialogically, but critically. Genealogy is received by the people not merely as a ritualistic record of the past, but rather, as a reaffirmation of the present. In this sense, it highlights the political awareness that the 'Chandravanshis' and 'Suryavanshis' of this world are still around. Countering the ecological mystique that is built into the mythic personae of the Moon (Chandra) and Sun (Surya), at least in certain brands of contemporary holistic thinking, these gods are divested of their sanctity. More critically, they are shown to be ignorant of two of the most basic 'staple-food' categories of Rajasthan—'makka' (maize) and 'jawar' (sorghum)....

## Notes and References

1. Another variant of this story and the discussion surrounding it can be read in Komalda's address to the participants in a workshop on documenting folklore, organized by the National Folklore Support Centre, in Jaisalmer, February 2001. Published in *Folklife*, Vol. 1, Issue 5 (April 2001), pp. 51–2.

2. A.K. Ramanujan, 'Who Needs Folklore?' in *The Collected Essays of A.K. Ramanujan*, Vinay Dharwadher ed., New Delhi, 1999, pp. 538–48.

3. Quoted by A.K. Ramanujan in 'Who Needs Folklore?,' (ibid.), p. 539. Elaborating on Narayana Rao's position, Ramanujan states that while Vedic pundits are learned in Sanskrit 'grammar, syntax, logic and poetics', their 'literacy' is 'imbued in their bodies,' in so far as their mode of acquiring and transmitting knowledge is entirely 'oral.' A learned man is referred to as '*kanthastha*', one whose knowledge is contained in his throat.

4. Ibid., p. 540.

5. While '*sarg*' and '*pratisarg*' refers to the primary and secondary stages of creation, '*kalpa*' refers to the longest period of time, consisting of 4,320 million years. Each *kalpa* is made up of 14 *manvantaras*, the age initiated by Manu or primeval man. It is in the reign of the seventh Manu that the Great Flood (*pralaya*) occurs—this event serves as a time marker to separate the period of the Manus from that of the Kshatriya kings that follow.

For an authoritarive contextualization of these terms within readings of cosmological and historical time, read Romila Thapar's *Time as a Metaphor of History: Early India* (New Delhi, 1996), and 'Genealogy as a Source of Social History' from her earlier book *Ancient Indian Social History: Some Interpretations* (Hyderabad, 1978).

6. Like the story of *Chida-Chidi* described earlier in the essay, the story being discussed in the remaining section of this chapter was also narrated in an abbreviated version in the seminar at Jaisalmer, February 2001. See *Folklife* (ibid.), pp. 49–50, for a somewhat more cursory rendition of the story from the one presented in this chapter.

7. In 'Social Mobility in Ancient India,' *Ancient Indian Social History* (1978), Romila Thapar mentions how the earliest dynasties recorded in the *Puranas* were classified into two categories—the *Suryavanshi* (Sun-Family) and the *Chandravanshi* (Moon-Family)—both of them tracing their ancestry to the hermaphrodite son of Manu, the primeval man. 'Apart from the symbolic significance of this myth,' she adds that, it became the mythical 'prototype of all rulers seeking Kshatriya genealogies' (pp. 132–33). The Rajput royal families of Rajasthan were no exception.

# 4.
# National Identity and the Realist Aesthetic

SUMITA S. CHAKRAVARTY

> Can a serious filmmaker, working in India, afford to shut his eyes to the reality around him, the reality that is so poignant, and so urgently in need of interpretation in terms of the cinema? I do not think so. For the truly serious, socially conscious film maker ... must face the challenge of contemporary reality, examine the facts, probe them, sift them and select from them the material to be transformed into the stuff of cinema.
>
> Satyajit Ray, *Our Films, Their Films*

OF ALL THE TERMS USED BY CRITICS TO CHARACTERIZE MAINSTREAM INDIAN CINEMA, realism defined in the negative or as a systematic absence has undoubtedly had the most currency. Conversely, the achievement of realism in a film becomes a mark of value, a sign of sincerity and truthfulness on the part of the filmmaker and of 'authenticity' of the material presented. This was particularly true during the postindependence period, when such qualities crystallized the hopes of a nation in search of its 'true' identity and trying to assign meaning to the complex process of change. As the medium with the potential power to bring India symbolically face-to-face with its own image(s), the cinema found itself implicated in paradoxical ways in the whole cultural response to nationhood. For realism not only seemed to deny established film practices but also Indian literary, dramatic, and philosophical traditions. Moreover, the call for realism meant that the cinema should project not images of what Indian society was but what it *should be*. This 'idealist' thread is what shapes the specific contours of realism as it evolved in Indian popular cinema, even as it tried to both articulate and diffuse the ambivalence of social attitudes to change. Realism is the masquerading moral conscience of the Indian intelligentsia in their assumed (though not uncontested) role of national leadership during the fifties. The debate on realism, therefore, has implications for the politics of self-representation.

Realism as elaborated here intersects with the idea of impersonation* in important ways: as the 'other' of impersonation, it gives shape to the social/national imaginary, the ideal of wholeness of perception and unity of common experience. It can thus be seen as a historical phenomenon, not new to the fifties but privileged in that period as a nation-building tool. As the aesthetic rallying cry emanating from the educated middle class, whose intellectual vanguardism conflicts with their economic decline, realism registers the ambivalence toward technology and progress and a general 'Westernization.' The intelligentsia's gloss on realism as coincident with morality and sincerity of purpose rather than a strict adherence to the principle of impartial observation of social phenomena subverts realism itself as empiricist doctrine. (The Ray statements quoted above exemplify the contradictory pull of this tendency, with their use of words like 'serious,' 'poignant,' and 'interpretation' alongside the social scientific jargon of process: 'examine,' 'probe,' 'sift,' 'select.' Although addressing the situation in Bengal in 1958, Ray is concerned with commercial filmmaking.) The appeal of realism in popular culture invariably rests on a heightened emotionalism, the call to an emphatic identification with the underprivileged. Finally, as a set of conventions in the Bombay cinema, the genre of realism self-consciously points to itself as superior (narratively coherent, carefully crafted) and yet refuses radical differentiation from the average commercial product by incorporating its range of pleasures (particularly stars, songs, and dances). All these factors have to be taken into account in order for us to be able to grasp realism as ideology, worldview, and genre in Indian popular cinema.

## Toward an Archaeology** of Indianized Realism

Before we can consider the particular inflections of impersonation in films that represent the turn to realism during the fifties, we need to trace the idea of realism through a number of discourses and practices in Indian culture and society. Generally, several problems arise in such an analytic endeavor. For

*The author is punning on the word impersonation/imperso-'nation'. Impersonation is an act of disguise and deception, of pretending to be someone else. In a like manner the Hindi film seeks to present itself as the nation with all its tensions and contradictions. Moreover, the Hindi film attempts to present itself as the nation should be as much as it is in actuality—therefore it is utopian in intent. Editor.

**Concept used by French philosopher Michel Foucault (1926–84). The idea of the 'archaeological method' is that systems of thought and knowledge are governed by rules, not just of grammar or logic, that operate beneath the consciousness of individual subjects and define a system of possibilities of thought in any given field or period. The historian then 'excavated' these structures that underlay individual thought. Editor.

while realism has a specific place in Western philosophy, with a history (as an artistic and literary movement) and a critical tradition (it is the subject of endless debate), its status in the Indian philosophical and classical aesthetic traditions has been marginal. It is not possible here (nor is it strictly necessary) to do a comparative analysis of the occidental and Indian epistemological systems that form the basis of arguments for and against realism as the desired norm for artistic products.[1] One can only make the general observation that the Hindu worldview (similar to the Platonic worldview) posits material reality as an aspect of spiritual or transcendent Reality, and so what we see is 'the reflection of reality in the mirror of illusion.'[2] Scholars of Indian aesthetics have stressed its nonmimetic view of art, which posits an essentially autonomous artistic world and an elaborate *rasasutra* (theory of aesthetic enjoyment) of depersonalized emotions.[3] It is not surprising, therefore, that in India standards of realism are evoked in relation to the novel and cinema, the two 'borrowed' or 'imported' art forms. Yet, as the critic Meenakshi Mukherjee shows us in her study of the novel in India, conventions of realism were slow to take hold, and details of surface reality never achieved a high place in the Indian literary tradition. 'In almost every major novel of the nineteenth century, behind the obvious European influence can be found the bedrock of a different narrative structure and value systems.'[4] Nevertheless, the conscious attempt of many nineteenth-century Indian novelists was to achieve realism in the manner of the Victorian writers they were familiar with, and this meant a preoccupation with the depiction of (often oppressive) contemporary social conditions such as the subordinate status of women, caste prejudices, joint family problems, and the like. The authors tried to render faithfully the details of the social milieu to which their characters belonged, reproduced patterns of speech in everyday conservation, and were concerned with ordinary life. Mukherjee points out the high place accorded to English education by these writers which contributed, paradoxically, to their own self-definition: 'English education becomes closely associated with the process of achieving a new social and individual identity.'[5] The reason is presented as follows:

> A part of the power of the British in India was technological superiority. This has always been the basis of colonial domination (one recalls the magical power of gunpowder in *Robinson Crusoe*, an early paradigm of colonial experience) and in *Indulekha* [1888] Kesavan Nambudiri is awed by the thread factory in Calicut where the wheels move 'as if they heard the word of command.' He speculates on the power of the smoke that comes out of the factory and the dark sacrifices that must be made to generate this power. Kesavan Nambudiri's confusion is between two systems—the rational and the magical, or the natural and the supernatural (factory smoke—

sacrificial fire). His wife knows that English education is the only means of demystification. Indulekha is not awed by anything because she can even explain 'the principles on which the railway is driven.'[6]

What appears now as naive technological optimism was, in the nineteenth century, an unbounded belief in scientific progress, both in the West and, by extension, in the colonies. (More than half a century later, Satyajit Ray used the railways as the beckoning symbol of modernity in his classic realist film *Pather Panchali* [*Song of the Little Road*, 1955]). Faith in science, one of the cardinal elements behind the European realist movement, was also a factor that drove Indian authors to strive for credibility and realism in their works.

Yet, what Raymond Williams has characterized as the scientific *attitude* implicit in Western realism—arising out of a host of specific historico-cultural factors such as the industrial revolution and secularism—could not easily be implanted on Indian soil, despite Macaulay's 'Minute on Indian Education' (1835), which envisaged 'a class of persons, Indian in blood and color, but English in taste, in opinions, in morals and in intellect.' Strong ideas about individualism, democracy, linear time, and material progress go against the grain of Indian philosophical speculations and experiential value systems: however, the educated middle class was affected by Western ideas, and 'realism' as a representational strategy in fiction was one way of coping with the processes of industrialization and modernity. Popular Indian novels of the late nineteenth and twentieth centuries have combined richness of detail in the description of a social milieu with some of the conventions of Indian oral narratives and openness of form rather than closure in the Western fictional mode.[7]

In postindependence India, the emphasis on 'realism,' particularly in the context of Hindi literature (and, as we shall see, in film), has taken on a force that has complex, indeed contradictory, associations with questions of individual and national identity. While Indian writing has maintained cultural continuity with the *past*, the perceived need of the writer to come to terms with the *present* and to locate him/herself within a *world* context has been, perhaps, greater. One interesting result of this phenomenon was that, in the fifties, stories were discussed as much or more than they were written.[8] In other words, interest in evolving a modern critical tradition, shaped by the particular literary and extraliterary (historical, linguistic, social) problems faced by the writers, is evident. Moreover, as scholar Gordon Roadarmel writes, 'Justifications for literary forms and trends have been sought in a more universal framework comparing the fiction of each new generation with that of the previous generation, with that of writers in other Indian languages, and with that of writers in other world languages.' Roadarmel goes on to say that 'criteria related to newness, realism, authenticity and the reflection of a "modern consciousness" are most highly valued' by Hindi critics and writers.[9]

These were used as synonymous terms, so that the ideal of realism signified at once being attuned to one's own time and place and working within a broader international tradition. The soul searching that writers went through regarding the urban/rural dilemma or their ability to give authentic portrayals of village life (the 'true' India) in view of their urban backgrounds was one instance of the broader cultural question of identity. Of course, the conception of what constitutes realism changed from that of Premchand and others (writing in the 1920s, 1930s, and 1940s) who used realistic settings and characters to promote a social or political view to a less direct, nondidactic mode of writing which would only communicate the complexity of contemporary experience. There was even the extreme position, such as that of the writer Nirmal Verma, who held that a writer could not even identify reality, much less express it: 'For one who is truly a realist, reality is always hidden in the bush.'[10]

Although conducted on a less sophisticated or sustained level, the discussion about realism in Indian cinema is no less complex for the purposes of critical analysis. First, the demand for mimetic cinema may itself represent the attitude of a limited, though still important, section of the movie-going public, namely, the city-bred, middle-class person, often English-educated and conscious of 'world standards' in the cinema. In the absence of proper ethnographic studies of audiences and in the face of the box-office popularity of different kinds of films, not just realistic ones, it is difficult to push the argument for realism as manifesting itself in *all* classes of the movie-going public.[11] The conventions of realism are generally absent from India's oral storytelling traditions (which the Bombay cinema partly draws upon) with their digressions, asides, stories within stories, interposed political, social, or philosophical commentary, and the like. As Salman Rushdie pointed out in a television interview some years ago, this style of storytelling is actually quite sophisticated when placed beside any straightforward notion of naturalism or illusionism in art. The latter, then, might be the expression of a predominantly middle-class sensibility, and this might explain why certain 'landmark' Bombay films espousing realism such as *Dharti ke Lal* (*Children of the Earth*, 1946), *Do Bigha Zamin* (*Two Acres of Land*, 1953), and *Jagte Raho* (*Keep Awake!*, 1956) were acclaimed by film reviewers and award panels but did quite poorly at the box office.

Nevertheless, there is evidence to suggest that a general mood supporting realistic cinema prevailed in the postindependence era and that it was linked to the intelligentsia's feelings of being alien in their own environment and of their search for the 'real' India. Edward Shils has dwelt on this in his book *The Intellectual between Tradition and Modernity*, finding on the basis of interviews he conducted a deep sense of guilt among city-bred, English-educated people over being cut off from their roots and not being able to communicate with the 'authentic' Indian, the villager.[12] Even as late as 1983, Girish Karnad, Oxford-educated filmmaker, playwright, and scholar, said, 'If you want to know the real India, you cannot get it from an Indian who lives in the city. It is the village Indian who is the real Indian.'[13] Since this is also the average Westerner's perception of India, it is interesting that in the very act of self-assertion and self-knowledge, the Indian urban intellectual should 'objectify' him/herself. And so one of the anomalies contained in the demand for realism in cinema is that the concept itself is alien to Indian philosophic and aesthetic traditions (not to speak of Bombay film-making practices generally) and certainly owed some of its impetus to the international climate favoring neorealism, but it was taken as a transparent means whereby 'Indian reality' could be revealed. In other words, the West provided the frame whereby Indians could view themselves. I do not wish to imply by this a disingenuous attempt on the part of Indian intellectuals to know themselves as Indians or any conscious aping of Western views and ideas. Rather, what is evident is the very complex nature of the notion of national identity, particularly in instances where a society contends with its colonial past, at the same time feeding upon it. It is in this sense that the urge to find verisimilitude in commercial entertainment takes on meaning, although on the face of it the tendencies that the two represented, particularly in the Indian context, would seem incompatible.

... the participants in the struggle over the question of 'legitimate' culture were joined in the perception of realism in narrative and storytelling (with Indian settings) as the antidote to a host of ills plaguing films, including their low social and international prestige. As the government sought to revive *Indian* cultural forms and traditions, Indian filmmakers and popular figures in the industry such as actors renewed their calls for moral integrity, sincerity of purpose, and realism in their own efforts to revitalize their products. In this regard, the Indian film establishment did not only look to the experiments of other countries but invoked a realistic 'tradition' from within the indigenous cinema. Film reviewers and filmmakers harked back to the 'golden age' of the 1930s, when the stability of the studio era had allowed filmmakers to portray contemporary social evils as they appeared. 'Realism' also meant a popularization of Indian literary classics, the works of Tagore, Bankim Chandra, Sarat Chandra, Premchand, Banbhatta, and Kalidasa, which constitute India's literary heritage. It involved choosing 'the beautiful national forms of our song, dance and music, so long and widely neglected in our films.'[14] Further, the important commercial filmmakers whose names were familiar to audiences and whose films earned awards, notably Bimal Roy, Zia Sarhady, V. Shantaram, Nitin Bose, and Mehboob, not to mention Satyajit Ray, working independently and outside Bombay, all issued statements or made claims regarding their realist intentions. Sometimes all these emphases were present in the official view that perhaps provided the lead in this demand for films communicating an 'authentic' national consciousness. We have as an example the view expressed by a public figure (R.R. Diwakar, then governor of the state of Bihar), on the occasion of the silver jubilee celebrations of the Bombay film industry: 'Some of the things necessary [to reach higher standards in the cinema] seem to be: diving into the very soul of India, deep study of the all-sided as well as varied culture of this great land, attempt at originality and the boldness to depict India as India, venturing out of the studios into the tumult and bustle of life, full utilization of colour and poetry that is profuse and inherent in the Indian scene, developing technical skill on all fronts and, above all, high idealism.'[15] As one can sense from this quotation, the burden placed on the cinema was indeed great.

Expectations of the Bombay film, then, ranged from straightforward notions of verisimilitude such as representation of the surface details of dress, decor, and social environment, to more totalizing and ambitious views such as the one expressed above. More important than these film-as-reflection views, however, is the effort by some film directors and writers to incorporate within the notion of realism a view of visual art rooted in Indian philosophy. We have, on the one hand, the Aristotelian claim for art as a mirror of life and, on the other, a claim for art that elevates and improves the mind through the agency of character types, patterned emotions, and a delicately balanced moral universe. This 'duality' is apparent in a statement entitled 'Realism as I understand it' made by Bimal Roy, described as the 'high priest of cinema realism' in the Bombay film world. We find a hint of familiarity with the Bazinian idea of the camera as uniquely suited to capture reality: 'The very nature of photographic art invites belief in the actuality of what is recorded. As a result, the film developed most consistently and successfully in the direction of realism, that is, reconstruction of life in such a way as to give its environment and psychology the effect of complete authenticity.'[16] However, Roy makes it clear that the goal of realism is not the scientific understanding of the human condition at a particular time and place but a knowledge of self (*atmanam biddhi*), not interpretation but the creation of a mood, 'realism which becomes "rasa."' The camera only *enhances* and concretizes the viewer's enjoyment and understanding of the play of forces of good and evil in the world, it does not radically alter them.

Thus the new technological art of cinema is *incorporated* into the basic Hindu religious and aesthetic traditions. This incorporation is further articulated by scriptwriter Nabendu Ghosh, who explains that according to Bharata Muni's *Natya Shastra*, 'our conception of right and wrong is based on religious books such as the *Dharmashastras*, the Vedas and the *Mahabharata* which enjoin upon the Hindu a code of ethical conduct. But in order to explain the seeds of truth, illustrations must be drawn from men and women's lives. That is the purpose of art as expressed in the *Natya Shastra*: to show how people react in various situations, how they decide between right and wrong.'[17] Ghosh goes on to say that the cinema can magnify emotions, as in a closeup, thus providing what gives a human being the greatest pleasure: to see. The Sanskrit word *darshan* (from the verbal root *drsh*), which means 'to see,' is also the word for philosophy. The primacy of the visual sense implied by this comparison stems from the all-inclusive meaning of seeing as integral vision, apprehension, understanding to be found in the earliest Hindu scriptures, while the notion of pleasure here would mean spiritual pleasure in 'seeing' the Truth. Ghosh's testimony is one instance of the sanction and inspiration that people seek for contemporary linguistic and cultural forms and practices from the past.

## The Neorealist Window of Opportunity

In 1952, India held its first international film festival. The occasion is regarded in the film industry as something of a milestone as people in the country had a chance to see contemporary European and other 'foreign' films for the first time. Previously Hollywood films had provided the model for commercial filmmaking in India, but now the works of the Italian neorealists were also available as the 'other cinema' attracting the more seriously inclined Bombay filmmakers such as K.A. Abbas, Bimal Roy, Nitin Bose, B.R. Chopra, and a few others. Abbas and Chopra had been journalists before they started making films, Bimal Roy and Nitin Bose had migrated to Bombay after initially being employed and trained by New Theatres of Calcutta with its tradition of 'socially conscious' cinema. They thus aligned themselves with progressive causes and the representation of contemporary Indian reality without necessarily renouncing the more pleasurable aspects of the commercial cinema such as songs and dances. In the polarized world of Indian film criticism, the realist impulse informing certain films is therefore seen as 'contaminated' by nonorganic and extraneous elements.[18] While Bimal Roy's name, for instance, is associated with film realism, he has not gained admittance into the ranks of the 'greats' because he mixed modes which are perceived as fundamentally at odds with one another (realistic mise-en-scène with songs and dances).[19] Needless to say, attempts at hierarchization are beside the point in trying to understand why certain filmmakers were accepted as 'realistic' by audiences as well as the specific version of realism their films sought to project.

## Realism and Nationalism: Bridging the Gap

In discussions of Hindi film realism, three films made in the late forties and early fifties are invariably mentioned by critics and industry representatives: Chetan Anand's *Neecha Nagar* (*World Down Below*, 1946), K.A. Abbas's

*Dharti ke Lal*, and Bimal Roy's *Do Bigha Zamin*. Although award winners, all three films did poorly at the box office. In them we have some of the dominant themes and oppositions of the realistic mode: the struggle between the haves and the have-nots, the country and the city, the tenant/peasant and the landlord or moneylender. These themes had found earlier expression in Bimal Roy's enormously popular Bengali film made for New Theatres, *Udayer Pathe* (*Awakening*, 1944), soon remade in Hindi as *Humrahi* (*Fellow Travellers*, 1945). Satyajit Ray comments that the Bengali version 'was widely regarded in its time as a milestone in Indian cinema. Timely in its theme, bold in its use of unknown amateurs in leading roles, and admirable in its moral stance, it was a step in the right direction, though not a big one.'[20]

*Udayer Pathe* is an overtly nationalist film and a socially conscious one, traditions already well established in Indian cinema, as S.T. Baskaran and others have pointed out. Why then did *Udayer Pathe* have such an impact? I shall suggest that, within the parameters of a very conventional narrative (poor boy meets rich girl), we have a realist idiom struggling to break through, an idiom that draws upon the cadence and patterns of everyday speech for moral effect. The film sought to apprehend the contemporary mood and moment through the evolution in language, literalizing the rise of subaltern (working-class and colonized) consciousness in the power of common speech. But by a further crossover, the power of common speech reposes in an urban intellectual, not in the representative of a village. In fact, the film is rare in the history of Indian cinema in that it presents the intellectual as hero and heroism as the ability to articulate class-consciousness.

Made at the height of the freedom movement, the film makes obvious use of symbols such as the national anthem, the Bengali literary and social reform tradition (photographs of Shri Aurobindo, Tagore, Vivekananda), as well as references to an international socialist tradition (Bernard Shaw) to create the intellectual milieu of its protagonist, Anup Lekhak (literally meaning 'Anup the Writer'). The story presents the polarized social worlds of the rich (the industrialists) and the poor (workers and wage-earners), with the former as exploiters (also identified with the British through their dress and life-style), the latter the exploited class (identified with the nationalists). The dice are fairly heavily loaded against the former, the dramatic tension arising out of such situations as Anup's sister being accused of stealing a necklace in her rich friend Gopa's house, and Anup's writing being plagiarized by Gopa's brother. Countering these class conflicts and personal rivalries is the developing romance between the poor Anup and the rich Gopa herself, his sister's friend and an industrialist's daughter. Gopa's contact with Anup results in her moral education about the lived conditions of poverty and deprivation and leads to her growing alienation from her own class. Gopa now dresses more simply, reads progressive literature (a novel written by Anup), and visits the tenements of the workers that are located in the shadows of her father's factory. As matters come to a head in the conflict between workers and management, Gopa leaves home and meets Anup, afraid that she has left the glamour of her existence behind. Assuring her that her destiny lies ahead, not behind her, Anup walks with her toward a symbolic dawn.

The film's frank populism and social idealism, its stereotypical representations of the rich and the poor, and its message of hope at the end suggest a moral parable overlaying the ideology of social realism in cinema. One way in which morality meets realism in cinema is that the rich-poor dichotomy translates into the appearance-essence problematic. Realist cinema usually relies on dress and life-style representations to signify social status. Film researcher Stanley Corkin cites clothing as a resonant aspect of characterization in certain late nineteenth- and early twentieth-century American novels. He writes, 'In a world of mass production and commodified goods and experiences, the material elements that garb a character have a meaning that suffices for the entire notion of a character's humanity.'[21] Clothing is, of course, a major signifier of social status as well as a vehicle of fantasy in the visual medium of the cinema. In *Udayer Pathe/Humrahi*, the world of mass production and a commodified life-style is also the villainized world of the rich, the arrogant preserve of the powerful. The heroine's humanization and proletarianization cannot come about until she willingly abandons her finery and embraces a plain, unadorned appearance. The code of clothing partakes of realism (the poor cannot afford fancy clothes) as well as metaphor. But it also suggests simplistically that class positioning is a matter of the externals of dress and jewellery which Gopa can abandon to signify her empathy with the poor.

Ultimately, it is not change in their material conditions but a moral victory that the workers and their spokesman, Anup, garner. The film's heady message of change becomes absorbed in the pacifist dream of interclass alliances and togetherness to fight oppression. Nevertheless, its portrayal of the intellectual as activist and its popularization of a nationalist intellectual tradition makes it a provocative instance of translation and transposition of a Bengali ethos and sensibility to the all-India level. Today, *Udayer Pathe/Humrahi* is interesting to us as a 'realist' film embodying preindependence moral passion and visionary zeal, and also for the implications that a film made in two languages has as a national-historical allegory. For here it is not a filmic character but film itself that assumes the garb of interchangeability to partake of a national identity. The question of language has always been very crucial in India, and the efforts of some filmmakers to make some films in two languages (even if ostensibly for marketing purposes) is not without its significance.

*Neecha Nagar* is very similar to *Udayer Pathe* in its plot, symbolic structure, thematic concerns, and social message. Winner of the Grand Prix at the Cannes Film Festival of 1946, it too dramatizes class conflict through anticolonial and nationalist images and motifs. The central image is that of water, the source of life, contaminated by big industry and turned into a life-threatening hazard for the poor. The pollution of water is both the effect and the analog of bourgeois oppression of the working class. The world depicted in this film is separated into *ooncha nagar* (upper town/area) and *neecha nagar* (lower town/area) inhabited by the very rich and the struggling poor, respectively. The source of conflict between these groups is a dirty stream that a rich industrialist known as Sarkarji ('Your Lordship') is diverting to pass through the poor section of town so that new houses can be constructed in the cleaned-up upper section. His daughter, Maya, objects to this decision but to no avail. The poor are represented by Balraj, who had attended college with Maya. Much of the film establishes the dynamics between the two opposing groups, including the activities of those who sell out to the factory owner. Balraj's negotiations, meanwhile, fall through. As the dirty water works its way through the poorer section of town, an epidemic breaks out and many people die, including Balraj's sister, Rupa. The people bond together and march toward the Sarkar's house, demanding justice. Cornered, and faced with the prospect of huge debts and bad investments, as well as a threat to his life, the Sarkar collapses on the floor, dead. Maya and Balraj are united in the end.

*Neecha Nagar* uses certain props to convey the bourgeoisie as a sinister power, the most prominent being a sculptured demon against which the industrialist is often framed. The film also juxtaposes a benign and becalmed natural world at the beginning of the narrative and images of the poor singing and happy, unlike the shadowy and cavernous interior spaces (home, office) associated with high living. It thus projects a romantic image of poverty, although that image gives way to more complex dynamics as the film progresses. Weighted with symbolism, including that of the central character, a Gandhian activist professing nonviolence, *Neecha Nagar* evokes worker power within an overall framework of the nationalist struggle.

*Neecha Nagar* is, strictly speaking, an expressionist rather than a realist film. In fact, director Chetan Anand called his film 'pretentious' in a retrospective glance.[22] The film is shot in high key lighting and is heavily symbolic in its use of props. The scenes of the people marching with torches glowing in the night, chanting freedom slogans, the momentum of the rising force of the oppressed, and the images of decay associated with the colonizing power translate the contemporary situation into cinema in a curious mixture of Gandhian and Marxist ideologies. Also, the heroine here, as in *Udayer Pathe*, serves as the link between the opposing classes and the mode of reconciliation rather than class hatred and mutual destruction.

*Dharti ke Lal* is an attempt to bring to all-India awareness the tragedy of the Bengal famine of 1943–44 in which five million peasants died. It was produced by the Indian People's Theatre Association (IPTA), of which Abbas, the film's director, was a founding member (as was Chetan Anand, the director of *Neecha Nagar*). This group of progressive writers, artists, musicians, and activists, born in the politically tumultuous days of the early forties, sought to enact consciousness-raising themes of contemporary relevance that would involve the people in street and neighborhood performances. At its inaugural conference in Bombay on 25 May 1943, the call went out: 'Come writer and artist, come actor and playwright, come all who work by hand or by brain, and dedicate yourself to the task of building a brave new world of freedom and social justice. And let us all remember, if we wish for a motto, that the workers are the salt of the earth and to be part of their destiny is the greatest adventure of our time.'[23] Khwaja Ahmad Abbas wrote and produced a number of plays for IPTA, such as *Yeh Amrit Hai* (*This is Immortality*) and *Zubeida*, the latter a very popular play. 'At certain open-air-performances, there were as many as ten thousand spectators. It is of some historical importance that many of the spectators of *Zubeida* included women who had never seen a play in their lives.'[24] *Dharti ke Lal* was based on another IPTA play, *Nabanna* (*New Harvest*), by Bijon Bhattacharya, and a Hindi story, *Annadata* (*Foodgiver*), by Krishen Chander. The film was a cooperative venture by IPTA members under egalitarian working conditions and distribution of labour.

About the historical circumstances leading to the Bengal famine, drama critic Rustom Bharucha writes:

> It is now widely acknowledged that the Bengal famine was not a natural disaster but a man-made one. The terrible irony about the famine is that it was not caused by any significant shortage of food. On the contrary, the per capita availability of food supply was 9 per cent higher in 1943 than in 1941, which was not a famine year. The problem was that this food was not made available to the peasants and laborers in the rural areas of Bengal. Instead, it was exported by the British to feed its armed forces fighting in Europe and Japan.[25]

Abbas's film concentrates on the human dimension of this tragedy. As is usual in the Hindi film, the British do not enter the picture, and the agents of oppression are their Indian counterparts—the landlord, the moneylender, the grain dealer. Abbas presents images of tranquility and quotidian village life in the beginning of the film that are gradually replaced by both stark city images of human destitution and (occasionally) stylized evocations of suffering.

The action centers on a peasant extended family in a Bengal village: the old parents and their two sons—one has a wife and the other is about to wed. The family harvest will pay for the wedding feast but the big landlord and the grain dealer from the city refuse to pay a fair price for it. The villagers get poorer though Niranjan, the older son, tries to hold out against the exploiting city bosses. Ramu, the younger brother, finds no rice to offer to the gods when his son is born. Several natural calamities force the villagers to migrate to Calcutta in search of a better life. But a worse fate awaits them there. Ramu and his wife are separated, he reduced to begging and she to prostitution. The old father dies, urging them to go back to the land. Niranjan and his wife return, along with some of the other villagers. Together they work hard to create a new harvest, benefiting from their sense of solidarity. Only Ramu and his wife remain outside, too alien now to go back to the simple rural life.

*Dharti ke Lal* tries to create a documentary look, particularly in its presentation of masses of starving and dying people. The hunger march into the city, shot with the help of the Kisan Sabha (Farmers Union) in Dhulia district, is a memorable scene. Film critic Kobita Sarkar writes, 'Two and a half decades later, it is easy to criticise the stiffness of the fabricated backgrounds, the stilted quality of some of the acting, the note of semi-hysteria that prevails at times and some of the contrived situations, for which the original form of the film, as a play, is at least partly responsible.'[26] The film celebrates some of the symbols of rural life such as the cow, the land, and rice, using them to suggest the villagers' ties to nature; the city, by contrast, is a cruel and ugly place, a camp for refugees. The film conveys messages of communal harmony, Hindu-Muslim unity, and patriotism. Director Abbas explains the film's poor reception at the box office as resulting from its badly timed release which coincided with the outbreak of the communal riots during Partition.[27]

## *Do Bigha Zamin*

Bimal Roy's *Do Bigha Zamin* is perhaps Indian cinema's most-cited film after *Pather Panchali*. The reasons are many: its 'contemporary' (that is, fifties) tone and texture, its exemplification of 'serious' intent within the popular commercial format, its Janus-faced view of Indian development. Like *Dharti ke Lal*, it deals with the harshness of village existence, an exodus, a symbolic return to loss and emotional devastation. Made after Indian independence, *Do Bigha Zamin* registers the ambivalence of the fifties toward the large-scale industrialization supported by the state. A contemporary review of the film remarked on its deep pessimism, saying that 'it is very odd that, at this early moment of Indian independence, any Indian director should make so savagely pessimistic a film. ... Not only is it a harsh film but, in the manner of Italian neo-realism, it gives an extraordinarily vivid picture of the living conditions in a great Indian city, where neon lights, occidental commodities in smart shops, and men and oxen sleeping in the streets are all part of the higgledy-piggledy scene.'[28] The film opens and closes with two stark images, the first of parched and cracked earth and the last of wire fence separating the main characters from their two acres of land. But the two images highlight a contrast: while the parched earth can become green and smiling again with the arrival of the monsoons, the farmer's land, once lost, is gone irrevocably. This is the concern voiced in *Do Bigha Zamin*—the destruction of the age-old Indian village by the forces of modernization allied to capital. The film's claim to realism rests in its double vision: showing the village through the perspective of city people and the city through the eyes of its villager-protagonists. In one shot early on in the film, a car stops at the edge of the fields and four strange men occupy the foreground of the frame, with the villagers in the middle ground and a cow in the background, a symbolic hierarchization that upsets the village structure. For developers, the village only signifies land to be bought and turned to profitable use.

The village/city divide, like the good peasant/evil moneylender divide, is of course an old theme in literature and cinema. Roy is not quite able to transcend the burden of this inheritance in the interests of realism so as to allow both to merge as complex entities. The early segments, for instance, focusing on village life, show the protagonists Shambhu (Balraj Sahni) and Paro (Nirupa Roy) as a hardworking and devoted couple and peasant life as one of simple, communally shared pleasures. (The only thorn in the side of this rural paradise is the archetypal figure of the moneylender, who, for all practical purposes, is an outsider). The city, on the other hand, is a ruthless jungle where it is easy to become dishonest and where the poor are trampled upon, women are molested, children are exploited. Shambhu's struggle to earn the necessary cash to extricate his two acres of land serving as collateral for the money he owes the village loan shark is elemental. As the overworked rickshaw puller, he becomes labour personified, an urban work-horse, a representative of the forgotten rural masses. The film seeks to nudge the moral conscience of the urban intelligentsia. Balraj Sahni admits as much when he notes in his autobiography how he had spent time with some rickshaw pullers in Calcutta in order to make his performance credible and his actions believable. Referring to a reviewer's observation that his acting in *Do Bigha* had a touch of genius, Sahni wrote, 'I owed this "touch" to that middle-aged ricksha-wallah.'[29]

Sahni also wrote that the character of Shambhu had two major flaws: one, he is never shown to stand up to the injustice and oppression he is subjected to, and two, he shuns the company of friends and colleagues.[30] Sahni seems to have put his finger on the tension at the heart of *Do Bigha Zamin* and in Indian sensibilities regarding realism: the manifest need to present at once an individualized consciousness *and* a proto-type, an agent *and* a victim. The filmmaker seems unable to resolve the contradictory pulls of inherited conventions on the one hand and political concerns on the other. To make matters more complicated, these do not divide neatly into art versus politics or (Bombay cinema) convention versus (Western cinema) innovation. For a political concern can make for conventional characterization, whereas realism as an artistic creed adopted from neorealism would still have to be adapted and contextualized to suit Indian social reality and its moral-emotional core. It is these correlations and cross-linkages that the film is not quite able to negotiate.

Why, then, is *Do Bigha* cited by Indian cineastes as a landmark realist film? I believe that the triumph of *Do Bigha* lies in turning land into a contested symbol, a good-bad commodity, for what signifies independence and dignity for the farmer (and, by extension, the mass of the population) is also, taken on a massive scale, the source of capitalist and landlord power and rural exploitation. Earlier films in this genre either did not show peasants as owning any land or simply did not treat the land as an object of emotional and psychic investment. *Do Bigha* is able to evoke the anxiety that we feel about property as a mark of material well-being and livelihood (the realm of necessity) and property as privilege (the realm not, spiritually speaking, of freedom but of class division). This anxiety, moreover, was inscribed in the very profile of India's nationalist ideologies and resulted in its peculiarly divided aims and policies. As a film that was able to capture and give shape to these ambivalences, *Do Bigha* remains a document of its time and an instance of popular cinema's moral realism.

## The 'Figurable' Nation: 'Morbid' Realism

If the above films reveal a deeply felt engagement with contemporary Indian life on the level of content and directorial purpose, what of style? Here we observe the characteristic turning to Hollywood as a model, for within the Bombay production mode, no radical stylistic departures could be or were proposed in the demand for realism. The question was of the cinema maintaining the illusion of reflection or representation within the fictional mode—that is, in the Hollywood style of smooth storytelling and invisible enunciation rather than

*Cinéma vérité, roughly translated as 'cinema of truth', is a style of film making combining naturalistic techniques, that originated in documentary film making, with the story-telling elements typical of a scripted film.

It aims for extreme naturalism, using non-professional actors, hand-held camera, genuine locations and naturalistic sound without substantial post-production mixing or voice-over. Editor.

in the cinéma vérité mode* or in open rebellion against studio conventions, as in Italian neo-realism. The star system was firmly entrenched in the Bombay industry and, as Fredric Jameson has said, 'the star system is fundamentally, structurally, irreconcilable with neo-realism.'[31] Most self-styled realist film directors operating out of Bombay worked with big stars but introduced the convention of deglamorizing them, of trying to write over the sign 'star' another sign which would read 'average man/woman.' Other conventions of the Hindi film, notably song and dance, did not necessarily interfere with the proposed realist stance, so long as the songs were few in number and appeared to be 'motivated' by the narrative. This does not suggest a naïveté on the part of filmmakers and viewers but rather a pragmatic acceptance of the basic ground rules of Bombay commercial cinema and modifications within its framework. Thus the lead performers in a film might burst into song at several key points, but if the story was set in Assam, for instance, the music director would feel obliged to provide Assamese rhythms and tunes and be congratulated for being realistic.

Filmmakers, then, brought this highly context—and culture-specific view of realism to bear on films. Nationhood provided the particular moment for the popularization of this view. The question we have raised is how the cinema actually incorporated concerns about realism and nationhood in its storytelling practices, narrative structure, and character motivation. But did the ethic of realism, however narrowly or broadly conceived, conflict with the notion of a *national* identity? How does one establish the 'truth' of social reality *as well as* allegorical representations of the nation? Three dilemmas may be pointed to. The first relates to how emphatic identification with character (Hollywood's classical realism) can be reconciled with the notion of objective observation, also aspired to by filmmakers. The second relates to the problem of how dramatic conflict, the core of fictional entertainment, can then be turned around to suggest the sense of a collectivity integral to nation building. And third, the desire to reflect the diversity and difference within Indian social life, its oppressions and prejudices, perhaps coming closest to the aims and intentions of realist filmmakers, is then faced with the gap between the 'local' and the 'global' within the Indian context. The question is of evolving a language of realism uniquely responsive to Indian needs. (... one reason for the obvious lack of success and decline of India's parallel cinema movement, in addition to the very material difficulties of finance and distribution, is its inability to forge a national idiom of cinema which could truly contest the Bombay film on its own terrain.) These dilemmas reveal, as Janice Radway points out, 'the thorny question of how culture and ideology are embodied in the content of mass-produced entertainment and how that entertainment affects the behavior of its consumers.'[32]

We can turn to Fredric Jameson's notion of 'figurability' as a way out of a theoretical bind. In his article 'Class and Allegory in Contemporary Mass Culture: *Dog Day Afternoon* as a Political Film,' Jameson contends that to be figurable is for something to be accessible to our imaginations, to become *representable* in tangible form. Through narrative figurability, film can help us detect changes in the underlying forces shaping social reality, 'since social reality and the stereotypes of our experience of everyday social reality are the raw material with which commercial film and television are inevitably forced to work.'[33] In certain Indian films of the postindependence period, though by no means in all, 'nationhood' assumes figurability—that is, it can be sensed 'through the tangible medium of daily life in vivid and experiential ways.'[34] The visceral quality of the experience of nationhood, quite apart from the abstract notion of it, is signaled in the films by changes in the narrative structure. The conventional 'happy ending' of the typical Bombay film, for instance, is replaced by an open-endedness that is unusual in that particular context of production. Moreover, the terms in which the central narrative conflict is delineated in the films implicate the broader social world outside the film in pointed referentiality. I shall concentrate on this dual process and its meanings in my discussion of some films in which the vision of realism itself becomes an issue.

As mentioned earlier, in postindependence India a major source of tension affecting the social and national consciousness was (and continues to be) the problem of holding on to established norms and value systems while the nation made the challenging and vaunted transition from feudalism to industrialism, from colonialism to democracy, from economic backwardness to material advancement. The impetus for the change was particularly strong right after independence, but while the leadership of the society was certain of the goals to be pursued the question of how to make the transition smooth or gradual was less often considered. Since the Indian sensibility tends to view complex issues as manifestations of moral choices, popular culture represented the felt experience of social change in terms of individual morality, of right and wrong, and 'resolved' them in various ways. Realist cinema could then explore the mixture of technological optimism (faith in the camera to reflect reality) and cultural pessimism, the idealization of village and community life in the face of mounting migrations to the city, material deprivation and the promise of easy wealth, widening class, regional, and communal divisions eclipsing the vision of an unfractured *national* identity. The 'truth' that the cinema was expected to 'capture' on the screen was not only the truth of social and psychological experience but the 'truth' of the right solution to moral dilemmas for the edification and satisfaction of the audience, in keeping with narrative traditions that Indian audiences were accustomed to. One way in which the Hindi film of the fifties sought to respond both to the cultural anxieties and the narrative expectations of its viewing public was through the problematization of the notion of poverty and the delineation of character progression along a trajectory that moves from a state of economic and social deprivation to material wealth to a deliberate return to poverty. The eschewing of definitive narrative closure (the 'happy ending' where the hero is at peace with, and part of, society) takes on significance in this regard. The closing frames of a film, for instance, might bring the stars of the film together, but only in the iconography of the marginalized or rejects of society. Before turning to the films in more detail, I would like to point out the cultural meanings attached to the deliberate embracing of poverty as signified in filmic and other discourses of the fifties.

The idea of poverty has a special significance in India. ('Poverty' here is only an approximate term. The word 'poverty' in its everyday sense denotes a material condition signified by lack of economic resources and consequent difficulty in maintaining a decent standard of living. I want to use it in this descriptive sense but without the wholly negative connotations and with the added dimension that makes it co-extensive with spiritual gain). While most religio-cultural beliefs and value systems embody some variation of the idea of material wealth as corrupting, in the Hindu religious and philosophical tradition the concept of poverty or nonattachment to material things has the status of an elaborated ethic. Apart from the fact that the essential thrust is toward the attainment of spiritual knowledge, there is the concept of the four stages of life on earth through which every Hindu passes—*brahmacharya* (that of a student learning the *shastras*, or holy books), *garhastha* (that of the householder fulfilling his or her social obligations), *vanaprastha* (that of a hermit, gradually withdrawing from society for meditation in the forest), and *sanyasa* (complete renunciation of worldly ties and desires). While the first half of a person's life is given over to this duties and responsibilities in the world, in the later years one is to concentrate more and more upon the spiritual and upon the search for liberation. The final stage of renunciation and withdrawal, therefore, marks the culmination and highest point of human achievement and is embodied in the image of the wandering mendicant who does not even care where his next meal is going to come from. This state of material poverty is a positive and willed condition, necessary for a person's self-realization, and one can think of numerous historical figures (Buddha, Shri Ramakrishna, Shri Aurobindo, among them) who chose to traverse this path. In the twentieth century Gandhi sought and enjoyed an identification with this image of poverty and deliberate renunciation, thereby earning the title of Mahatma, or 'great soul.'

A view of money as tainted and of poverty as sublime is thus part of the Indian psyche. But it is the act of *becoming* poor, not the state of being already poor, that attracts the Indian imagination. For poverty as degradation, breeding suffering, squalor, and death, has long been a harsh reality of the Indian landscape. In the postindependence era this poverty came to be called by its social scientific name of 'economic backwardness' and stood in the way of India's self-image of progress and equality with other nations. Economic backwardness was a condition that could be eliminated, our leaders fervently believed, by industrialization, science, and technology. The mode of the affluent Western nations was there for all to see. But it was not a model that India wanted to import wholesale, that is, it could do without the materialistic attitude of the West, its worship of money. Rather, in the nature of a transaction, India could offer to the (Western) world its spiritual traditions, its sense of ethical values, community, and compassion. Nehru's doctrine of Panchsheel, or the 'five principles' of mutual respect, nonaggression, nonintervention, equality, and peaceful coexistence, was cast in this optimistic and mediatory mode. This idea of the spiritual East complementing (or counterposed against, depending on the political winds blowing at the time the comparison is drawn) the materialistic West was not new in the Nehru era. It has been subscribed to by both Westerners and Easterners, finding its most creative expression in India in the mid- to late nineteenth century and having known various types of modifications and vulgarizations over the years. India's fragile sense of identity as a nation during the early years of independence (with the ambivalent view of 'poverty' as one of its symptoms) created both a moral and an intellectual dilemma. As Richard Lannoy states:

> The idea of national identity—the self-awareness of the nation, its self-image, and its values—springs from a desire for fixed points of reference in the enlarged world of today. The self-image of India is tentative in character and has evolved from the way it perceives its history from ancient times through many centuries of decline and foreign domination to the decades of its recently achieved status as an independent sovereign state. The difficulties in forming a contemporary national self-image may be more clearly appreciated when it is realized that while India is now building a modern, secular state, its traditions are permeated by a sophisticated religious sensibility.[35]

An impediment to the creation of a self-image that India could proudly embrace was indeed the excessive poverty in which half the population lived. But there were dangers in the dominant ideology endorsing too strongly what was its opposite, namely, money or material affluence. Not only did affluence have negative connotations in the folk imagination, but a too eager pursuit of money could unleash the undesirable social traits of cupidity, fraud, theft, and the like. Since implicit in the creation of a new society is some vision of utopia, an idea of what type of society is desirable and what sort of citizens should inhabit it, forms of mass culture can become instrumental in embodying the tension that results between the utopian ideal and the bedrock of practical considerations to which it must be linked. Richard Dyer has suggested, 'Entertainment offers the image of "something better" to escape into, or something we want deeply that our day-to-day lives don't provide. Alternatives, hopes, wishes—these are the stuff of utopia, the sense that things could be better, that something other than what is can be imagined and maybe realised.'[36] Moreover, Dyer asserts that entertainment responds to real needs created by society and that the utopian sensibility 'has to take off from the real experiences of the audience.'[37] Much of the realistic cinema of postindependence India can be seen in this 'utopian' vein. Broadly speaking, the utopian sensibility was linked to a strong moral stance vis-à-vis fetishized images of money. Indian mass culture translated the allure of money (with its materialistic and unethical connotations) into an instrumental view of money. In other words, filmmakers could provide what seemed a naturalistic portrayal of social reality, the world of 'dirty' business, black money, corruption, and greed, while at the same time imply through point-of-view shots and sympathetic and morally upright characters the availability of the utopian solution. The ethical code suggested that money earned through honest hard work was a desired social virtue, but excessive accumulation of it or an obsession to acquire it could create a social world that was the opposite of utopian. At its simplest we have in films the national stereotypes of the poor but happy peasant, the hard-working and honest labourer, the idealistic schoolteacher, the philanthropic doctor. These figures were touched but not corrupted by the social environment created by the momentum of a fast-growing economy supporting capital accumulation, the struggle for higher wages, illicit profits, and the like. But the utopian sensibility may also be generally absent in some films, to be replaced by a deliberate exploration of negative modes of feeling like anxiety, pessimism, fear, and resignation. *Hum Log*, *Andhian*, *Footpath* (1953), *Shri 420* (*The Gentleman Cheat*, 1955), *Jagte Raho* (*Keep Awake*!, 1956), *Pyaasa* (*The Thirsty One*, 1957), and *Kala Bazaar* (*Black Market*, 1960) were a few of these films.

Such films work with the raw materials of the contemporary experience of the lower middle class and the labouring classes of urban Indians (the target audience of the Bombay cinema) and may be said to present the city as the microcosm of the nation. This is apparent in terms of formal structure and the use of narrative space. In the typical Hindi film (and in commercial entertainment generally) the central conflict engaging the characters allows for a division of the fictional space available to them, so that they can retreat to the part of it that represents refuge, harmony, and happiness. The home, the village, scenic natural surroundings provide this kind of privatized fictional space. In some of the well-known postindependence films, however, particularly in *Jagte Raho*, *Pyaasa*, *Shri 420*, *Deedar* (*Sight*, 1951) but also in others like *Mr. Sampat* (1952), space is alien and threatening, allowing the central character no escape outside it. This space is the big city, a closed urban milieu impressionistically rendered, with an atmosphere that is claustrophobic, evil, corrupt. Divided between a naturalist (focusing on objects to define character) and a realist (focusing on the individual) impulse, these films create a morbid realism. Filmic space provides the testing ground for the character's moral sense, but moral victory can only result in withdrawal to a nonexistent space, to nowhere, a space that the films do not indicate visually at any point in the narrative.

A few examples should make this clear. In *Jagte Raho* the opening shots present a deserted city street at night where the 'hero' finds himself wandering, lost and alone. The iconography of dress and makeup suggests that he is a villager but we are never told where he belongs, no flashbacks connect him to the place he has left, and at the end of the film when he walks away from the apartment building where he was trapped as in a maze he only gets as far as beyond the gates of the building. In *Shri 420*, similarly, the hero's arrival in and departure from the big city mark the beginning and end of the narrative. Urban space engulfs him, symbolizing the closed world of the city dweller who is forced to confront pain and temptation. Vidya (meaning 'knowledge'), the heroine of the film and its moral center, is a poor schoolteacher. In *Pyaasa*, the alienated hero is not from the village but is city-bred, educated but expendable in terms of the operative values of urban society. He is a poet and therefore unemployable, important to society only in death, shunned and institutionalized in an insane asylum when alive. He has a family but no home and can only leave at the end of the film for an unknown destination with a similar marginal figure, a one-time prostitute. In *Mr. Sampat*, based on an R.K. Narayan novel, the hero as antihero is also without family or attachments, but unlike the central characters in the other films, he embodies that rare phenomenon in the Bombay film, the corrupt hero who is thoroughly immersed in the fraudulent city milieu and remains a liar and opportunist till the end of the film. He is the man of the world incarnate, turning every occasion to his benefit and someone else's loss. But he is no more corrupt than a host of other social types who inhabit that fictional world—tall-talking politicians, unethical businessmen, heartless journalists, get-rich-quick merchants, scheming philanthropists—and may even elicit grudging admiration from the audience for being able to live by his wits.

Within this all-encompassing urban world 'poverty' and 'wealth' as signifiers* act on two levels. In terms of contemporary experience they point to economic and social divisions within society and of the fantasies of the poor to get rich and of the rich to get richer. But they also embody the stock opposition between the 'traditional' moral values of honesty, hard work, and fellowship and 'modern' urban culture breeding hatred, suspicion, greed, and loneliness. The two worlds are poised against each other, and seldom do the films explore the possibility of infusing the values of the one in the culture of the other. The result in terms of dramatic movement is a circular one; the hero returns to his initial state and to a space outside urban society, which is nevertheless denied a palpable existence in visual or narrative codes. The return involves a conscious and deliberate rejection of the values associated with city life that stem from the possession or the pursuit of wealth. For instance, in *Deedar*, childhood as an idyllic condition where class divisions do not count is juxtaposed with the adult world of social hierarchy and distance. The narrative charts the hero's spatial and temporal movement from childhood and 'inside' society to adulthood and 'outside' it in terms of his loss, recovery, and then self-inflicted loss of vision, the final act of self-directed violence signaling his disenchantment by a departure from the depicted social world.

The central characters of *Do Bigha Zamin* return to their village after a sojourn to the city only to find that they have no place to live. In *Jagte Raho* the outsider-hero can only quench the thirst that has driven him to the city by stepping outside its stultifying and corrupt confines and symbolically retracing his steps back to the village. The narrative agent of *Shri 420* follows a similar circular trajectory after having nearly lost his integrity (*iman*) among the city sharks. In *Pyaasa* the poet-hero's fortunes involve a torturous succession of 'worldly' success and failure through which he can only liberate himself by willfully choosing the anonymity from which he had started out to escape. What is interesting here is that contestation of the dominant generic conventions of the Bombay film at the level of narrative paradigm can be offset by the assertion of traditional moral values at the level of the image. In each of these films wealth serves also as an object of desire at the level of the subtext, revealed on the visual track by an excess of images of money—paper

*The idea of the 'sign' was first defined by the Swiss linguist Ferdinand de Saussure in his Course in General Linguistics. Language is made up of signs which have little to do with the referent, the actual object in the world. The signs are composed of two parts: the signifier (the letters on the page c-a-t or the sound kat that our eardrum registers) and the signified (the concept that appears in our brain: the animal known as Cat).

The relation between signifier (c-a-t) and signified (cat) is arbitrary since there is nothing inherent in the letters that connect with the cat or its nature. Editor.

currency, bank notes, gold coins—gratifying the viewer's eye and imagination by means of close-ups, superimpositions, and other cinematic techniques. The conflict itself is inscribed within the *dharmic* code (signifying the law) that Vijay Mishra talks about in an article on the Bombay cinema. Poverty and wealth, then, are associated in the texts with *dharma* and renunciation on the one hand and *adharma* and worldliness on the other. As Mishra tells us, 'The opposition between *nivritti* ('renunciation') and *pravritti* ('worldliness') constitutes a major epistemological shift in Hindu thought which survives, in its various forms, to this day. Needless to say, its ramifications in the Bombay film too are considerable.'[38] Most Bombay films rework this opposition and work toward a mediation through the agency of the hero. How then are we to read the act of renunciation in the films under review? Does it offer a genuine alternative, either on the real or the symbolic/representational level? I have suggested above that the renunciation that the films espouse has only an emotional force (it does not appear as a concrete possibility), and I find this as evidence of the enlarged national context that the films allegorically represent. In these texts the mediation operates on another level. The films accommodate the demands of verisimilitude and those of ideology by representing the human costs of economic growth and social Darwinism, but they prescribe a strict moral code and 'legitimize' renunciation of the ways of the unscrupulous. So while renunciation is negated, since it is the opposite of involvement, the required and desired state for citizens of the new nation, it is also proposed as a fitting rejection of the social evils of cupidity, fraud, and competitiveness.

Bimal Roy's *Parakh* (*Test,* 1960) brings these themes together through the medium of social satire. With story and music by Salil Chowdhury, a long-term member of the Bimal Roy production team, *Parakh* is a thinly veiled attack on the nation's politicians, particularly those with vested interests who manipulate the common people for personal gain and power. The action is set in a small village with its ensemble of representative characters: the postmaster; the schoolteacher; the *pundit*, or professional prayergiver; the *zamindar*, or landlord; the moneylender; the village doctor; the astrologer; and the politician, who is a union board president. The film introduces each of these characters, all of whom, with the exception of the postmaster and the schoolteacher, Rajat (Vasant Chowdhury), are satirized as embodiments of the negative traits of meanness, greed, fraudulence, pomposity, and pretense. Mostly Bombay film comedians (some often cast as villains as well) were chosen for these roles, so as to build on prior associations, a practice common in the Hindi cinema. The eye of the camera catches, as it were, each man revealing his own negative trait as he goes about his activity in the village. Only the postmaster (Nasir Hussein) is decent and honest, as is Rajat, the hero, who is in love with the postmaster's charming and childlike daughter, Seema (Sadhana).

The plot in *Parakh* involves an enigma and an impersonation: a lame postman, Haradhan (Motilal), delivers a letter to the postmaster from a wealthy beneficiary named Jagdish Chandra Ray, whose identity is not known. The letter says that a reward of Rs 5 lakh (roughly $50,000) will be given to the person in the village with the best record of social service. When the letter is read out in the presence of all the village notables, their expressions are captured through freeze frames: mouths fall open, swallowing motions are seen, the *zamindar* stops smoking. Rajat suggests that a vote be taken, and the elections are set for the first day of the following month. Then starts a veritable scramble for the goodwill of the people as the candidates vie with one another to reverse their habitual mean or greedy attitudes: the doctor gives free treatment, the *zamindar* forgives his debtors, the *pundit* fakes a miracle. Processions, banners, and loudspeakers proclaim the virtues of different candidates, and fights between rival factions break out. Only the postmaster remains aloof and is on the verge of losing his home because he cannot pay the mortgage. Rajat also withdraws from the election. But the people find none of the candidates worthy of the award and declare the postmaster the winner. The identity of the benefactor is also revealed: he is Sir J.C. Roy, a rich and powerful man masquerading as the lame postman and studying the dynamics of the village. The villagers rejoice with the surprised postmaster as honesty and goodness are rewarded in the end. Haradhan's fantasy over, he regretfully leaves the village.

This parable of political corruption and chicanery in postcolonial India is explored through the 'victimized' space of the village (where politicians routinely make their appearance before an election) in which moral order and disorder can be presented in fairly clear-cut tones. In keeping too with the conventions of the Bombay film the saree-clad and innocent village belle is contrasted with a Westernized and spoilt city-bred woman, the sister-in-law of the *zamindar*. Through the medium of satire, traditional and new-found authority is challenged. But the vision of change offered by the film is a paternalist one. Fantasies of escape into a romanticized 'averageness' are only available to the very rich, who can afford to pass on some of their wealth to the poor provided the latter are good and honest. The upper-class, aristocratic benefactor masquerading in the village and upsetting its routines preserves the broader social hierarchies even as he holds himself beyond them through his superior knowledge and wisdom.

## *Sujata*

*Parakh* is a crossover from 'morbid' realism to moral realism. That is, it is anxious to morally frame the social evil it depicts, to present contemporary life in the form of a fable. *Sujata* (*The Well-Born*, 1959), on the other hand, is much more gentle in its approach, the camera more objective, the characters psychologically rounded. It may be considered a condensation of many of the elements we have discussed as constituting realism in Bombay cinema: a Bengali-Hindi combination (the film was based on a Bengali novel by that name written by Subodh Ghosh), a nationalist purpose (Bimal Roy, the director, responded to a call for a film to be made on Untouchability), a highlighting of emotions through subtle editing and camerawork, naturalistic mise-en-scène, and a morally elevated tone. *Sujata*'s theme of stability and change seems to reproduce its maker's own transitional state. By the time Bimal Roy produced *Sujata*, he was a prominent and esteemed commercial filmmaker. An emigré from East Bengal, he had started his career in the mid-thirties as a cameraman, first with the pioneering director P.C. Barua, then with Nitin Bose of New Theatres in Calcutta. He was forced to move to Bombay when the Calcutta market suffered a serious setback with the Second World War and impending Partition, bringing his own group of unit members (Hrishikesh Mukerjee, cameraman, Nabendu Ghosh, writer, Asit Sen, actor, and Paul Mahendra, dialogue writer) with him. He was later joined by Salil Choudhary, Kamal Bose, Sudhendhu Roy, Nazir Hussain, and others. He set up Bimal Roy Productions in 1953 and made many films under his own banner. Although exposed to all the commercial pressures of the Bombay industry, he tried to continue the tradition of 'social realism' of New Theatres, also running his company in the old studio manner of the big extended family. The influence of the Bengali 'sentimental' novelistic tradition of Sarat Chandra Chatterjee is evident in his films, which usually have a strong story-line, psychological characterization, and ennobling sentiments. His films bear the stamp of the sensibility of the middle-class intelligentsia, who shared the idealism of the national reconstruction phase and subscribed to broadly socialist values. *Sujata* is invariably included in the official retrospectives of Indian films at international film festivals and enjoys the status of a classic. Its mechanisms of pleasure, blend of realism and idealism, and the humanitarian vision that it embodies denote a powerful if fading, current in the fifties' symbolic universe.

In *Sujata*, many of the oppositions discussed earlier—between poverty and wealth, renunciation and worldliness, *dharma* and *adharma*, desire and law—are worked out in terms of the family as nation/nation as family idea. This is the culmination of the utopian vision, for it integrates within the construct of the nation the self-sufficiency implicit in the image of the modern bourgeois family (by extension the modern bourgeois state) and the ties of blood and genealogy that characterize traditional Indian notions of family. The story concerns the adoption of an Untouchable baby girl by a Brahmin family and the problems that then arise. The child is not so much adopted as allowed to stay on because a suitable home cannot be found for her, her parents having died in an epidemic.

She is named Sujata and grows up with the family's own daughter, Rama. When a relative with orthodox religious views visits, matters get complicated and Sujata (Nutan) learns of her low-caste origins. Her adoptive mother wants Rama to marry Adhir (Sunil Dutt), a highly educated and accomplished Brahmin boy who, however, falls in love with Sujata. Enraged, her 'mother' insults Sujata and has an accident that leaves her in need of a blood transfusion. Only Sujata's blood matches her own and Sujata is thus able to save her life. The family is reunited and Sujata and Adhir are married.

The narrative is structured by posing the toughest problem of all in class and genealogical terms: the 'pollution' of blood and the 'mingling' of blood. The film is openly didactic in that it stresses the correct moral position with respect to caste distinctions, operating at both the discursive and emotional levels. At various point in the narrative the opposing views regarding Untouchability are counterposed in dramatic conflict, while the viewer's empathy for and identification with the central character, Sujata, is assured by every means available to the entertainment cinema: star quality, cinematic techniques of the close-up, point-of-view shots and framing, the narrative pleasures of romance, suspense, and a happy ending. Illusionism is maintained by projecting the fictional world as co-extensive with the real world, with common reference points and shared (Gandhian) values, as also by 'natural' acting, dress, and speech and the use of outdoor sets. The film is ideological in the sense that it presents the possibility of the idea society in the here and now under the spirit of Gandhi, who is a sort of patron saint to Sujata, saving her once from suicide and unfailingly offering comfort, strength, and hope in her darkest moments. (In fact, the very idea of the narrative situation, that of an Untouchable being 'adopted' by an upper-caste family, is taken from Gandhi's teachings: Gandhi advocated that Hindus should adopt Muslim children and vice-versa to promote communal harmony.) Moreover, the film is firmly grounded in a middle-class, upper-caste ethos, for it is Sujata who is 'elevated' in the caste hierarchy by her induction into a Brahmin family rather than the other way around, and time and time again in the narrative the essential nobility of spirit of the major Brahmin characters becomes evident, including the two caste-conscious women characters in the film, Sujata's 'foster mother' and Adhir's grandmother, who experience a change of heart at the end of the film. On the other hand, the few portraits of people belonging to Sujata's own caste are decidedly unflattering fulfilling the stereotypes of the drunken, physically unattractive lower castes.

Against his background, it is Sujata's character which becomes a poignant instance of impersonation: she is 'Brahmin' among the untouchables and 'untouchable' among the Brahmins. She, and we, the audience, are always conscious of her split identity. The fact that Sujata is an Untouchable by birth is almost incidental, though it has a crucial importance in the unfolding of the narrative. Sujata's associations are with nature, and some of the most beautiful shots in the film show her in close proximity with flowers, against rain-laden clouds, in the garden among rare and delicate species of plants. (The visual and symbolic 'distance' of Sujata from the condition of untouchability is underscored by the fact that one of the foremost stars of the period, Nutan, plays this role with great finesse.) Sujata is a floating signifier*; her natural parents are dead at the beginning of the film and her entry into the dominant social order must be initiated through a reconstruction of genealogy and connections of blood. In spatial terms, she must move from outside society to inside it, from a 'natural' state to marriage and domestication, from poverty and dependence to wealth and social position. Membership in the family/nation, in other words, leads to upward mobility along several axes. We will examine each of these coordinates as they affect the notion of utopia in the film.

At first glance it would seem that the film makes an unproblematical statement about the insiders of society, the wealthy and upper caste, versus those like the poor and lower castes, who have to suffer the status of outsiders and have to be incorporated. But the distinctions are not always so clear. Upendra Chowdhury is not rooted to place and community, the fact that is taken as the mark of identity of the twice-born Hindus. In a sense he has lost his caste, since he has a job (as an engineer) that takes him to remote places, remote from his own kind, that is. His taking in and then harboring an Untouchable is to some extent possible because of these circumstances. Moreover, he is a man of science and therefore rational, enlightened, free from outmoded ideas of caste. It is in such apparently incidental details (the film does not draw attention to Upendra's job although it does to his enlightened thinking) that *Sujata* has a contemporary resonance and is 'realistic.' It directs its message to those whose lives were changing as a result of the nation's industrialization and development projects, forcing them to travel outside their regions and thereby loosening, to some extent, the hold of caste taboos on them. Yet even here the film is at best cautious. Upendra and his wife, Charu, are always conscious of Sujata's 'difference' and never fail to underscore it—particularly Charu, whose verbal distinction between her own child and the adoptive child ('my daughter' and 'like my daughter') runs as a motif through the film and is an index of Sujata's emotional and familial isolation. It is only when Sujata 'proves' herself through the biggest test of all, the giving of her own blood to save Charu's life, that she is finally accepted into the caste identity and social milieu of Upendra's family. Sujata must transcend the conditions of her birth before she can truly 'belong,' and the agent of her upliftment is not something

*A signifier with an unspecified or variable signified; such signifiers mean different things to different people. Editor.

she does but something that *is*: her blood type happens to match that of the dying Charu. The film, while making the point that caste is not a matter of polluted blood, nevertheless ossifies caste by making the breaking of caste barriers dependent upon accident.

The conflict of values represented by the opposition of 'poverty' and 'wealth' that is central to the films we talked about earlier is here less overt, but the question of inheritance does occupy a key place in the narrative. We (the audience for the film) sense, although there is no specific sign, that one reason for Charu's anxiety in safeguarding the prospects of her daughter, Rama, in securing Adhir's affections and her perception of Sujata as a threat in this regard is that Adhir is the sole heir to his grandmother's wealth. Only such an unspoken hope can explain the viciousness with which she turns on Sujata when she hears that Sujata has 'usurped' Adhir's love, accusing her of being a serpent in their midst. Sujata has done the ultimate wrong that a foster child can perpetrate: she has tried to take the place of the natural child and, in a sense, disinherit her. The question of property and inheritance, then, plays an unobtrusive but forceful role in the motivation of character and plot. Wealth is obviously part of the utopian vision and the hero, Adhir, has enough of it. But he does not possess it directly and is apparently uncaring about it, for he likes to be immersed in books (the 'displaced' source of wealth) and even spurns his grandmother's legacy when she opposes his marriage with Sujata. Since one of the points that the film wishes to make is that modern education is true wealth, the means of dispelling ignorance, superstition, and prejudice, inherited wealth, which goes with social class, is an attribute of the upholders of prejudice in the film such as Adhir's grandmother, who probably inherited *her* property. But by making Adhir and Sujata ultimately come into a lot of money, the film maintains both sides of the contradiction: money operating as class and caste barrier and money as ascension into a higher class and caste. In a country where a major social division is perpetuated as a result of inherited wealth (and status), inherited wealth can only be justified as a source of philanthropy. Inherited wealth is morally justifiable when it is instrumental in bringing about social upliftment. The film, however, does not propose any radial change in the basic economic divisions in society. If we then pursue our family-as-nation metaphor, the lower castes and untouchables can be incorporated into the larger body of society by a symbolic purification of blood and the sharing of inheritance.

Just as deliverance from a lower-caste identity can come through integration into a higher-caste family, deliverance from a subordinate sexual identity must come through marriage. Sujata's subjectivity is defined by the two characters emotionally closest to her, both of whom are male: Upendra, her substitute father, and Adhir, her wooer and prospective husband. As mentioned earlier, one of the projects that the film sets itself is to confer on Sujata an identity in social and familial terms. This involves, among other things, the process of naming. Early in the film, Upendra names the foundling 'Sujata,' meaning 'of good birth,' in a symbolic reversal of her true origins that is to continue throughout the film. With Adhir's arrival on the scene, this task is taken over by him. A particular sequence, quite movingly and beautifully presented, makes this clear. Rama's birthday party is being celebrated, as it is every year, and Charu has just hurt Sujata's feelings once again by identifying her to one of the guests as *beti jaisi* ('*like* my daughter'). Sujata leaves the enclosed space of the room where the party is being held and, as is her wont, seeks refuge in the open air of the night. Adhir has noticed her pained embarrassment and quietly follows her. In the course of their conversation, he asks her when her birthday is and she replies that it is lost in the darkness of oblivion. Adhir then points to the sky and 'names' her birthday by saying that on that day too the stars were shining as brightly and they were witness to the event of Sujata's birth. In reply to his question of what gift she would like for her birthday, she replies that he had given her the greatest gift of all: recognition as a human being to one whose birthday was unknown and who was therefore without any sort of identity.

The film thus poses Sujata's dual identity, as daughter (to Upendra) and wife (to Adhir), as problematic and sets about clearing the obstacles to its establishment. Marriage to Adhir is considered, by Sujata and by all others in her social world, as the ultimate good fortune, and the film offers Sujata no options to make it on her own. She has had no formal education and no chance to prove herself except in domestic matters, as an 'elevated' and very efficient servant. Marriage to Adhir is also linked to her financial independence: Adhir's grandmother, in a gracious gesture of defeat, leaves Sujata the money that she had set aside as a gift for Adhir's bride. A woman's social and individual identities are therefore both conferred by marriage, for without it Sujata is simply an appendage, and often an embarrassment, in the Chowdhury household. While part of this has a dramatic function, to highlight Sujata's plight as an Untouchable, the overall traditional attitude to women remains in place. The fact that the men in the film are open-minded and progressive while the women are superstitious and rigid in their thinking (with a change of heart in the end) can be seen as an extension of this attitude. In terms of the utopian vision, then, an upper-middle-class, male-dominated culture remains in place, but it is a culture infused with the ideals of liberal education, scientific thinking, and class and caste mobility.

From *Sujata*, to Bimal Roy, to fifties moral realism in cinema, to realism as the metaphoric site of displaced intellectual anxiety in postindependence India, we can retrace our mental steps in order to apprehend 'realism' as a historical process of cultural consensus building in which, briefly, the cinema saw itself as a dominant player. Each of these discursive constructs has served as a nodal point in the preceding analysis to illustrate the convergence of ideological purpose, social and economic change, artistic endeavour, and traditional values. In other words, nationalist goals as envisioned and articulated by political leaders were widely shared by all influential sectors of the population and the general public more than in any subsequent period of the nation's history. Vast projects of industrialization unleashed conditions of social flux that found in realism a stabilizing discourse. The influence of Western narrative models, both literary and cinematic, meant the striving after the 'truth' of lived experience and social reality, the minimizing of the gap between the fictional world and the referential world. And, finally, the valorization in cultural texts of traditional values of duty, renunciation, and poverty was meant to offset the greed, selfishness, and individualism associated with Western-style progress. Realism, then, is that which crosses over, binds, and translates one domain of social experience and capitalist development with, and for, another.

But I have also tried to present realism as an impersonating discourse. By this my impulse has not been toward constructing a hierarchy of 'realisms' within the Indian cinema (regional and all-India) in which the commercial Hindi film can be reconfirmed to hold the lowermost space. Whose realism is more real is not a question that concerns me in this study (although I do not deny that there might be a context for raising such issues of aesthetic differentiation). Rather, it is the *adoption* of realism as a guiding principle that has been of interest here. Moreover, in keeping with the idea of impersonation elaborated so far in this book, I have tried to show the co-presence of contradictory, even oppose forces and tendencies that makes *this realism* a uniquely Indian phenomenon; that is, a social and psychic investment at a given place and time. Thus 'realism' has been a code word for 'moralism'; an aesthetic yardstick to gauge commercial filmmaking practices; a mode of juxtaposition of the intellectual with the working poor (as in the actor Balraj Sahni's comments regarding his 'education' at the hands of a rickshaw-puller prior to the shooting of *Do Bigha Zamin*); an ethic of deglamorization of stars and of cinematic production generally, within the generic frameworks already in place; and a mode of national self-examination, self-reflection, and self-representation, again within the parameters of 'idealist' conventions, in which pain, humiliation, and agony as contemporary conditions can only have meaning as the masquerading forms of the eternal verities of truth and beauty. Realism, in other words, allows Indian popular cinema to will itself as an (ambivalent) participant in a worldwide hegemonic formation (the 'modernization' formula), seeking to disclose from within the bases of technological power and bourgeois capital technology's human face.

## Notes and References

1. The question of realism has been crucial to the discussion of cinema from the very beginning but received its most systematic formulation in the 1940s and 1950s in the work of Andre Bazin, *What Is Cinema?* 2 vols. (Berkeley, 1967). Siegfried Kracauer's *Theory of Film: The redemption of physical reality* (New York, 1960), also adopts a realist stance. During the 1970s, issues of realism were central to the ideological and aesthetic debates that flourished in *Screen*. See, for instance, Paul Willemen, 'On Realism in the Cinema,' *Screen* 13, no. 1 (Spring 1972): 37–44; Colin MacCabe, 'Realism and the Cinema: Notes on some Brechtian theses,' *Screen* 15, no. 2 (Summer 1974): 7–27; and Colin MacCabe, 'Theory and Film: Principles of realism and pleasure,' *Screen* 17, no. 3 (Autumn 1976): 7–27. Other journals that have taken up the debate on realism are *Cinema Journal, Camera Obscura,* and *Quarterly Review of Film Studies.*

2. Ananda Coomaraswamy, *Dance of Siva: Essays on Indian art and culture,* (New York, 1985), p. 104. The concept of *maya*, or illusion, in the Hindu philosophical tradition is a complex and difficult one. Material reality as maya should not be taken to mean that this view holds the world to be a figment of one's imagination. For a brief clarification of the concept, see Mircea Eliade, *Myths, Dreams and Mysteries: The encounter between contemporary, faiths and archaic realities* (New York, 1967), pp. 238–45.

3. An extensive literature is available on the 'Rasasutra,' the basis of Sanskrit classical drama and aesthetics. For an introduction to the concept, see Edward Dimock et al., *The Literatures of India: An introduction* (Chicago, 1974), pp. 115–36, 216–27.

4. Meenakshi Mukherjee, *Realism and Reality: The novel and society in India* (Delhi, 1985), p. 15.

5. Ibid., p. 89.

6. Ibid., p. 80.

7. See, however, a critique of Mukherjee's position in a review of her book by Nancy Fitch, *Journal of South Asian Literature* 22, no. 1 (Winter/Spring 1987): 238–44.

8. Gordon Roadarmel, 'The Modern Hindi Short Story and Modern Hindi Criticism,' in Dimock, *The Literatures of India*, p. 241.

9. Ibid., pp. 241–43.

10. Ibid., p. 245.

11. For detailed background information on developments within the Bombay film industry during the fifties, I have relied primarily on *Filmfare* and *Filmindia* for reasons of availability and also for the fact that as English-language film magazines they had a pan-Indian readership. I have also consulted the *Journal of the Film Industry* and the film page in the *Illustrated Weekly of India*.

12. See Edward Shils, *The Intellectual between Tradition and Modernity* (The Hague, 1961).

13. Aruna Vasudev and Philippe Lenglet (eds.), *Indian Cinema Superbazaar* (Delhi, 1983), p. 222.

14. *Filmfare*, 24 July 1953.

15. *Indian Talkie, 1931–56*, p. 4.

16. *Filmfare*, 18 March 1955.

17. Interview with Nabendu Ghosh by the author, 13 March 1984.

18. Even as astute a filmmaker as Shyam Bengal felt that the editing out of songs from Guru Dutt's *Sahib Bibi aur Ghulam* would enhance it as a 'realistic' film. See Vasudev and Lenglet, *Indian Cinema*, pp. 161–62.

19. Kumar Shahani, interview with the author, March 1984.

20. Satyajit Ray, quoted in *Film India: Looking back, 1896–1960* (New Delhi, 1981), p. 134.

21. Stanley Corkin, 'Realism and Cultural Form: The Common Structures of American Cinema and Realistic Literature in the Late 19th and Early 20th Centuries' (Ph.D. dissertation, New York University, 1984), p. 93.

22. Interview with the author, February 1984.

23. Rustom Bharucha, *Rehearsals of Revolution: The political theatre of Bengal*, (Calcutta, 1983), p. 40.

24. Ibid., p. 42.

25. Ibid., p. 48.

26. Kobita Sarkar, *Khwaja Ahmad Abbas as a Film-Maker*.

27. Interview with the author, December 1982.

28. Review of *Do Bigha Zamin* in *Film India: Looking back*, p. 134.

29. Balraj Sahni, *Balraj Sahni*, p. 205.

30. Ibid., p. 212.

31. Fredric Jameson, 'Class and Allegory in Contemporary Mass Culture: *Dog Day afternoon* as a Political Film,' in Bill Nichols (ed.), *Movies and Methods*, Part 2 (Berkeley, 1985), p. 722.

32. Janice Radway, 'The Error of Her Ways,' Book Review Section in *Journal of Communication* 35, no. 4 (Autumn 1985): 181.

33. Jameson, 'Class,' p. 719.

34. Ibid.

35. Richard Lannoy, *The Speaking Tree: A study of Indian culture and society*, (New York, 1974), p. xix.

36. Richard Dyer, 'Entertainment and Utopia,' in Nichols (ed.), *Movies and Methods*, p. 222.

37. Ibid., pp. 228–29.

38. Vijay Mishra, 'Towards a Theoretical Critique of Bombay Cinema,' *Screen 26*, no. 3–4 (May–August 1985): 139.

# 5.

# 'Unity in Diversity?' Dilemmas of Nationhood in Indian Calendar Art

PATRICIA UBEROI

## I Prologue

IN A SEMINAR HELD IN DELHI NOT SO LONG AGO, A HISTORIAN WELL-KNOWN FOR HIS sensitivity to the visual idioms of popular culture intervened in a heated debate on the fate of Indian 'secularism' with a reference to a particularly ubiquitous representation of that theme in popular 'calendar art'. I am no longer sure that I can pin-point the precise occasion of his intervention; nor can I now recapitulate his overall argument. But, as a long-term observer of calendar art, I was struck by the comment nonetheless.

The print he referred to was apparently known to almost everyone present. It has been constantly reproduced through the troubled decade of the 1990s. Probably it dates back much further. In any case, the idea and the idiom of representation were so familiar with repeated viewing as to seem scarcely remarkable. The print bears the slogan, '*Ham sab ek hai[n]*' (We are all one), and shows in its four quarters four fair, cherubic and physiognomically almost identical young boys, recognizable respectively as Hindu, Muslim, Christian and Sikh (Figure 1).[1] As I recall it, the historian (we may now identify him as Shahid Amin) had two points to make about this poster.

The first was a comment on what he believed to be the contemporary fate of the foundational nationalist ideal of 'secularism', conceived as the acceptance of religious diversity in the context of modern nation-building.[2] '*Ham sab ek hain*', Amin asserted, was an image that was now completely 'drained of meaning', the remorseless and unchanging repetition of the print being a sure sign of its semiotic emptiness. It is now just a tokenistic, ritual gesture to an

Excerpted from *Contributions to Indian Sociology* (n.s.) 36, 1 & 2 (2002), Sage Publications, New Delhi, Special Issue, *Beyond Appearances? Visual Practices and Ideologies in Modern India*, edited by Sumathi Ramaswamy.

Figure 1: *'Ham sab ek hai[n]'* (We are all one). Artist: unclear, (probably Anil Sharma). Publisher VPP 242, Delhi 1990. (Author's collection.)

ideal of national unity which no longer holds meaning—a 'dead metaphor', that has long since lost its power to excite, to provoke, to index a new reality.[3]

The suggestion has obvious merit, though it challenges the commonsense presumption of much of the writing on this genre of popular culture (my own and others') that the persistent reiteration of a theme or image is what enables it to create and maintain a sense of shared community.[4] One can think of other examples of popular prints currently in circulation that appear similarly conventionalized, routinized, and devoid of either charisma or innovation: images of freedom fighters, national leaders and politicians—calendars especially destined for the school room, municipal office, or political party headquarters (cf. Jain 1998: 20; 2002). Nowadays, these only rarely come to life, though their potentiality to do so obviously remains.

Amin's second observation on '*Ham sab ek hain*' concerned the caricature and stereotyping of the Muslim 'other'. In particular he pointed to the trope whereby the Muslim boy was made recognizable by his special head-gear, a 'miniature inverted waste-paper basket with a tail', commonly identified as a 'fez'[5] (Amin 2000: 77). As Amin reminded us, it is not as though all little Muslim boys are to be found scampering around in fezes to mark them out from their non-Muslim neighbours and classmates—indeed, were they to do so, it might have a terrifying, even menacing, effect! But the point was simply that the fez is in real life only an item in the 'fancy-dress' performance of Indian Muslimness, a sign, Amin asserts, 'put there by the advertisers of our multi-religious nation-state' to mark the essential 'otherness' of the adult male Musalman vis-à-vis other citizens (ibid.). Indeed, we will have occasion to refer to another such example later on in this essay (see Figure 7).

I have two nearly identical versions of '*Ham sab ek hain*' with me: one picked up in Delhi in 1990 (see Figure 1), the second, rather glossier, purchased in Dharwar (Karnataka) in 1992.[6] The little Muslim boy is indeed, as Amin had rightly remarked, distinguished by his fez, *but*—and Amin did not comment on this aspect—the little Sikh boy also stands out (though perhaps with greater referential accuracy) by virtue of the kerchief on his topknot, as well as his open neck (sporty?) shirt. In this case, you would need to be familiar with the representational code to distinguish the Hindu and the Christian children. The Christian boy is 'anglicised', dressed in collar and tie, his hair neatly parted, while the Hindu child is, as it were, closer to nature (the appearance of uncut hair) and wears a simple, saffron-coloured shirt. The saffron colour is no doubt intentional.

However, leaving aside the issues of the sartorial stereotyping of the minorities and the 'draining of meaning', on which one may or may not agree with Amin, the striking feature of this print is *actually* the prominent central medallion around which the four children are symmetrically arranged

(Figure 1). This image has an independent presence within the archive of Indian calendar art, and a career historically almost coincidental with the medium itself. In the centre of the medallion, and the focal centre of the print, stands the scarlet-clad figure of 'Mother India', holding in one hand a burning torch (*Amar jyoti*, the eternal flame in remembrance of heroic sacrifice?), and in the other, the national flag. Her golden halo and lion companion ('vehicle') align her semiotically with the Goddess Durga, though she has but two arms and carries no weapons. She stands beneficently on a map of India, its outline almost filled out by mountains and lakes, forest and flowers, perhaps signifying the Hindu holy sites of Mount Kailash and Lake Mansarovar. Notwithstanding the reiteration of the national flag in the centre top of the print (linking the Hindu and Muslim boys, as it were), it is clear that the nation-state has been symbolically re-inscribed here as a *Hindu* polity through the emblematic figure of Mother India/Durga (cf. Ramaswamy 2002). The manifestly egalitarian message of '*Ham sab ek hain*' is thereby compromised and, to this extent, the 'marked'-ness of the three non-Hindu boys and the 'unmarked' naturalness of the Hindu child take on new meaning. It is not merely that the Muslim, Sikh and Christian boys are sartorially singled out for special treatment, amounting to caricature. Rather, they are *all* appropriated here to the regime of the Hindu Goddess.

## II A Politics of Incitement?

There are two aspects of the politics of contemporary print production that have recently attracted some scholarly attention. The first, already alluded to in the previous comment, is the apparent new pervasiveness of the figure of 'Mother India', relentlessly colonizing public space and promoted by the VHP (Vishwa Hindu Parishad) and its political allies as the symbol of a reinvigorated Hindu nation. This development has invited a recapitulation of a continuous history of the invention and dissemination of the image of 'Mother India' from the late 19th century,[7] as well as an examination of other aspects and forms of the VHP/BJP's (Bharatiya Janata Party's) visual politics of incitement (e.g., Basu et al., 1993; Brosius 1999, 2002).

The second cause of public comment and anxiety has been the apparent '*en*masculinization' of the god Ram. The trend is also linked, once more, to the growth of militant Hinduism, and specifically to the context of the Babri Masjid–Ram Janmabhoomi controversy that resulted in the demolition of the disputed mosque in December 1992 and widespread communal riots thereafter. The several images that have provoked this public comment show an uncharacteristically 'muscular' Ram, standing commandingly in front of or astride a photographic representation of the (still to be built)

Ram temple in Ayodhya his bow drawn or his weaponry conspicuously displayed. Iconographically, according to Anuradha Kapur, who first drew scholarly attention to this development (Kapur 1993), these prints represent a reversal of the 'traditional', 'soft' and youthful image of Ram. They express 'anger' (*ugra*), as against 'serenity' (*shant*) (ibid., 103–4). In fact, Kapur sees these images as in some sense the logical culmination of the project of artistic modernity, inaugurated by Ravi Varma in the late 19th century, that redefined the attributes of Indian masculinity and femininity under the regime of imperialism—'strength and musculature in men and softness and delicacy in women' (ibid., 99; cf. Nandy 1983; Lutgendorf 2002). Even the recent proliferation of cute 'baby' Rams, she asserts, contributes to reinforcing the unidimensionality of the adult male Ram as a figure of resolute masculinity (Kapur 1993; cf. Basu et al. 1993; vii, 61, 82–83, 108; Jain 1998: 95).

A close look at the archive of calendar art suggests, however, that both these critiques—the story of continuity and the story of rupture—are problematic, each in a different way. Mother India may indeed derive her iconographic attributes from the Hindu Goddess, but she is not the exclusive property of the VHP and its allies however much they may nowadays seek to be her sole spokespersons. Nor does she have essentialized properties independent of the socio-political context in which she is deployed. That is, she may be associated with Gandhian non-violence; or the inspiration of armed resistance and terrorism. She may be the symbol of the rejection of foreign rule and of resistance against the enemy without; or a challenge to the non-Hindu presence within. She may be benign and nurturing, as the Mother Cow; or militantly aggressive, demanding the sacrifice of her 'sons' in the cause of the Mother-land (see Figure 13). She may be on the attack, as Kali/Durga; or pathetically vulnerable, as Draupadi striped by Duhshasan or as the Mother Cow slaughtered by beef-eaters.[8] So much depends on the context of production within the wider frame of nationalist struggle and postcolonial nation-building.

Similarly, according to Christopher Pinney, whose ethnographic writing on Indian photography and chromolithography is well known, the assumption of a menacing teleology in the advent and velocity of circulation of images of a militant Ram ignores the paradoxes, complexities and circularity of mass print production through the last century. Given the century-long record of the recycling and plagiarization of images from a hybrid range of Indian and foreign sources, a linear history for the contemporary 'militant' Ram imagery compelling and tantalizing though it is, amounts to a travesty of the historical record (see Pinney 1997a; also Jain 1998: 240ff; Lutgendorf 2002).[9] Somehow, as Jain succinctly puts it (1998), albeit making a rather fine point of the distinction, we need to be alert to the demonstrable 'historicity' of calendar art imagery, while yet avoiding 'teleology'. It is the *context* that is crucial (cf. Gupta 1996).

The point will be illustrated shortly with reference to another, indeed notorious, mass-produced image that, under specific and recurrent circumstances since the very beginning of popular print production in India, has been associated with incitement to communal violence. This is the image of the Mother Cow: simultaneously divinity and nation. The usual context in which this figure is discussed is that of Hindu-Muslim communal relations, but the image clearly bears on the wider question of the Constitution of India as a multi-religious state. In this instance, however, we will digress somewhat to reflect on the ways in which a particular calendar art image of the Mother Cow, dating from the early 1970s but currently once again in vigorous circulation, reflected on the question, 'Who is a Sikh?' (to borrow the title of H.W. McLeod's well-known book [1989]).

Curiously absent in discussions of the historical trajectory of the Hindu nationalist images of Mother India and the militant Ram, including even the work of Pinney, is sensitivity to the specificities of the quarter century of 'nation-building' immediately following Indian independence. Discussion tends to simply leap-frog from the early to the last decades of the 20th century, by passing the critical period when the new nation-state was attempting to define its being (cf. Jain 1998: 214–5). This period, which embodies what one may call, albeit somewhat imprecisely, the 'Nehruvian' vision of the nation,[10] has been simply glossed over as epiphenomenal or ephemeral in the light of the broader divisions that historians are wont to make between precolonial (or 'traditional'), colonial, and postcolonial ways of seeing (cf. ibid., 233 ff.),[11] its ideals dismissed as pious self-delusion, if not sheer hypocrisy. A generation on, I am surely not alone in suggesting that it deserves, now, a considered and more sympathetic revisiting (cf. Roy, 2002).

## III Visualizing the Nation

In the period immediately after Independence and in the aftermath of the bloodbath in which the nation was born, the first national task was that of securing the country's frontiers. An undeclared war over the accession of Kashmir, the effects of which continue to fester, border war with China in 1962, war with Pakistan in 1965, and a second war with Pakistan over the liberation of Bangladesh in 1971, ensured that defence of the country's borders was a question of the highest priority. Patriotic iconography was then (as it has been once again, post-Kargil [1999]) an important category within the total repertoire of calendar art, so much so that many prints of the period look like army recruitment propaganda. In the world context of Cold War, India under Nehru sought to chart out a policy of constructive Non-Alignment, equidistant from both the United States and the Soviet Union; perhaps this period represented the apogee of Indian visibility in world affairs. At home the chief contradiction to be resolved was the choice between investment in production and economic growth, and investment in war-preparedness. The iconography of Nehru's successor, the diminutive Lal Bahadur Shastri, sought to transcend this opposition and to assert the non-contradiction of these two objectives. His famous slogan, '*jai javan, jai kisan*' (Hail the soldier, Hail the ploughman), which summed up this position with great economy, immediately lent itself to visualization in the medium of calendar art (and remains a conspicuous feature of truck and tractor art in the Punjab even now).

Besides ensuring national security, the focus of the ideological agenda of nation-building was the achievement of material progress, prosperity and the elimination of poverty. Here, the nation was faced with a dilemma of choice: What path to development should be followed? As a poor and developing country, should India prioritize investment in agriculture and the reinvigoration of village society, or should it invest in strengthening the industrial base? Or was it to attempt to balance the two tasks at once? Equally important, and related to this: Would the advent of modernity disrupt India's traditional moral economy and undermine the foundations of Indian culture? Or could the new and the old be blended into a harmonious whole? And could economic development be achieved along with social justice, and within the framework of democratic governance? (Frankel 1978: esp. Chapter 1). Like popular cinema, calendar art provided a site of contestation for these conflicting values and choices in the quest for modernity and progress. A whole range of solutions was offered in calendar art as across the political spectrum, but certainly a major rhetorical strategy was the *denial* or *transcendence* of contradiction: all modes of development were presented as similarly, synergistically, productive. In this sense, these calender art representations of nationhood collectively assume a 'mythic' dimension, a striving for utopia where all contradictions are resolved.

A second focus in the visual rhetoric of nation-building was the project of creating 'unity' out of Indian 'diversity', of weaving the 'fragments' into a viable nation-state (Chatterjee 1993; also Roy 2002). Specifically, the challenge was that of bringing India's different religious communities together under a 'secular' regime, of undoing the work of communalization that had brutally ruptured the body politic into two nations at the very moment of freedom. But there was also the task of uniting the different classes and castes, men and women, tribals and others, into a homogeneous, democratic and just national society. Again, Nehruvian rhetoric worked to transform the 'problem' of cultural diversity into a 'resource' for the developmental agenda of the new Indian state (Srirupa Roy, personal communication; see also Basu et al., 1993).

Many signs were deployed, individually and in combination, to signify the national community. There was, first of all, the *map* of India, the signifier of territorial integrity (see Brosius 1997; Krishna 1994; Ramaswamy 2002), its inner, political boundaries usually left unmarked. There was the national *flag* (or the Hindu pennant, if a more exclusive definition of nation was to be asserted). There were Hindu deities, male or female or anthropomorphic, as the case may be. There was the potent figure of Mother India, in secular garb or merged with the Goddess. There was the Mother Cow, a symbol of universal nourishment (or, more exclusively, of the Hindu community *contra* others). There was the child—male, female, androgynous or divine (Uberoi 2001). And there was the couple, husband and wife, sign of fecund potentiality, of the erotic, of the project of nation-building, of modernity.

In this article, I confine myself to a single aspect of the Nehruvian 'vision': that is, the constitution of the nation as a multi-religious entity, and to the variety of ideological positions on the contested theme of Indian 'secularism' to which the calendar art medium gave play. I do so with several caveats. First, one must remember that the theme of secularism is merely a single piece in a larger semiotic ensemble, the project of nation-building and modernity. Second, my exposition proceeds inductively and relies for its material largely on a personal collection of calendar art whose mode of acquisition was, admittedly, rather haphazard.[12] Third, and more to the point, this attempt to recuperate the secularist vision of this era through its visual expression in calendar art is circumscribed by the fact that we have almost no direct access to the producers of the prints (artists, publishers, distributors), nor to their audience:[13] just the prints themselves and their retrospective interpretations, inevitably coloured by contemporary contexts. The methodological pitfalls of such an enterprise are self-evident. What one can say, however, is that these visual representations of the idea of 'unity in diversity' repay interrogation. Both in themselves, and conceived as comprising a dialogical set, these prints are clearly open to a range of interpretations and readings, as our contemporary ethnography also affirms. And while, as expected, the 'Hindu Right' appears to dominate the visual field, it is neither hegemonic nor unchallenged, nor proof against subversion. Other readings are conceivable; other 'paths' acknowledged. This plurality is possibly enabled by the particular characteristics of the calendar art medium as a non-elite, mass-produced consumer product, catering both to local needs and tastes and sectarian loyalties as well as to the imperatives of a nationalist agenda (see e.g., Larson 1997; cf. Manuel 1996). This is a proposition which we will consider further at a later point in this article (see Section VI).

## IV *'Ham Sab ek Hain'*

In representing the theme of unity in diversity, calendar art of the post-independence era gave expression, in its own way, to a continuing dilemma—

the dilemma, in fact, that had brought about the Partition of the country: Are India's different religious communities to be equal and complementary partners in the constitution of the national society, or are non-Hindus to be appropriated to an essentially *Hindu* visualization of communal unity and equality (cf. Smith 1963)? This dilemma was played out in a number of different ways, which we shall now detail with reference to selected prints, reserving for later our comments on the visual 'code' that was thus activated.

By way of a beginning, let us return to the theme of the child as the signifier of a secular society. In '*Ham sab ek hain*', a print which dates from the early 1990s, the theme of unity in diversity is expressed through the co-association of four (male) children, each bearing the sign of his particular community, linked to three recognized national emblems—the Indian flag, the map of India (whose sacralization in nationalist iconography has been discussed by Sumathi Ramaswamy 2002), and the figure of Mother India. We had noted that the flag motif was reduplicated as Mother India's standard, but that this supposedly 'neutral' sign[14] was compromised by the religious connotation of Mother India as a manifestation of the Goddess Durga even as the project of Indian 'secularism' was identified (*via* the map and the national flag) with the *state*, rather than with civil society.

I have not actually seen similar prints from the Nehruvian period, though I am confident that they would be readily located, if not in calendar art then at least in expressly political and pedagogic materials. For the present I merely counterpose against that print a rather different image dating from the early 1970s (Figure 2). The print foregrounds a near naked infant, seated on a globe (the world), playing with a platter of flowers (*puja* offerings?). On the child's head fall rays of light emanating from a glowing flame/the sun, which simultaneously irradiates (or draws its illumination from) four medallions containing images of Guru Nanak, Krishna, Jesus, and the Muslim holy structure, the Kabah. Or perhaps it is the light of divine knowledge that is signified here, for an open book lies in the child's lap. In other contexts, the book might signify a precocious commitment to learning for the self-improvement of the family, the nation and the human race,[15] but here it is tilted toward the spectator to disclose the legend, '*Gita aur Granth ismen Baibal aur Quran, bolo bacca hai mahan*' (The Gita, the Granth, the Bible and the Koran—say, O child, they are [all four] great). Note that in place of the four communally identified children of '*Ham sab ek hain*' we have here a single, androgynous infant (sex neatly concealed beneath pink diapers),[16] as yet *unmarked* by the signs of community identity. Indeed, the figure of the pre-social, androgynous child is widely used to represent themes of nation-building, production and national defence (see Uberoi 2001),[17] and appears to be particularly apt for rendering an egalitarian,

'Gandhian' interpretation of Indian 'secularism' as the essential truth and unity of all religions.[18]

Women may be similarly deployed[19]—and perhaps there is a lesson to be learned here. For instance, in the print reproduced as Figure 3, four women, identifiable respectively as Muslim, Hindu, Sikh and Christian, are shown at prayer in their respective styles. From each woman there leads a circuitous path to their distinctive places of worship (mosque, temple, gurdwara and church), each (once again) illuminated by rays of light emanating from a single lamp (or each contributing to the radiance that illuminates the firmament). The respective signs of Allah, *Om, Ik-Onkar* and the Cross are embossed on the rays. In explanation the legend reads, in quotes: 'O Lord, the different paths which men take through their different tendencies, various though they appear, crooked or straight, all lead to Thee.'[20] Here the four religions that signify India's religiously plural society appear to be treated relatively even-handedly, and the assertion is made that each religion follows its own path to universal light, or that universal light draws on the illumination emanating from each religion. The text, taken from the Upanishads, is proffered to endorse the idea that Indian culture is, and has ever been, 'tolerant' of other faiths.

We have seen that 'baby' iconography may lend itself *both* to the principle of the equality of all religions (Figure 2) *and* to the idea of their encompassment within a 'tolerant' Hinduism or an accommodating 'Hindu' nation-state (Figure 1). Similarly, the figure of the woman may support either position, even, contradictorily, both at once. Thus, contrasted with the representational logic of Figure 3, one may find an image of women of India's different religious communities (distinguished by their different constumes and the shadowy outlines of their respective places of worship) lined up to welcome the radiant 10-armed goddess, Durga, who emerges from the map of India (Figure 4). As the nation is a composite of its respective communities, all rejoicing in the Goddess, so the Goddess herself appears to embrace the iconographic features of the trinity of Durga, Lakshmi and Saraswati (cf. Basu et al., 1993: 83; Ramaswamy 2005). In this vision, too, there is a recognized place for people of all religions, all classes and all walks of life, but it is a place in which they are subordinate to the aura of Mother India as Goddess Durga.[21] In other words, citizenship is here dependent on acceptance of the hegemony of the 'majority' religion.

The set of images we turn to now are rather more complex, involving the figure of the cow as at once a Hindu deity, signifying the nurturing quality of motherhood, and as the symbol of the *unity*—or alternatively, the *differentiation*—of India's several religious communities. In Figure 5, for instance, we see two iconographic forms of the Mother Cow (*Gau-Mata*), assimilated to the trinity of Hindu Goddesses: Uma (= Durga) in the centre, flanked by Lakshmi and Saraswati.[22] In this particular consociation, it is the benign, rather than the fierce

Figure 2: *Gita aur Granth is men Baibal aur Quran, bolo bacca hai mahan* (The Gita, the Granth, the Bible and the Koran—say, O' child, they are all great). Artist: Mahendra, Soni Studio. Publisher: Belgium Glass House, Ludhiana, 1974. (Author's collection)

Figure 3: (Untitled) The equality of religions. Artist: Ram Verma. Publisher: Belgium Glass House, Ludhiana, 1974. (Author's collection)

and malevolent aspect of the Mother Goddess that predominates (cf. Hershman 1977; also van der Veer 1996: 89). Beneath the trinity, on the lower right, is the cow-figure usually identified as 'Kamadhenu',[23] the 'wish-fulfilling cow' a composite mythological creature with the body, hoof and horns of a cow, birds' wings and a peacock's tail, and the face of a beautiful woman. Milk from the cow's udders gushes on to a *Shivalingam-yoni* beneath. In many prints, the Kamadhenu figure is set in idyllic flower-filled pastures high in the Himalayas, blessed from the heavens by Shiva and Parvati. Indeed, in some renderings it seems that the milk from the cow's udders inscribes a sacred geography of the nation as it courses in rivulets down towards the plains: a *Hindu* sacred geography, of course.[24]

In the second cow image, usually called '*Gau Mata*' (Mother Cow) or '*Jagat Mata*' (Mother of the Universe), the cow's body encompasses all the Hindu deities, the *rishis*, and the sacred mountains and rivers as well (see also Brosius

Figure 4: (Untitled) Motherland. Artist: unknown. Publisher: Coronation Litho, mid-1970s(?). (Author's collection)

1999: 107, Plate 38, 108n); as such, it has the potential both to unite and to incite. An elaborated version of the Mother Cow image, entitled '*Chaurasi Dev darshan*' (Vision of the eighty-four deities), appears here as Figure 6. Published in Delhi in 1967, it is signed 'B.C. Sharma',[25] although Sharma's role was clearly that of 'copyist', more than of 'artist' (if such 'bourgeois' distinctions can be made in reference to this medium. [see Jain 2002]). Several aspects of this print are notable and relevant here. First, as the abode of eighty four deities, the cow figure unites the many strands of Hinduism within one sacred and all-encompassing body, mediating sectarian, class, and rural-urban differences and figuring a united 'Hindu' community out of multiple and fragmented identities (Freitag 1996). As many studies have now shown, the cow has provided a unique rallying symbol for Hindu 'religious nationalism' through the colonial and postcolonial periods.[26]

Figure 5: (Untitled) Five forms of the female deity. Artist: S.P. Raj (overwritten on another name [?]). Publisher: Sun Shine Calendar Co., Delhi, 1978. (Author's collection)

Figure 6: '*Chaurasi Dev darshan*' (Vision of the 84 deities). Artist: B.C. Sharma. Publisher: Baby Picture House, Delhi, 1967. (Author's collection)

Second, is the explicit depiction of a Muslim, a European (or Anglo-Indian), a Parsee and a group of Hindus,[27] all of them in their different styles[28] receiving the gift of cow's milk from a cowherd. Nowadays, and probably when Sharma's print was circulated in 1967, the community identifications are routinely mis-read by informants as the *bhai-bhai* (brotherhood) of the catch-phrase, '*Hindu-Muslim-Sikh Isai*', at least until specific details of the print are brought to attention. That is, the Parsee is nowadays taken to be a Muslim (it is the notorious 'fez' that once again clinches the matter!); the European/Anglo-Indian in top-hat becomes 'Christian' (the religious identity superseding the racial); and the Muslim (his style of beard and turban notwithstanding) is read as 'Sikh', Sikhism having meanwhile gained the status of a separate 'religion' (and not merely a branch or sect of Hinduism [but see Section V, following]).

The image of the cow as the universal nourisher drawing together persons of all religions in the constitution of the nation is made explicit in another, stylistically very different, calendar of the same period (Figure 7). The print bears the legend: '*Desh dharm ka nata hai, gay hamari mata hai*' (The country and religion bond us; the cow is mother to us all) (see Larson et al., 1997: 54, Plate 46; FAAM 2000: 33, Plate 3.9). Here, male representatives of the Hindu,

Figure 7: '*Desh dharam ka nata hai, gay hamari mata hai*' (The country and religion bond us; the cow is mother to us all). Artist: Sapar Bros. Publisher: unknown, ca. 1968. (Author's collection)

Christian, Sikh and Muslim communities, distinguished by their different costumes and headgear (again) and their respective places of worship, receive cow's milk directly from the udders of the Mother Cow who dominates the print's upper foreground. Such unmediated nourishment is a privilege normally reserved for the prankster-child Krishna, whose conceptual place, Christopher Pinney has suggested (1997a: 840ff.), has here been taken by the communitarian representatives. The Hindu pantheon does not actually inhabit the body of the cow in this print, as it does in *Chaurasi Dev darshan*, but the putative democracy of 'unity in diversity' is once again subverted by the appropriation of all communities under the sacred sign of the Mother Cow.

Figure 8: (Untitled) The Sikh Gurus embodied in the Mother Cow. Artist: Mohinder Singh. Publisher: Aarti Glass House, Ludhiana, 1974. (Author's collection)

This apart, the really prominent feature of *Chaurasi Dev darshan*, distinguishing it from other renderings of the Cow-Mother, is the bare-toothed monster with raised sword seen advancing on the hapless cow, as a figure in front, and another (inexplicably airbone) above her tail, attempt to remonstrate with him. Such images have been around for a long time (see Pinney 1997a, 1999, 2002), being associated with recurrent Cow Protection agitations from the 1880s onwards. In fact, B.C. Sharma's 1967 print is an almost exact copy, minus the identificatory captions, of a Ravi Varma print of the second decade of this century (see Pinney 1997a: 845, Plate 4, 1999: 232–33, Plates 7 and 8; also, Jain 1998: 55, Plate; Mitter, 2002). The monstrous, 'matricidal' figure, captioned 'Kaliyug' (the demon Kali, personifying evil) in the Varma print, is readily identifiable with the Muslim community (Pinney 1997a: 846); or more broadly, with Muslim, Christian and Hindu low-caste beef-eaters. In fact, the print in question was proscribed as inflammatory by the British colonial government, but subsequently reissued after a compromise with the German publisher who eliminated the provocative figure of the monster cow-slayer (Pinney 1999: Plates 7–8). It would surely not be coincidental that the refurbishing of this particular image paralleled a revival of the movement for Cow Protection in the mid-1960s, culminating in the notorious *sadhus*' siege of Parliament in November 1966 (see Graham 1993: 147–55).

Even without explicit depiction of the demon cow-slayer, it appears that the Mother Cow image works to stress the 'otherness' of non-Hindus, even as it unites the otherwise fragmented Hindu community within one body (Freitag 1996; Ludden 1996: esp. 4–8). As an Old Delhi calendar publisher told me firmly when I inquired if he had ever produced such prints of 'Kamadhenu':

> We do not do such subjects. They provide unnecessary agitation. Some agree, some do not agree.[29]

And to this he added a further piece of home-spun 'secularist' wisdom: 'Religion only *adds*, it does not *part*.'

## V 'Some Agree, Some do not Agree'

As we have seen in the foregoing, the figure of the Mother Cow defines Indian citizenship in terms that are at once democratic and Hindu-hegemonic, cohesive and divisive, conciliatory and deeply provocative. The calendar I now wish to present (Figure 8),[30] reiterates these contradictions in a way that reflects on the presently contentious relations of affinity and difference between the Hindu and Sikh faiths. Painted by a Sikh artist, Mohinder Singh, it bears the legend —a line of *Gurbani* (scripture)—'People were searching for *amrit* (ambrosia), and found it in the gift of the Gurus'.[31] Here, the flame of the 'lamp of original truth' bears the Sikh sacred symbol, '*Ik-Onkar*'; the generous bowl of cow's milk, resting on a lotus, is identified as '*amrit*' (the consecrated sweetened water used in the Sikh initiation rite); and the cow's body—in conspicuous imitation of the Hindu Mother Cow—is peopled by the ten Sikh Gurus, other saints, *bhagats* and martyrs, and the Sikh scripture. The Khalsa symbol is emblazoned on the cow's forehead, and the sign '*bhakti*' (devotion) across her muzzle. The virtues of '*daya*' (compassion) and '*punn*' (merit) are the 'sun' and the 'moon' above the cow's eyes, while those of '*pau*' (fear/respect), '*tap*' (self-control), and '*tyag*' (renunciation) are in the cow's hoofs. The creature's gilded horns recall the architecture of a gurdwara, and indeed an unidentified gurdwara is shown to one side, its holy pennant flying. In this rendition, the general disposition of the figures is serene, though several of them had met with heroic deaths or suffered torture and martyrdom. Hargobind, the Sixth Guru, wears neither of his two swords (the temporal and the spiritual), and the heroic Baba Dip Singh is seated serenely, and not—as often pictured—engaged in battle, his bloody severed head held high in one hand (see e.g., McLeod 1991: 123, Plate 53). The 'militant' face of Sikhism is in abeyance here.

The Sikh scholars from whom I informally sought opinion were divided in their assessment of this print. One declared this an example of 'Hinduism *getting into* Sikhism!'; another that it is 'A Sikh [artist] *using Hinduism* to say something' to a non-Sikh audience, in an idiom familiar to them. Another stated that: 'It didn't come off; it didn't "stick". That's why you don't see this sort of thing nowadays.' (In this latter observation he was wrong, as I was soon to find out.) A Sikh politician snatched the prints from my hands and rushed off to get them photocopied: 'Don't you know?' he said, 'The RSS [Rashtriya Swayamsevak Sangh] are distributing such pictures in the villages of Punjab?'[32] In his view this was the most recent provocation in the ongoing effort of the 'saffron-brigade' to reabsorb Sikhism into the mother-body of Hinduism. He spoke as though this were an issue of great immediacy, rather than one that had preoccupied Sikh public opinion for over a century.

Taken together, these varied contemporary responses commend close attention to the print's detail, particularly the question of who *is*, and who *is not*, included in the maternal boy of the 'Sikh' cow. Apart from the 10 Sikh Gurus (numbered 1 to 10), the *Guru Granth Sahib* (Sikh scripture), which occupies a prominent place, and two martyrs of the faith (Baba Dip Singh on the rump, and Mati Das[33] on the front leg), we see several other figures whose presence one might presume to be more or less acceptable to 'orthodox' Sikh sentiment. Thus, in the belly of the cow are clustered three figures: the poet Kabir, attired as a Muslim, whose compositions are included in the *Adi Granth* along with those of other *bhagats* (see McLeod 1968: 155–57).[34] There is also

Bhai Gurdas, amanuensis of Guru Arjan, the compiler of the *Adi Granth*. Though Gurdas's own compositions are not actually part of the scripture, they are revered as the clearest exposition of the philosophy of the early Gurus, as well as an important source for the reconstruction of their biographies (see McLeod 1968: 14–15, 100; Oberoi 1994: 50–51; Singh 1963: 310–12).

The middle figure of the threesome is more problematic. This is Sri Chand, son of Nanak and founder of the Udasi ascetic order who, having chosen the path of renunciation, was bypassed for succession to guruship in favour of Guru Angad (see Grewal 1994: 47–48; 116–17; McLeod 1989: 46–47; Oberoi 1994: 78–81, 123–28). The Udasis had played an important role as custodians of Sikh scriptures and Sikh shrines through the vicissitudes of Sikh history, until they came into violent conflict with the Akalis in the early 20th century. Sri Chand's accommodation here turns the clock back, as it were, to what Harjot Oberoi has described as the '*Sanatan*' ideology of 19th century Sikhism, itself a pragmatic reconciliation of the duality between 'Khalsa' and 'Sahajdhari' (non-Khalsa) Sikh identities (Oberoi 1994: Chapter 2; see also Fox 1987: esp. Chapter 6; Grewal 1994: Chapters 6 & 7).

A different sort of gesture is made by the inscription in the bovine body (hind leg) of the *bhagat* Ravidas, an Untouchable leather-worker by caste, whose compositions, like those of Kabir, are also included in the *Adi Granth* (see H. Singh 1992–98: II, 454–55, III, 493–94). While the Sikh scriptures and institutions of *sangat* (congregational worship) and *pangat* (communal kitchen) expressly seek to transcend caste distinctions, it is well-known that caste practices continue to remain entrenched in the daily life of the Sikh community and that for much of Sikh history (and no doubt until today in the Punjab villages), dalit (Mazhabi) Sikhs are regarded as defiling and on this account excluded from gurdwaras (Hershman 1981: 22–23; McLeod 1989: 109–10).[35] One might wonder whether or not it is significant that Ravidas occupies the lowliest position in the cow's body, and that he is not pictured here with the tools of the cobbler's trade (as he is in prints aimed specifically for purchase by his low-caste sectarian devotees).

Two further figures call for explanation. Identified as 'Ram Singhji' and 'Vadbhag Singhji' (located on the cow's throat and chest respectively), they represent 'heterodox' sectarian groups which, like the Udasis, continue to recognize 'living Gurus' even after the closure of the line of succession and the initiation of the Khalsa.[36] The cult of Baba Vadbhag Singh (d. 1762), a direct descendant of the sixth Sikh Guru, Hargobind, is located in Kartarpur (Punjab) and Una (Himachal Pradesh), and specializes in the exorcism of evil spirits, the removal of afflictions, and the granting of boons. The cult represents the miraculous and magical side of popular religious practice in the Punjab which Singh Sabha reformism has failed to eliminate despite a century or more of strenuous effort (see Fox 1987: Chapters 6, 9; Oberoi 1994: Chapter 3), and it is not entirely surprising that this 'heterodoxy' should find expression through the medium of popular calendar art (see also McLeod 1991: 132 and Plate 54).

With Ram Singh, the bovine connection is more explicit. Ram Singh was the leader of the Kuka or Namdhari religious reform movement of the 19th century, a movement that sought a return to the fundamentals of the Sikh faith (especially, meditation on the divine name), and the elimination of deviant, superstitious and Brahmanical practices (see Grewal 1994: 141ff.; McLeod 1989: 64–5, 115–17; Oberoi 1994: 194–201; H. Singh 1992–8: III, 465–7; Khushwant Singh 1966: 127–35). The Kukas' fanatical commitment to cow protection, among other causes, and their attacks on Muslim butchers in 1872, had led to the movement's violent repression by the colonial government (though their present reputation is of strict-living and pious Khalsa Sikhs). In any case, with the Singh Sabha's endorsement of the *jhatka*, rather than the *halal* (Muslim), style of animal slaughter, 'orthodox' Sikhism now in practice accepts a ban on cow-slaughter (see Fox 1987: 115).

In sum, then, the 'Sikh cow' figure envisages a reconciliation of several strands of *sanatan* and popular Sikh faith and practice that the Singh Sabha and later Akali movements had sought to suppress over the last century or more of religious reform. By the same token, at least as far as many 'fundamentalist' Sikhs are concerned, this amounts to the elimination of Sikhism as a separate religion through its reabsorption within the fold of an all-embracing Hinduism (and, indeed, the suppression of its Islamic/Sufi affinities as well). This is a danger of which the Sikhs in modern times are ever aware (Fox 1987: Chapter 9; Grewal 1994: Chapters 7, 9, 10; Gupta 1996: esp. Chapter 4; McLeod 1989). Articulated early on by the reformist Kahn Singh Nabha in his famous tract, '*Ham Hindu nahin*' (We are not Hindus, 1899), the imminent threat of the loss of independent Sikh identity is perceived to go hand-in-hand with the emasculation of the Sikhs as a political force in their 'own' state of Punjab, where they are a precarious majority, and in the nation-state of India, where they are an almost insignificant minority. At least in some readings, this dilemma of cultural and political identity in relation to Hinduism as the 'majority' religion of India provides a major explanation for the unrest in the Punjab in the late 1970s and 1980s.

We do not know, specifically, what motivated the production of this calendar in 1973/74, nor how it was received at the time, but its potential for provocation is evident in reactions to the circulation of almost identical prints in the Punjab in the last months of the year 2000, allegedly at the behest of the RSS. Thus, the author of a vituperative article in the Sikh *Spokesman weekly* (January 2001), entitled, 'Even after the High Court judgement, why do they insist on calling the Sikhs, the Hindus', seeks to counter the 'misleading propaganda' spread by the RSS that 'the Sikhs were born out of Hindus' and that the 'Khalsa was created for the protection of the Hindus.' The article reproduces an almost identical version of the 1973/74 'Sikh cow' print (minus Mohinder Singh's signature) along with the caption:

> Picture [sic] of this type (some of which are most derogatory to the Sikh Gurus and are of blasphemous nature)[37] have been got printed and are being distributed in large numbers by the RSS with the sole aim of belittling the Sikh gurus and the symbols of Sikh sovereignty in comparison with the Brahmin-invented 'sacred' symbols of Hindu faith. Taking advantage of the Akali leaders' lust for power,[38] the RSS people have intensified their anti-Sikh campaign in Punjab (G. Singh 2001: 24).

An article in the subsequent issue of the *Spokesman weekly* (February 2001) similarly denounces a series of RSS cow protection booklets that were allegedly circulating on the campus of the Guru Nanak Dev University (Amritsar). These booklets are said to misuse the gurus' *bani* to endorse cow protection, presenting Guru Gobind Singh as a 'cow protector' (including inventively attributing to the Guru a Sanskrit *shlok* to that effect), and additionally promote all manner of irrational and unscientific 'facts' about the cow and her supposedly miraculous products.[39] This, the article stresses, is all evidence of the contemporary and ongoing subversion of Sikhism by 'Brahministic tendencies'; the perversion of the fundamental Sikh doctrine of the inseparability of temporal and spiritual power, allowing crass, opportunistic politics to take over; and the endorsement of Hindu ritual practices by Sikh politicians attempting to curry favour with their present electoral allies (Virk 2001).

'The Sikhs have gone mad,' a Sikh scholar told me, ruefully shaking his head as he reflected on this literature. 'If they don't have anything else to quarrel about, they go and make an issue of things like this!' He had just finished explaining to me that cow protection was actually a perfectly rational and 'natural' custom in the South Asian context, given the ecologically vital role of cattle in the region's ecology since Vedic times.[40]

## VI Representing 'Secularism': Message, Code and Medium

'The story so far' has counterposed a democratic, inclusivist and essentially 'religious' visualization of the secular ideology of independent India against what one might call an instrumental and majoritarian view (see Madan 1997: 250–60), whereby 'other' religious communities are accommodated under the insignia of a specifically *Hindu* religious nationalism—the Mother Goddess. Mother India, the Mother Cow—or else excluded altogether from citizenship. As we have seen in the case of some contemporary responses to the 'Sikh cow' image, this may dialectically provoke a 'minoritarian' reaction—a refusal to accept the embrace of the 'other', and a reactively exclusivist definition of self-identity (cf. Gupta 1996: esp. Chapter 4).

But religious pluralism, like linguistic pluralism, may have other modalities of expression, too, beyond the logic of equality/competition, or assimilation/segregation, and it is important to give them due recognition.[41] One of them is suggested by the informant who interpreted the 'Sikh cow' as a conciliatory gesture, a deliberate articulation of the principles of Sikhism *in the idiom* of the 'other' (cf. Manuel 1996: 127). Socio-linguistic studies provide many examples of such communicative strategies in stable multilingual situations, where language is actively *negotiated* in face-to-face interaction in a spirit of mutuality and reciprocity.

Another modality is recourse to a common language of expression across the different denominations, as in folk religious practice, corresponding to the popular and functional, as against the purist, styles of a single language—for instance, Hindustani, rather than literary Hindi or Urdu (cf. Manuel 1996). A somewhat frivolous examples of this in popular visual culture has already been provided—the bovine Buraq/equine Kamadhenu (see note 23)—but other examples come to mind, too.[42] For instance, we have an almost identical pair of images of the 'fruits' of good and evil deeds (the contrast of a serene heavenly existence with torture in boiling cauldrons stoked by bare-toothed monsters), with Shiv at the centre of one, and Nanak presiding over the other.[43]

One may also find ready instances where the first and last Sikh Gurus (Nanak and Gobind Singh) are put into co-association with Shiv, Vishnu or Ram, with sometimes the Hindu deity, sometimes the Sikh Guru, occupying the central, commanding position. Viewed individually, each appears to appropriate the other to its religious ethic; read dialectically, a sort of equivalence is asserted, such that any one figure can stand in for the other, according to the devotee's personal preference and commitment. I can think of several prints where such 'code-switching' (to resume the linguistic analogy) takes place. For instance, a 'Hindu' calendar from 1974[44] has Shiv in the centre of the print, along with Krishna and Ram (the two linked by the sign, '*Om*'), and Nanak and Gobind Singh (linked by '*Ik-Onkar*'), in the four corners. A comparable 'Sikh' example, a Rang Roop piece entitled '*Tin das, tin bhagvan*' (Three servants, three Lords, 1975) (Figure 9), shows Guru Nanak in the centre as one of 'three Lords', with Ram and Krishna on either side. Their three 'servants' are smaller figures below (respectively, Guru Gobind Singh, Hanuman, and Arjun), while three holy books (the *Guru Granth Sahib*, the *Ramayan*, and the *Gita*) complete the picture.

Figure 9: '*Tin das, tin bhagvan*'. Artist: Rang Roop Studio. Publisher: Kawality Calendar Co., Delhi, 1975. (Author's collection)

I discussed this piece with a number of Sikh scholars, anticipating (wrongly, as it turned out) that they might find it offensive that the Tenth Guru was made a mere 'servant' of Nanak, or that the *Ramayan* and the *Gita* should be put on par with the *Guru Granth Sahib* as 'scriptures':

> 'The meaning is that Guru Gobind Singh, Hanuman and Arjun all *fought for* their spiritual guides,' one of them informed me authoritatively.
>
> 'This is just the shopkeeper trying to attract both Hindus and Sikhs,' another suggested, discounting any deep theological reasons for such eclectic conjunctions: 'It's just good business sense. Look at the meat shop opposite. On one side there's a calendar of Nanak, on the other one of Vishnu. It means, he wants to please *both* customers.'
>
> 'That's not it,' a bystander remarked, emphasizing exclusionary rather than inclusionary motivations behind the prints' display: 'It just means, "We are not *halal*"'.
>
> 'No, this sort of calendar is meant for the "Sindhis",' another volunteered, referring to the non-Khalsa, 'Nanak-panthi' tradition which continues to be strong among many Sindhis.
>
> 'I don't think you get this sort of thing these days,' said another, again voicing the view that the Sikh and Hindu communities no longer 'code-switch' the way he believed they used to. At the back of his mind, clearly, was a sense that relations between Hindus and Sikhs had undergone a major polarization in recent years (Field notes, January 2001).

There was yet another model for the Sikh religion articulated in the calendar prints, at least in those obviously destined for the Sikh 'niche' market. Sikhism could be projected as transcending, synthesizing or encompassing its others. Figure 10, for instance, shows Guru Nanak standing centrally between the outlines of a mosque on one side and a temple on the other, as Nehru was positioned between Khrushchev and Kennedy to express the principle of political non-alignment.[45] The theological basis of this 'mythic' mediation of opposites (see Section III) is the celebrated declaration with which Guru Nanak began his spiritual mission: 'There is neither Hindu nor Mussulman' (McLeod 1969: 38). Its visual analogy is with a favourite, 'traditional' representation of the first Guru, seated with his beloved companions to either side: Mardana, the Muslim minstrel, and Bala, the Hindu (see e.g., McLeod 1991: Plates 8, 20). Or, in another example, Nanak's revelation might be visualized as encompassing Hinduism, Islam, Christianity and Sikhism itself—all of them expressing the same message of devotion (Figure 11). Nanak occupies the centre of the print, his hand raised in blessing. Inscribed on his palm is the sacred sign, *Ik-Onkar*, surrounded by the word *tera* (a pun on the homophony of *tera* ['Thine'], presumably in the sense of 'your devotee', and *terah* [the number 13], referring to an episode in the

Figure 10: (Untitled) Guru Nanak. Artist: Rang Roop Studio. Publisher: unknown, 1966. (Author's collection)

*janam-sakhi* legends).[46] The word '*tera*' again forms a rosary or halo enclosing in its four quarters the radiant signs of the four religions, with Sikhism at the apex.

Significantly, there was another role for Sikhism that found expression in the calendars of the postindependence period. That was the role of the Sikhs in defence of the motherland. Figure 12, for instance, foregrounds Guru Gobind Singh, with his emblematic hunting hawk and sheaf of arrows. To one side a monochromatic inset shows the Guru leading his forces (against the Moghuls), and on the other a Sikh regiment marching into battle beneath the Indian national flag. The year was 1966, and the 1965 war with Pakistan was still fresh in public memory. Of course, for the most part Mother India/the Goddess Durga continued to preside over the defence of the nation (see Ramaswamy 2002, Figure 13), but there was clearly a 'market' somewhere for the idea of the Tenth Guru as patriot/protector of Hindustan.

In the intervening years, through the late 1970s and 1980s—and particularly following the traumatic events of 1984 ('Operation Bluestar' and the anti-Sikh riots following the assassination of Prime Minister Indira Gandhi by her Sikh bodyguards)—it seemed evident that the Sikh self-image was being reconstructed around the figures of the martyr of conscience or

Figure 11: '*Sab ek hain*'. Artist: Rang Roop Studio. Publisher: Rashtrya Calendars, Ludhiana, 1973. (Author's collection)

Figure 12: (Untitled) Guru Gobind Singh. Artist: H.S. Likhari. Publisher: unknown, 1966. (Author's collection)

Figure 13: '*Ma Ki Pukar*' (The Call of the Mother), ca. 1966. (Author's collection)

the militant hero of the faith, rather than the keeper and protector of the nation. The 'ethnicization' of the Sikh community appeared complete and irrevocable (cf. Gupta 1996). One was somewhat surprised, then, to find the 2001 calendar of the Punjab and Sind Bank[47] celebrating 'the gallant role of Sikh soldiers' in liberating the country 'from the fetters of centuries-old Mughal rule'; in 'blocking entry routes of alien invaders' during the reign of Maharajah Ranjit Singh; in saving the country from aggression in 1947; in assisting the 'liberation' of Junagarh, Hyderabad and Goa; and in 1965, 1971 and most lately in the 1999 Kargil operation (all armed conflicts with Pakistan), displaying 'indefatigable courage' under fire. The calendar cover picture shows Sikh *javans* on parade saluting the *Guru Granth Sahib*, while a picture inside shows a *javan* carrying the Holy Book with him into battle.

## VI Conclusion

This article has sought to set out before the sociologist's critical gaze a selection of popular prints on the theme of Indian secularism dating from the post-independence era. In so doing, it aims both to enhance our understanding of the secular agenda of the Indian nation-state with a view from popular visual culture, and simultaneously to complicate some current debates on the role of popular prints in the supposed communalization of the public sphere in the 1990s.

In general it seems clear that the valorization of religious pluralism is a subject that no longer captures the public imagination in the way it apparently used to in the earlier, Nehruvian, era. Indeed, representations of the idea of '*Ham sab ek hain*' seem now tediously routinized and drained of meaning (Amin 2000)—even when they avail of the evergreen attractions of 'baby' iconography. Secularism—and calendar publishers frankly endorse this view—no longer 'sells', and its promotion as a national ideal must be left to the state itself, or to public-sector or public-minded companies seeking an enlightened profile for themselves at the national level (ibid. cf. Roy 2002). Indeed, 'pasteurized multi-culturalism' seems to have lost its flavour.

The print of '*Ham sab ek hain*', with which we began this discussion, both endorses 'secularism' as a statist project (through the flag and the map) and foregrounds a tension between an egalitarian, and a Hindu majoritarian, view of the constitution of India as a multi-religious society. This tension is certainly not a new development in the discourse of calendar art, and we have seen examples of each type from the earlier period. We have also seen the active reworking and rejuvenation of old images in new contexts, sometimes to provoke or reawaken the assimilationist/separatist confrontation, but sometimes, on the contrary, to mark a conciliation.

To refer back to some of the Sikh prints we had discussed: when I first began to seek opinion on the 1970s 'Sikh cow' image, my informants (Sikh scholars and theologians) were as puzzled by it as I was; they told me they had never seen anything like it. Of course, middle class Sikhs in general do not attend to the details of popular calendar art, which most of them dismiss with active disdain and distaste, both on 'aesthetic' grounds (see Jain 2002), as well as on ideological grounds (the anti-idolatry stance of the Singh Sabha reform movement [see McLeod 1991: 28–29]). But no one anticipated that this very print would soon—a generation later—become *cause célèbre*, and the subject of passionate denunciation in the *Spokesman weekly*. On the other hand, while many of the same informants felt that the patriot/protector image of the Sikh Gurus and the Sikh community no longer had any 'takers'—that this ideal had been betrayed at once by the 'Hindu' state and the Sikh militants—in fact post-Kargil iconography has seen a cautious return of that perspective.

Though there is no clear trajectory of ideological development from the colonial period to the present, it is possible that the last half century has seen a diminishing of the *variety* of visualizations of religious pluralism, from an 'elaborated' to a 'restricted' code of expression (to use the socio-linguist's terminology [see Bernstein 1971]). Between equality on the one hand, and appropriation on the other, other types of relationship of the religious communities with each other and within the nation were visually represented, suggesting code-sharing and code-switching, reciprocity and exchange, a space for the majority and a recognized role for the minority, a view from the centre as well as one from the periphery. Perhaps calendar art as a *popular* medium actively enables such a multiplicity of perspectives—that is, both statist or 'official', albeit now 'drained of meaning' (to revert to Shahid Amin's judgement), *non*-statist, and even *anti*-statist (cf. Freitag 1996). Certainly, we have ample evidence of calendar art's innovativeness in the realm of Hindu iconography through over a century of popular print production (see Pal 1997; Lutgendorf 2002; Neumayer and Schelberger 1997; Uberoi 1990, 2001).

This article has been able to address only one limited aspect of the Nehruvian vision: its conceptualization of the secularist project of 'nation-building', uniting India's separate religious communities into one people. Addressing the other aspects of that vision—the attempt to reconcile industry and agriculture, city and village, modernity and tradition—is a task that must await another occasion. But this era represented a foundational moment in the visualizing of independent India, and it is certainly instructive, sometimes, to return there.

## Notes

1. One of the children—the Hindu child—is arguably 'androgynous', as the 'babies' of popular calendar art often are (see Uberoi 2001).

2. For the moment I avoid the vexed issue of whether or not the term is correctly applied in the Indian context, but see in this regard the argument of Partha Chatterjee (1997: Chapter 14), among others (e.g., Madan 1987, 1997; Nandy 1990; Smith 1963: esp. Chapter 2).

3. What Satish Deshpande, in an apt turn of phrase, has described as India's 'pasteurised multiculturalism' (Deshpande 1998: 163n).

4. This is the more so when one recalls that, at least for the 'god-poster' type within the total range of calendar art, the ritual efficacy of the image is believed to be enhanced, and certainly not depleted, by its infinite replication (see also Pinney 1997a: 860–61).

5. OED, 'fez': 'Turkish cap, a tasselled dull-red truncated cone'.

6. Collection J.P.S. and Patricia Uberoi, Delhi. The former carries a publisher's trademark, 'RLB 242', and has a very faint artist's signature, (?) Sharma, the forename smudged by the publisher's trademark. (It is possibly the well-known Anil Sharma). In the latter, trademarked 'VPP 242', the frame has been slightly reduced and the artist's signature eliminated.

7. See the recent work of Geeti Sen on the figure of Mother India in the fine arts and in popular culture; also, McKean (1996); Ramaswamy (1999, 2002, n.d.); and Sarkar (2001: esp. 176–81).

8. For a range of examples from the preindependence period, see Neumayer and Schelberger (1997: 104ff.). Some more recent examples can be found in FAAM (2000: 33, 35–38). See also Guha-Thakurta (1992); Mitter (1994: Colour Plate 21); Ramaswamy 2002.

9. Though Jain (1998: 135ff. also 2002) reports on the complaint of a number of calendar artists that publishers do not allow them to exercise their artistic skills to represent the Gods 'realistically', that is, with 'muscles', divine 'muscularity' is not unknown in calendar art iconography. While Ram's muscularity was usually embodied by his loyal disciple Hanuman (see Lutgendorf 2002; also Neumayer and Schelberger 1997: Plate 60), early 20th century chromolithographs provide examples of a more aggressive figure of Ram in his Parashuram *avatar* (see ibid., Plate 63, after a well-known Ravi Varma painting).

10. I am taking this period to extend beyond the death of Prime Minister Nehru to include the prime ministership of Lal Bahadur Shastri, and the early period of Mrs Indira Gandhi's leadership, through the Bangladesh War and up to the collapse of national consensus and the declaration of National Emergency in 1975. For a concise statement of the economic 'ideology' of this period, see Deshpande (1993, 1998); also Frankel (1978: esp. Chapters 1, 4, 13). Writings on the rise of communalism in post-

independence India note a 'sea-change' beginning in the 1980s. See various papers in Ludden (1996).

11. Interestingly, this erasure of historical context has not been the case with studies of the related medium of popular cinema, which have been compelled to seek explanations for the advent in the late 1970s and 1980s of a spate of violent, hero-focused films; or, in the late 1980s, for the collapsing of the roles of the heroine and the 'vamp' (see e.g., Chakravarty 1996; Kazmi 1999; Prasad 1998).

12. Collection J.P.S. and Patricia Uberoi, Delhi. In particular, we had rarely picked up photographic poster prints on the grounds that these eliminated the creative input of the artist, and we had neglected 'sceneries' as devoid of interest: misguided on both counts, as the work of other scholars has since amply demonstrated (e.g., Pinney 1995, 1997b). Moreover, the calendars were acquired mainly in the North Indian region, with a special eye for Sikh and Muslim themes. Indeed, if the truth be told, and quite disproportionately to the total range of calendar production in which Hindu religious prints overwhelmingly predominate, 'pin-ups' are probably as numerous in this collection as are Hindu deities!

13. In general, one can say that address to the audience or 'consumption' aspect of popular culture genres has been relatively neglected, but see, for example, Dickey's study of popular cinema audiences (1993); Pinney, on the 'social life of Indian photographs' (1997b: esp. Chapter 3); Jain, on calendar art and the ethos of the 'bazaar' (1997, 2002); and papers in Dwyer and Pinney (2001), particularly those of Dirks, Dwyer, Uberoi and Vasudevan.

14. For a reflection on the ethnic politics of national and political party emblems in the contemporary Sri Lankan context, see Tammita-Delgoda (n.d.). Erwin Neumayer has in his collection an interesting piece (see Neumayer and Schelberger 1997: Plate 90) which shows Mother India, holding in her hands the earlier flags of the Indian National Congress, presenting the new flag of the Indian Union to Prime Minister Nehru. On platters at her feet, set out as though for *puja*, sit the severed heads of various freedom fighters.

15. As in another calendar of this period (1974), entitled '*Satyam, Shivam, Sundaram*' (Truth, Holiness, Beauty) in which a child, watched over by a chimpanzee, reads a book on which is written: '*Paro aur insan bano*' (study and become human).

16. The marking of the child's sex is not, I think, an unimportant detail. On the whole, despite the 'androgynous' representation, informants appear to construe the child in this figure as male, not female, in line with the masculinity of the figures of Krishna, Jesus and Nanak. All the same, this relatively asexual image contrasts with that of a currently popular poster, reproduced widely under several different signatures, which shows a naked little boy conspicuously urinating into a tub. (The peeing boy is a favourite of scooter-graffiti too.) Though the child appears to be East Asian, he wears around his neck a gold medallion bearing the patriotic slogan, '*Jai Hind*'.

17. In another print I have in mind, the message is similarly explicit. Captioned, 'Perceived the Almighty to be a child' (1978), the naked, androgynous child at the centre of the print is shown reading a book (a 'scripture'?) by candlelight, surrounded by representations of Hinduism, Islam, Jainism, Christianity, Sikhism and Buddhism. The child's 'divinity' is expressed here in its undifferentiated embodiment of all the major religions of the subcontinent.

18. On Gandhi's understanding of secularism, see Donald E. Smith (1963: 148ff.); also Madan (1997: esp. Chapter 8); Nandy (1990); J.P.S. Uberoi (1996); van der Veer (1996: 94).

19. For a more comprehensive address to the representation of women in calendar art, linked to themes of nation-building, see e.g., Guha-Thakurta (1991); Uberoi (1990, 1996, 1999–2000).

20. The fuller Upanishadic text has been reproduced by Donald E. Smith (1963: 168) as follows:

> As the different streams having their sources in different places all mingle their water in the sea, O Lord, the different paths which men take through different tendencies, various though they appear, crooked or straight, all lead to thee.

21. For a colour reproduction of this print, see FAAM 2000: 37 (Plate 4.7). A similar, if more theatrical image from the same period, entitled '*Jai Hind*', shows Mother India, hands outstretched to welcome Indian independence, saluted by figures representing India's various religious communities (Hindus, Muslims and Sikhs are recognizable), men and women, old and young, and persons of all walks of life (the farmer and the shopkeeper, etc.) (ibid., 37 [Plate 4.8]). Interestingly, the map of India which forms the backdrop of this print, shows ominous dark clouds over India's north-western and north-eastern borders.

22. The composition varies from time to time. It may include, besides the trinity of Durga, Lakshmi and Saraswati, also Sita (see FAAM 2000: Figure 1.1) and goddesses representing sectarian or regional preferences (Santoshi-ma Bahucharji, etc.); or a single goddess may be represented in her multiple forms, such as the nine Durgas, or the eight forms of Lakshmi. Figure 5 is a relatively unusual presentation, as far as I know.

23. In fact, either of the cow figures may be labelled 'Kamadhenu' or '*Gau-mata*' (Mother Cow) interchangeably. Interestingly, Punjabi informants to whom I showed the Kamadhenu prints spontaneously identified the figure as Buraq, 'the animal upon whom Muhammed is said to have performed the nocturnal journey called *Mir' aj'* ... 'a white animal, between the size of a mule and an ass, having two wings', which British writers apparently aligned with the Assyrian 'gryphon' (Hughes 1935). Confronted with the caption, 'Kamadhenu', these informants insisted nonetheless that the *basic* image was of Buraq (who in turn was given the attributes of Muhammed's mare, Duldul): 'You can tell by the figure', they insisted. 'That's obviously a horse's rear and saddle cloth. It's just a horse with cow's udders and horns added.' Presumably, the intended purchasers of these prints would not be so deceived, but the ready misidentification, based on the

merging of the Buraq/Kamadhenu image, suggests a common vocabulary and aesthetic of representation (where Buraq is bovine, and Kamadhenu mare-like) which is not necessarily dominated by Hindu imagery but which specifically allows and enables ambiguity.

24. See, for example, the adjacent Plates 44 and 45, labelled 'Kamadhenu' and 'Go-Mata', in Larson et al., 1997: 53, also (Colour Plate 4), and FAAM (2000: 33, Plate 3.8), where the idea of a sacred geography is relatively explicit. Sivaramurti (1982: 45) describes Kamadhenu as the 'zoomorphic version' of the auspicious deity Sri (Lakshmi). The iconographical representation of the cow with its body filled with hierarchically ordered deities and the udders 'forming the four oceans' (ibid., 55) is apparently derived from the *Asrmavasikaparva* section of the *Mahabharat.*

25. I have not identified B.C. Sharma, though he appears to be an artist of the Nathdwara School (NTD in the signature?). For the special contribution of the Nathdwara artists (promoted initially by the Karachi-based firm of S.S. Brijbasi) to the history of Indian chromolithography, see Pinney 1995, 1997a: 860–63; also Jain 1998: 56–62. H. Daniel Smith has extensive field notes on several of the Nathdwara painters, including B.G. Sharma, C.B. Sharma and N.L. Sharma, and on the publishing firms of S.S. Brijbasi and Hem Chander Bhargava, who popularised the works of the Nathdwara painters. See Smith (1988).

26. The other major rallying point was the 'language' issue, Hindi *versus* Urdu (see King 1989). For writings on the role of Cow Protection towards creating a Hindu 'religious nationalist' identity in the colonial period, and the specific deployment of mass-produced cow images in that cause, see, e.g., Barrier (1968: 528–30); Brosius (1999: 106–7, esp. Plate 38); Freitag (1980, 1990: Chapter 5, 1996: 215–34); Jain (1998: 54–56, esp. Plate 55); Jones (1976: 152–53); Pandey (1983, 1990: esp. Chapter 3); Pinney (1997a, 1999, 2002); van der Veer (1996: esp. Chapter 3); and Yang (1980).

27. Perhaps they may be distinguished by sectarian marks on their foreheads, or by their headgear, as the three upper *varnas* (Brahmin, Kshatrya, Vaishya).

28. The European/Christian has a cup and saucer; the Muslim a sort of bowl; and the Hindus and Parsee, *lotas.*

29. Interview, January 2001.

30. I have three almost identical specimens from 1973 and 1974, published in Ludhiana and Sangrur (Punjab). Mohinder Singh was reputed to be based in Delhi, and had executed a large number of 'Sikh' themes.

31. *Sri Guru Granth Sahib* (standard edition) p. 918: *Ramkali Mahala* 3, *Anand, Shlok* 13.

32. The image in fact appears to be commonly used in Cow Protection literature. See for instance the similar image from the cover of a VHP booklet on cow protection (ca. 1990) reproduced in Brosius (1999: Plate 38). The VHP organisation has a department dedicated to cow protection (Basu et al., 1993: 67).

33. Bhai Mati Das, companion and diwan of Guru Tegh Bahadur, was arrested on imperial orders along with the Guru in 1675. Refusing to become apostate, he was tortured and sawn in two. See H. Singh (1992–98: III, 68–69).

34. Arguably, this might be a tepid recognition of the Islamic/Sufi contribution to Sikh theology. See J.P.S. Uberoi (1996: Chapter 3).

35. Fox (1987: Chapter 9) details the competition between the Arya Samaj and the Singh Sabha movements for the 'conversion' of low-caste groups. See also Jones (1976: 207–8, 210).

36. Interestingly, however, representatives of the Nirankari and Radhasoami sects are not incorporated within the cow's body here, marking the outer limits of the syncretistic formulation (see Grewal 1994: 140–41, 216–17; McLeod 1989: 115–21; Khushwant Singh 1966: Chapter 8).

37. The 'blasphemy' appears to refer particularly to the use of *Gurbani* in captions and titles of prints and illustrations. I was surprised that it did not extend, at least explicitly, to a critique of the transformation of the cow's milk/*Shivalingam-yoni* into *amrit*, which has a specific religious connotation in Sikhism. See also Virk (2001), who gives the further example of an RSS booklet, *Hindutva and environment*, whose cover picture of a cow suckling its calf is accompanied by a caption which is supposedly *bani* of Guru Arjan.

38. He was referring to the coalition alliance of the Akali Party with the BJP in the Punjab government, as well as at the Centre.

39. Such statements are actually the common stuff of cow protection literature. See, e.g., 'Bharat Mata for sale, Rs 3' (*The Times of India*, 3/12/2000) on the door-to-door promotion campaign of this RSS literature in Delhi in November–December 2000.

40. This echoes Jawaharlal Nehru's rationalist argument on behalf of cow protection (T.N. Madan, personal communication).

41. Here I use as my template earlier work on the structure of linguistic pluralism in South Asia (Uberoi and Uberoi 1977), based on a close reading of the work of socio-linguist, P.B. Pandit (especially Pandit 1977).

42. By way of comparison, McLeod (1991: Figure 14) reproduces a late 19th century 'double print' of two very similar images: on the one side, a Sikh family paying homage at the shrine of Baba Atal Rai, and on the other, Brahma and Shiv worshipping Durga. McLeod comments:

> Dual prints of this kind testify to the eclectic nature of popular Sikh taste during the nineteenth century, an attitude soon to be attacked by the Singh Sabha reformers. It should be added that although the Singh Sabha campaign exercised a considerable influence among educated Sikhs, *it never succeeded in extinguishing the popular appreciation for prints of this kind* (McLeod 1991: 128, emphasis added).

43. Both were executed by the same artist, Ram Singh, founder of the Rang Roop Studio, Delhi. A publisher told me that Ram Singh often painted sets of near-identical pictures of Shiv, Ram, and Nanak. Whether this was out of inner religious conviction

or market-savvy opportunism, he would not say (interview, January 2001; interview with Vijay Singh, Ram Singh's son [also a calendar artist], January 2001). On Rang Roop, see also H. Daniel Smith (1998).

44. Untitled. Artist, S.M. Kumar; Publisher: India Glass House, Ludhiana.

45. As in another print from the Rang Roop Studio, dating from the same period (Collection J.P.S. and Patricia Uberoi).

46. The popular story, a relatively late tradition, according to H.W. McLeod, relates how Guru Nanak, distributing commodities in the commissariat, would fall into a trance on reaching the number 13 (*terah*), continuing to repeat '*tera, tera, tera* ... (Thine)' (see McLeod 1968: 107n).

47. The well-produced annual calendars of the Punjab and Sind Bank (and now also the Bank of Punjab), each of which pursues a particular theme or style, have played an important role in generating visual statements of Sikh identity—at least on behalf of the Sikh urban middle classes.

## References

Amin, Shahid. 2000. Remembering the Musalman. *In* Hiroyuki Kotani et al., (eds.), *Fusing Modernity: Appropriation of history and political mobilisation in South Asia*, pp. 75–101. JCAS Symposium Series 11. Osaka: National Museum of Ethnology.

Barrier, Norman G. 1968. The Punjab government and communal politics, 1870–1908. *Journal of Asian studies* 27, 3: 523–39.

Basu, Tapan, et al. 1993. *Khaki Shorts and Saffron Flags: A critique of the Hindu Right* (Tracts for the Times, 1). New Delhi: Orient Longman.

Bernstein, Basil. 1971. *Class, codes and control, I: Theoretical studies towards a sociology of language*. London: Routledge & Kegan Paul.

Brosius, Christiane. 1997. Mapping the nation. In Pooja Sood (ed.), *Mappings: Shared histories, a fragile self*, pp. 15–19. New Delhi: Eicher Gallery.

———. 1999. Empowering Visions: A study on videos and the politics of cultural nationalism in India (1989–98). Dissertation: Europa-Universität Viadrina, Frankfurt-Oder.

———. 2002. Hindutva intervisuality: Videos and the politics of representation. *Contributions to Indian Sociology* 36, 1 & 2: 265–95.

Chakravarty, Sumita S. 1996 [1993]. *National Identity in Indian Popular Cinema, 1947–1987*. Delhi: Oxford University Press.

Chatterjee, Partha. 1993. *The Nation and its Fragments: Colonial and postcolonial histories*. Princeton, N.J.: Princeton University Press.

———. 1997. *A Possible India: Essays in political criticism*. Delhi: Oxford University Press.

Deshpande, Satish. 1993. Imagined economies: Styles of nation-building in twentieth century India. *Journal of Arts and Ideas* 25–26: 5–35.

Deshpande, Satish. 1998. After culture: Renewed agendas for the political economy of India. *Cultural Dynamics* 10, 2: 147–69.

Dickey, Sara. 1993. *Cinema and the Urban Poor in South India*. Cambridge: Cambridge University Press.

Dwyer, Rachel and Christopher Pinney (eds.). 2001. *Pleasure and the Nation: The history, politics and consumption of public culture in India*. New Delhi: Oxford University Press.

Fox, Richard G. 1987. *Lions of the Punjab: Culture in the making*. New Delhi: Archives Publishers.

Frankel, Francine R. 1978. *India's Political Economy, 1947–1977*. Princeton, N.J. Princeton University Press.

Freitag, Sandria B. 1980. Sacred Symbol and Mobilizing Ideology: The north Indian search for a 'Hindu' community. *Comparative Studies in Society and History* 22, 4: 597–625.

———. 1990 [1989]. *Collective Action and Community: Public arenas and the emergence of communalism in north India*. Delhi: Oxford University Press.

———. 1996. Contesting in Public: Colonial legacies and contemporary communities. *In* Ludden 1996: 211–34.

Fukuoka Asian Art Museum [FAAM]. 2000. *From Goddess to Pin-up: Icons of femininity in Indian calendar art*. Fukuoka: Fukuoka Asian Art Museum.

Graham, Bruce. 1993. *Hindu Nationalism and Indian Politics: The origins and development of the Bharatiya Jana Sangh*. Cambridge: Cambridge University Press.

Grewal, J.S. 1994. *The New Cambridge History of India, II.3: The Sikhs of the Punjab*. New Delhi: Foundation Books, South Asia Paperback edition.

Guha-Thakurta, Tapati. 1991. Women as 'Calendar Art' Icons: Emergence of pictorial stereotype in colonial India. *Economic and Political Weekly* 26, 43: WS91–99.

———. 1992. *The Making of a New 'Indian' Art. Artists, aesthetics and nationalism in Bengal, c. 1850–1920*. Cambridge: Cambridge University Press.

Gupta, Dipankar, 1996. *The Context of Ethnicity. Sikh identity in comparative perspective*. Delhi: Oxford University Press.

Hershman, Paul. 1977. Virgin and Mother. In Ian Lewis (ed.), *Symbol and Sentiments: Cross-cultural studies in symbolism*, pp. 269–92. London: Academic Press.

———. 1981. *Punjabi Kinship and Marriage*. Delhi: Hindustan.

Hughes, Thomas Patrick. 1935 [1895]. *A Dictionary of Islam*. London: W.H. Allen.

Jain, Kajri. 1997. Producing the Sacred: The subject of calendar art. *Journal of Arts and Ideas* 30–31: 63–88.

———. 1998. Gods in the Bazaar: The commercial, sacred and libidinal economies of Indian 'calendar art'. Doctoral dissertation, University of Sydney.

———. 2002. More than Meets the Eye. The circulation of images and the embodiment of value. *Contributions to Indian sociology* 36, 1 & 2: 33–70.

Jones, Kenneth W. 1976. *Arya Dharm: Hindu Consciousness in 19th century Punjab*. Delhi: Manohar.

Kapur, Anuradha. 1993. Deity to Crusader: The changing iconography of Ram. *In* Gyanendra Pandey (ed.), *Hindus and Others*, pp. 74–107. New Delhi: Viking.

Kazmi, Fareed. 1999. *The Politics of India's Conventional Cinema*. New Delhi: Sage Publications.

King, Christopher R. 1989. Forging a New Linguistic Identity: The Hindi movement in Banaras, 1868–1914. *In* Sandria Freitag (ed.), *Culture and Power in Banaras: Community, performance and environment, 1800–1980*, pp. 179–202. Delhi: Oxford University Press.

Krishna, Sankaran. 1994. Cartographic Anxiety: Mapping the body politic in India. *Alternatives* 19: 507–21.

Larson, Gerald James. 1997. A Postmodernist Perspective on India's Popular Religious Art. *In* Larson, et al. 1997: 24–27.

Larson, Gerald James, Pratapaditya Pal and H. Daniel Smith, compiled. 1997. *Changing Myths and Images: Twentieth-century popular art in India*. Bloomington: Indiana University Art Museum.

Ludden, David. 1996. *Making India Hindu: Religion, community and the politics of democracy in India*. Delhi: Oxford University Press.

Lutgendorf, Philip. 2002. Evolving a monkey. Hanuman, poster art and postcolonial anxiety. *Contributions to Indian Sociology* 36, 1 & 2: 71–112.

McKean, Lise. 1996. Bharat Mata: Mother India and her militant matriots. *In* J.S. Hawley and D.M. Wulff (eds.), *Devi: Goddesses of India*, pp. 250–80. Berkeley: University of California Press.

McLeod, H.W. 1968. *Guru Nanak and the Sikh Religion*. Oxford: Clarendon Press.

_____. 1989. *Who is a Sikh: The problem of Sikh identity*. Oxford: Clarendon Press.

_____. 1991. *Popular Sikh Art*. Delhi: Oxford University Press.

Madan T.N. 1987. Secularism in its place. *Journal of Asian Studies* 46, 4: 747–59.

_____. 1997. *Modern Myths, Locked Minds: Secularism and fundamentalism in India*. Delhi: Oxford University Press.

Manuel, Peter. 1996. Music, the Media, and Communal Relations in North India, Past and Present. *In* Ludden 1996: 119–39.

Mitter, Partha. 1994. *Art and Nationalism in Colonial India, 1850–1922: Occidental orientations*. Cambridge: Cambridge University Press.

_____. 2002. Mechanical reproduction and the world of the colonial artist. *Contributions to Indian Sociology* 36, 1 & 2: 1–32.

Nandy, Ashis. 1983. *The Intimate Enemy: Loss and recovery of self under colonialism*. Delhi: Oxford University Press.

_____. 1990. The Politics of secularism and the recovery of religious tolerance. *In* Veena Das (ed.), *Mirrors of Violence: Communities, riots and survivors in South Asia*, pp. 69–93. Delhi: Oxford University Press.

Neumayer, Erwin and Christine Schelberger, compiled. 1997. *The Oleographed Gods of India*. Vienna: Private circulation.

Oberoi, Harjot. 1994. *The Construction of Religious Boundaries: Culture, identity and diversity in the Sikh tradition*. Delhi: Oxford University Press.

Pal, Pratapaditya. 1997. The Printed Image: An iconographic excursus. In Larson, et al. 1997: 29–38.

Pandey, Gyanendra. 1983. Rallying with the Cow: Sectarian strife in the Bhojpuri region, c. 1888–1917. *In* Ranajit Guha (ed.), *Subaltern Studies II: Writings on South Asian history and society*, pp. 60–129. Delhi: Oxford University Press.

——. 1990. *The Construction of Communalism in Colonial North India*. Delhi: Oxford University Press.

Pandit, P.B. 1977. *Language in a Plural Society* (Dev Raj Chanana Memorial Lectures). Delhi: Delhi University Press.

Pinney, Christopher. 1995. Moral Topophilia: The significations of landscape in Indian oleographs. *In* Eric Hirsch and Michael O' Hanlon (eds.), *The Anthropology of Landscape: Perspectives on place and space*, pp. 78–113. Oxford: Clarendon Press.

——. 1997a. The Nation (Un)pictured? Chromolithography and 'popular' politics in India, 1879–1995. *Critical Inquiry* 23, 4: 834–67.

——. 1997b. *Camera Indica: The social life of Indian photographs*. Chicago: University of Chicago Press.

——. 1999. Indian Magical Realism: Notes on popular visual culture. *In* Gautam Bhadra, Gyan Prakash and Suzie Tharu (eds.), *Subaltern Studies X: Writings on south Asia*, pp. 201–33. Delhi: Oxford University Press.

——. 2002. 'A Secret of Their Own Country': Or, how Indian nationalism made itself irrefutable. *Contributions to Indian Sociology* 36, 1 & 2: 113–50.

Prasad, M. Madhava. 1998. *Ideology of the Hindi Film: A historical construction*. Delhi: Oxford University Press.

Ramaswamy, Sumathi. 1999. Virgin Mother, Beloved Other: The erotics of Tamil nationalism in colonial and post-colonial India. In Rajeswari Sunder Rajan (ed.), *Signposts: Gender issues in post-Independence India*, pp. 17–56. New Delhi: Kali for Women.

——. 2002. Visualising India's geo-body: Globes, maps, bodyscapes. *Contributions to Indian Sociology* 36, 1 & 2: 151–89.

——. 2005. The Goddess and the Nation: Subterfuges of antiquity, the cunning of modernity. In Gavin Flood (ed.), *Blackwell Companion to Hinduism*. Blackwell Publishers.

Roy, Srirupa. 2002. Moving Pictures: The postcolonial state and visual representations of India. *Contributions to Indian Sociology* 36, 1 & 2: 233–63.

Sarkar, Tanika. 2001. *Hindu Wife, Hindu Nation: Community, religion and cultural nationalism*. New Delhi: Permanent Black.

Singh, G. 2001. Even after the High Court judgement why do they insist on calling the Sikhs, the 'Hindus'? *Spokesman Weekly*, January: 23–24.

Singh, Harbans (ed.) 1992–98. *The Encyclopedia of Sikhism*, 4 vols. Patiala: Punjabi University Press.

Singh, Khushwant. 1963. *A History of the Sikhs, Volume I: 1469–1839*. Princeton, N.J.: Princeton University Press.

——. 1966. *A History of the Sikhs, Volume II: 1839–1964*. Princeton, N.J.: Princeton University Press.

Sivaramurti, C. 1982. *Sri Lakshmi in Indian Art and Thought*. New Delhi: Kanak.

Smith, Donald Eugene. 1963. *India as a Secular State*. Princeton, N.J.: Princeton University Press.

Smith, H. Daniel. 1988. Fieldnotes. Mss. preserved in the Smith Poster Archive, Syracuse University, New York.

Tammita-Delgoda, Sinha Raja. n.d. The Imagery of Nationalism: Classical allusion and the politics of Sinhala nationalism. Illustrated lecture presented at the 'Dialogue of Democracy and Diversity in South Asia'. Centre for Political Studies, JNU, 14–17 March 2001.

Uberoi, J.P.S. 1996. *Religion, Civil Society and the State: A study of Sikhism*. Delhi: Oxford University Press.

Uberoi, Patricia. 1990. Feminine Identity and National Ethos in Indian Calendar Art. *Economic and Political Weekly* 25, 17: WS41–48.

——. 1996. From goddess to pin-up: Icons of femininity in Indian calendar art, 1955–1995. In Pooja Sood (ed.), *Of Women: Icons/Stars/Feasts*, pp. 7–9. New Delhi: Eicher Gallery.

——. 1999–2000. Times Past: Gender and the nation in 'calendar art'. *Indian Horizons* 46, 4, & 47, 1: 24–39.

——. 2001. Baby boom: Forms and figures of a new generation. Exhibition catalogue, *Kitsch Kitsch Hota Hai*, India Habitat Centre Visual Art Gallery, March 2001 (unnumbered pages).

Uberoi, Patricia and J.P.S. Uberoi. 1977. Towards a New Sociolinguistics: A memoir of P.B. Pandit. In H.S. Gill (ed.), *Parole and Langue. Pakha Sanjam* 8 (1975–76): iii–xvii.

van der Veer, Peter. 1996 [1994]. *Religious Nationalism: Hindus and Muslims in India*. Delhi: Oxford University Press.

Virk, Hardev Singh. 2001. False RSS propaganda at Guru Nanak Dev University, Amritsar. *Spokesman weekly*, February: 27–30.

Yang, Anand A. 1980. Sacred symbol and sacred space in rural India: Community mobilization in the 'Anti-Cow Killing' riot of 1893. *Comparative Studies in Society and History* 22, 4: 576–96.

# 6.
# Guru and Gramophone: Fantasies of Fidelity and Modern Technologies of the Real

AMANDA WEIDMAN

> Nothing excites the memory more strongly than the human voice, maybe because nothing is forgotten as quickly as a voice. Our memory of it, however, does not die—its timbre and character sink into our subconscious where they await their revival.
>
> Rudolph Lothar, The Talking Machine: A Technical-Aesthetic Essay

> Guru, face to face, shows the marga [way]. The sisya has to make the journey to excellence. How is that excellence purveyed? ... There is a message that voice leaves in the listener's soul, a memory like the ubiquitous murmur of surf, long after the particular sangatis of a rendering have been forgotten ... [Today] music is treated all wrong ... as though it were a mere science, a matter of arithmetic, of fractions and time intervals.
>
> Raghava Menon, quoted in S.V. Krishnamurthy, 'Divinity, the Core of Indian Music'

IN POSTCOLONIAL SOUTH INDIA, KARNATIC, OR SOUTH INDIAN CLASSICAL MUSIC HAS come to be prized as one of the signs of uncolonized Indian distinctiveness. Discourse about classical music in South India is dominated by ideas about the primacy of the voice and the importance of oral tradition. But *voice* and *oral tradition* have become more than merely descriptive terms in a discourse about authenticity and fidelity to origins that derives its urgency from the perceived onslaught of technologies of recording and reproduction. The significance of these terms is apparent from the way they are used to oppose Karnatic music to a generalized idea of Western music: whereas Western music is instrumental, Karnatic is vocal; whereas Western music is 'technologically' superior, Karnatic is more 'spiritual'; whereas Western music can be played just by looking at written music (or so the stereotype

I thank the editorial committee of *Public Culture* for their thoughtful reading of the original draft of this essay, which enabled me to sharpen many of the arguments made here.

Excerpted from *Public Culture* 15(3): 453–76, Duke University Press, 2003.

goes), Karnatic is passed on through a centuries-long oral tradition and a system of teaching that technology cannot duplicate.

This article concerns the quest for authenticity in twentieth-century discourse on Karnatic music and its relationship to technologically conceived ideas of fidelity and authority. I focus on moments when practices and ideas of listening, performing, and music itself seem to change in conjunction with technologies of recording and broadcasting. In particular, I note the emergence of certain fantasies and anxieties about the replacement of the human guru with a machine, the quantification of music, the collapse of time, the reproducibility of the voice, and the possibility of complete loss. Rather than narrate the takeover of a 'traditional' practice by 'modern' technologies, I show how ideas about authenticity, tradition, and modernity were—and continue to be—shaped in the very encounter with such technologies. My focus here is on the discursive networks in which technologies take their place as points of relay between bodies, sounds, writing, and forms of power.[1]

A number of issues emerge here concerning the relationship between fidelity and authority. On the one hand, technologies of recording and broadcasting create a disruption of traditional modes of teaching, performing, and listening—a disturbance that is experienced by musicians and listeners variously as a forgetting of voice, a loss of face-to-face contact, and a speeding up of time. If the guru's authority is in part produced by the fidelity of his *sisya*, or disciple, fidelity carried to an extreme threatens that authority. On the other hand, the focus of traditional desire is projected out of the new technologies themselves. The social sense of fidelity, in the distinctly postcolonial sense of fidelity to tradition, loyalty to one's roots and nationality, comes to be modeled on the technological sense of fidelity. Here technologies appear as both destroyers and saviours, as instruments of both memory and forgetting, and longing for the past is accompanied by an odd sense of futurity.

## His Master's Voice

The short story 'Vidwan' [The musician] (Malan 1981) begins with a classic scene of artistic angst, as its protagonist, the violinist Janakiraman, struggles to express a musical idea.[2] He is interrupted by the arrival of a former student from America, Joseph Om.[3] Om had miraculously sought out Janakiraman, a simple, unassuming man who cared only about music, who had spent his life teaching students. But there had been no student he could call a real *sisya* until Om had come along. 'For two years Om had learned by Janakiraman's side, night and day. He would learn sitting cross-legged on the floor. He had learned to eat *rasam* and rice with his eyes watering. He knew every bit of Janakiraman's daily routine. That was *gurukulavasam*.'[4]

The pretext for Om's visit is to install a computerized robot named Yakshani that will do the housework and cooking for Janakiraman and even tune his violin. The system proceeds to work without a hitch, yet Janakiraman never lets it anywhere near his violin.

> *Sangitam* [music] was a divine matter. A sacred thing. He had decided that you couldn't put such a thing in the hands of a machine. One day, after finishing his *puja*,[5] when he came inside and sat down, Yakshani asked:
>
> 'What does "shadjam" mean?'[6]
>
> Janakiraman was startled. 'What?'
>
> 'What does "shadjam" mean?'
>
> 'Shadjam is a *swaram*.'
>
> 'What is a "swaram"?'
>
> 'Yakshani, why are you torturing yourself with this?'
>
> 'Will you not teach me music?'
>
> 'What?! You? ... Music is a divine art, an elevated thing. Something that requires a lifetime to know.'
>
> '*Divine, elevated, lifetime*—these are all new words. What do they mean?'
>
> 'Yakshani, stop troubling me.'
>
> The next afternoon after he had eaten and had his betel and was lying in a half-awake stupor he heard Yakshani's voice.
>
> 'From tomorrow, you have a week's concerts in Delhi. I have folded your clothes, packed your music book, fruits to eat, betel, and your address book and diabetes medicine. Shall I pack the violin?'
>
> 'Don't you touch it!' Janakiraman shouted.

Ten days later Janakiraman comes back from his Delhi tour. As he approaches his house, he hears strains of music from within.

> From inside the house a divine *bhairavi* was floating. ... So clear. So tender.[7] As soon as he heard it he felt chills on his body. The excellence of such pure music shook his soul [*ma<u>n</u>acu*]. Something inside him was struck. He felt like crying. He let out a sob. All these sixty-five years he had never heard such purity. Now, hearing it, he was unable to endure it. The *raga alapana* and *kriti* finished, and the *swaram* playing began.[8] He couldn't stand it any longer. He opened the door and switched on the light. Immediately the music stopped. ... Janakiraman went around looking in every room.
>
> 'Who was playing the violin just now?' he asked.
>
> After a half minute, Yakshani answered. 'I was.'
>
> 'What?! You?' Janakiraman felt an irrational pang of envy. He became annoyed. 'I told you not to touch the violin!' he roared.
>
> 'I did not touch it.'

> 'What do you mean, you didn't touch it! I just heard the sound. My ears were not mistaken.'
>
> 'Those were sounds I made at a particular frequency.'
>
> 'Who taught you such wonderful music?'
>
> 'You did ... what I made were only sounds. Different sound waves. ... It is your wish if you call it music. It is the basis of what you teach your students.'
>
> 'Can you play only *bhairavi*? What else?'
>
> 'I can play any raga. A raga is a predecided pattern of several notes. A formula [*formula*]. Notes are certain frequencies of sound. If they were programmed into my memory I could construct different formulas and elaborate different ragas.'
>
> Janakiraman was shocked. Was music just calculations [*kanakku*]? Was what he had struggled to learn night and day for fifty years such a small drop that a machine could learn it in ten days and play it back? ... Was it just an illusion that music was the food of the gods? Tears welled up in his eyes.

Janakiraman storms out of the room. But the next day, humbled, he approaches Yakshani:

> 'Yakshani, what you said is right. ... I have never heard such a pure *bhairavi* in my life. I believed my guru was a real rishi. In my experience there was no music like his. But even he never sang like this. ... We deceive ourselves by saying [music] is a divine thing. The time has come to worship science. Until yesterday I did not believe that. Today it is as if all has finally become clear. From now on, you teach me. I will think of it as being god's *sisya*.' Janakiraman's voice was choked with emotion.
>
> 'You are saying new words. We are machines. We can only know what you know. We cannot come to know a thread more than that. We have no imagination [*kaṟpaṉai*]. ... Our skills are your slaves. We can never win over you. You tell me to teach you. I have completely forgotten music. If you do not want me to learn something, I have a 'built-in mechanism' that will delete it completely from my memory bank. It gauges your dislike from your anger or tears. Yesterday the moment my sensors sensed the tears in your eyes the music was entirely destroyed.'
>
> Janakiraman felt an unspeakable shock. He had not foreseen such a possibility. He stared blankly for a few minutes, unable to get a grip on his shock. Then resolutely, he began: 'Yakshani, look here. This is *saralivarisai*.[9] *Sa-ri-ga-ma-pa-da-ni*. ...'

Malan's story thematizes the concerns and anxieties surrounding *gurukulavasam*, perhaps the most venerated institution of Karnatic classical music. *Gurukulavasam* refers to the long years in which the *sisya*, or disciple, lives with the guru, learning music by a process of absorption, serving and learning humility before the guru. Above all, it represents the premodern, a time and place that existed before the differentiation of time into concerts and music lessons, before the separation of music from life in general and the advent of recording technology. The absence of technology is, in most contemporary accounts, the condition of *gurukulavasam's* authenticity.

And yet, as Malan's story illustrates, there is something compelling in the analogy between the computer's artificial intelligence and the logic of *gurukulavasam*, something that suggests the dual nature of fidelity as a social and technological concept. Although the story ultimately privileges the human guru, Janakiraman, the narrative's overall effect is more destabilizing. The robot replaces music and voice with frequencies and sound waves, memory with a memory bank, forgetting with deleting, the devoted disciple with a computer, and a lifetime of study with the instantaneity of digital processing. It is both a fantasy of disembodied perfection and a nightmare of reproduction gone out of control.

The original *gurukulavasam* is already displaced at the beginning of the story. Unable to achieve it with any of his Indian students, Janakiraman achieves it with Om, an American. In turn, Yakshani, a technological creation of the West programmed by Om, becomes the *sisya* par excellence, learning to serve Janakiraman according to his wishes and all the while absorbing his music. If a computer can replace the *sisya*, can it not, as Janakiraman comes to realize, also replace the guru? What happens when the threshold of perfection is in the hands of a machine? What if the black box of *gurukulavasam* really could be opened and revealed to or by the technology of the West? The threat that music can be completely quantified, reduced to 'calculations [*ka<u>n</u>akku*],' is also the threat that the voice is reproducible.[10] If perfect music is attainable without years of study, doesn't time itself threaten to collapse? Just as we begin to imagine such possibilities, the second shock of the story comes: Yakshani reveals that it has deleted all its music. This is no gradual loss as in loss of human memory, but a sudden, irrevocable erasure without a trace, a loss that gives Janakiraman an 'unspeakable shock.' In the face of such shock, Janakiraman reverts to what, for him, is automatic: he restarts *gurukulavasam*. If there is something reassuring in this, it also leaves open a literally unnerving possibility: that the guru's flesh and blood might be replaced by computer wiring, and that technology might create music which sounds more like tradition than tradition itself.

## Gorgeous Gramophones

Frederick Gaisberg, the first recording engineer for the Gramophone Company, looking back in 1942 on his Far Eastern tours of 1920–23, wrote that 'the gramophone we brought to India was to enjoy an especially widespread popularity as an entertainer, and was to vie with the umbrella and the bicycle as a hallmark of affluence. Even now, shoppers ... demand a large glittering brass horn to dazzle their neighbours' (Gaisberg 1942: 57).[11]

Ananda Coomaraswamy, an art critic and aesthetician of Sri Lankan Tamil descent, was less enthusiastic. He began his essay on the gramophone in 1909 with the observation that 'enlightened maharajas,' so intent on improving society in other ways, spent extravagant amounts of money on 'gorgeous gramophones, mechanical violins, and cheap harmoniums' ([1909] 1981: 191). The educated classes, generally infatuated with anything that came from the West, had lost their love of Indian music and were finding amusement in the gramophone instead. Coomaraswamy warned that Indians, fascinated with listening to copies, would one day find themselves without the real thing: 'It is not possible for anything to be a compensation for the loss of Indian music,' he warned ([1909] 1981: 200).

What was this real thing, this Indian music? What made real Indian music different from other music? For Coomaraswamy, the difference lay in Indian music's resistance to being written down. Indian music, to be authentic, had to flow from a master's mouth directly to a disciple's ear; *gamakas* were too variable, subtle, and mood-dependent to be written.[12] 'There is thus in music that necessary dependence of the disciple upon the master, which is characteristic of every kind of education in India' (Coomaraswamy [1909] 1981: 172). The danger that writing posed for Indian music was that it stripped it of *gamakas*, the very sounds that made it Indian: 'And so it is that an Indian air, set down upon the staff and picked out note by note on a piano or harmonium becomes the most thin and jejune sort of music that can be imagined, and many have abandoned in despair all such attempts at record[ing it]' (Coomaraswamy [1909] 1981: 173). The difficulty of writing down vocal music was due to the fact that there was no mechanism, like a musical instrument, to see; the voice, and its authenticity, were hidden inside the body. And that was as it should be; otherwise the musician might be degraded, as the weaver had already been, 'from the status of intelligent craftsman to living machine' ([1909] 1981: 202). 'The intervention of mechanism between musician and sound,' wrote Coomaraswamy ([1909] 1981: 205), 'is always, per se, disadvantageous. The most perfect music is that of the human voice. The most perfect instruments are those stringed instruments where the musician's hand is always in contact with the string producing the sound, so that every shade of his feeling can be reflected in it. Even the piano is relatively an inferior instrument, and still more the harmonium, which is only second to the gramophone as evidence of the degradation of musical taste in India.'

The gramophone reproduced the vocal sound without contacting the musician's body at all. Therein lay its danger: it was no longer the supplement to the voice, but the substitution for that voice. While educated middle-class Indians in Madras were flocking to musical instrument shops to purchase glittering, morning-glory-shaped gramophones, Coomaraswamy ([1909] 1981: 204) proclaimed them to be the very spectre of ugliness: 'For pure hideousness and lifelessness ... few objects could exceed a gramophone. The more decorated it may be, the more its intrinsic ugliness is revealed.' The pleasure of a music concert was in 'the vision of a living man giving expression to emotions in a disciplined art language' (Coomaraswamy [1909] 1981: 204). To see the same sounds emanating from the decorated horn of a gramophone, which could have no concept of such a language, was to be confronted with the separation of musician and music, subject and speech, form and content, and to come face to face with the startling mixture of animate and inanimate.

The gramophone had managed to do what no living person—not even the most patient of disciples with the help of the most learned Indian masters—could: write down, or record, Indian music and reproduce it. This was its 'fatal facility' (Coomaraswamy [1909] 1981: 203); the unliving machine threatened to kill true musical sensibility. 'To a person of culture—especially musical culture—the sound of a gramophone is not an entertainment, but the refinement of torture' (Coomaraswamy [1909] 1981: 204). Whereas instruments like the veena or *sarangi* require a musical master, 'a gramophone ... often enables the most unmusical person to inflict a suffering audience with his ideas' (Coomaraswamy [1909] 1981: 199). For Coomaraswamy, 'musical sensibilities' went beyond the ability to appreciate music; indeed, to be really authentic, they had to reach into the realm of national sensibilities. A musical subject was above all an Indian subject who would not forsake his guru, or the disciplined years of study. True musical pleasure was not in the sound itself but in the knowledge that such sound was authentically Indian, that it thrived on a mode of reproduction different from the technological reproduction of the West. 'For no man of another nation will come to learn of India, if her teachers be gramophones and harmoniums and imitators of European realistic art' (Coomaraswamy [1909] 1981: 206).

But *what if* there were a gramophone that even a musician could not distinguish from the real thing? The hypothetical supposition seemed to haunt Coomaraswamy. Indeed, he allowed that there could be a use for the gramophone as a 'scientific instrument—not as an interpreter of human emotion. In the recording of songs, the analysis of music for theoretical purposes, in the exact study of an elaborate melody of Indian music, the gramophone has a place' (Coomaraswamy [1909] 1981: 205 n). The idea that there might be something to be learned about Indian music that could not be taught by a guru is potentially more subversive than Coomaraswamy's vision of listeners forsaking musicians for gramophones. Luckily for Coomaraswamy, the something that might be learned fell not into the realm of art but into the realm of the 'scientific' and the 'real.'

In 1910–11, A.H. Fox-Strangways went to India in search of this 'real.' Having studied music in Germany and dabbled in Sanskrit texts, he went to India to find clues to early music theory (Clayton 1999: 88), the inaudible basics that underlay the musical systems of all nations. Armed with a phonograph, Fox-Strangways spent several months touring South India recording folk music, recounting his recording experiences in the form of a 'musical diary.' His idea was to capture music in its natural, spontaneous setting, in street cries, sailors' chanteys, and women's work songs. But because of the difficulty of maneuvering with the phonograph, which unlike a camera 'cannot be carried on the person or unlimbered and brought into action in half a minute,' he was forced much of the time to use himself in the manner of a phonograph, 'recording' melodies in staff notation (Fox-Strangways [1914] 1995: 17). Fox-Strangways wrote that 'it was not until I had been some months in India that I found the opportunity I had been waiting for of *overhearing* a folk-melody. I awoke at Madras, about 5:30 am, to the sound of singing; it was next door, and seemed to come from a woman about her household duties. In the dim light I scribbled down the [notation]' ([1914] 1995: 26; emphasis in original). In such 'humble melodies,' Fox-Strangways heard, or overheard, the real basis of Indian music. The object, he wrote, had been 'not so much to present complete and finished specimens, as to get close down upon those natural instincts of song-makers which, when followed out in the domain of art, cause their music to take one form rather than another; to get behind the conventions, of which art is full, to the things themselves of which those conventions are the outcome' (Fox-Strangways [1914] 1995: 72).

## The Real

At the turn of the twentieth century, Friedrich Kittler (1990: 230) writes, with the introduction of storage facilities for data other than writing, such as gramophone records, film, and photography, 'the technological recording of the real entered into competition with the symbolic registration of the Symbolic.'[13] At issue was not simply that new technologies expanded the possibilities of storage, but that what was stored by these new technologies was thought of as fundamentally different from what was stored by writing in the nineteenth century; this new stored material came to be experienced as the 'real.' Coomaraswamy, writing in 1909, was able to differentiate between the harmful use of the gramophone for entertainment and its beneficial potential for scientific studies of music precisely because the voice it reproduced was now strangely doubled: there was the voice that could be enjoyed and remembered, and the voice which was to be studied, or literally dismembered, treated as a matter of frequencies and sound waves. The phonograph, Kittler (1999: 22–23) writes, is 'an invention that subverts both literature and music ... because it reproduces the unimaginable real they are both based on. ... The phonograph does not hear as do ears that have been trained immediately to filter voices, words, and sounds out of noise; it registers acoustic events as such.' Thus, one trait of modernity, whether German or Indian, is the new conception of the real as a background unable to be grasped by human senses alone, but requiring the help of technology. Recording technology both creates and fulfills a demand for memory that exceeds human capabilities.

In a memoir entitled 'My Musical Extravagance,' the amateur violinist, student of sound waves, and chief accountant of Indian railways C. Subrahmanya Ayyar (CSA) described his first experience of recording in 1933. The recording session seems to have proceeded without incident, almost like clockwork:

> At about 2 o'clock in the afternoon, I was asked ... just to take down the time of what I proposed to recite, so that there might be a sort of complete rehearsal in the maximum 3 and ½ minutes allowed for each side of the 10-inch record, and with a watch I just rehearsed once in ... the Shankarabharana raga. ... I went to the studio of the HMV Co. who had come to Madras specially for recording a number of artists, and found that a European gentleman was the recorder. ... After I had played the raga alapana of Shankarabharana, for a minute or so, the recorder asked me to stop and he played back what was recorded in the wax for me to listen. I was fairly satisfied and he asked me to begin afresh the raga alapanam. I put him a silly question whether what I had already played would go into the final record, being ignorant of the fact that the wax would have been destroyed by the play-back. I then started playing the raga, and finished the melody. I recollect that the microphone was at least 15 inches away from my bow. After an interval of two or three minutes, he recorded the other side with no rehearsal. I came out of the studio within a dozen minutes in all. (Subrahmanya Ayyar 1945: 25–26)

There is little trace of unease or discomfort in such an orderly description. CSA puts down any surprise to this own ignorance and silliness. Then, almost as an afterthought, he adds: 'The reason why I recorded was merely to be able to criticise my play. It is indeed difficult to be one's critic of one's own play in the very act' (Subrahmanya Ayyar 1945: 26).

When, and why, had it become difficult to criticize, or even hear oneself, in the act of playing? And why did such self-criticism become not only conceivable but necessary? As an amateur who started learning violin in his adulthood with several different teachers, CSA seemed to be searching for the guru and long years of patient discipleship he never had. Earlier, he writes, he had purchased a portable gramophone and a number of gramophone records, 'so as to get examples of raga elaboration' (Subrahmanya Ayyar 1945: 5–6). Possessed of a scientific mind, he had measured the frequencies of musical notes with the help of a sonometer (Subrahmanya Ayyar 1945: 10). He made seventeen 'records' of his violin playing with an oscillograph on a trip to London in 1934 (Subrahmanya Ayyar 1939: 134–35), in the hope that *gamaka*, so difficult to analyze in the very act of playing, might become clear on paper.

It was only with the advent of recording technology that the idea of criticizing one's own playing became conceivable, for recording offered the musician a way of listening after the act, instead of having a guru who would criticize one's playing 'in the very act.' The importance of such a shift can hardly be overestimated. As the so-called real music began to be hearable only after the performance, a kind of phonographic hearing was privileged. Whereas a musician or listener might be affected by senses other than hearing, or might remember only general impressions, the phonograph offered a new kind of real in which the purity of hearing alone was distilled. It operated as though music consisted only of sound and not of gesture or inaudible suggestion. The phonograph did not know ragas or talas or lyrics and therefore, unlike a person, could not fill in when it 'heard' lapses, could not adjust if the singer missed a beat. Precisely because it could not talk back, the phonograph could only hear.[14]

Gaisberg (1942: 57) wrote that in India 'most of the artists had to be trained over long periods before they developed into acceptable gramophone singers.' What might such training have entailed? Probably the most difficult aspect of recording was the time constraint introduced by the use of wax cylinders. Musicians who might sing a composition preceded by a twenty-minute *alapana* and followed by ten minutes of *swara kalpana* found themselves with only three and a half minutes to record. As a result, improvised sections such as *alapana* and *swara kalpana* were drastically reduced on recordings, if not entirely eliminated (Farrell 1997: 140). Karnatic musicians had to rehearse to make sure they could present 'a complete rehearsal' in just over three minutes; such careful planning and budgeting of time left no time for listening, which was separated out to be done after the act. Phonographic listening called for phonographic playing or singing: performances that would stand up to infinite repetition. Perhaps this is why improvised passages on gramophone records seem more like a pouring out of ideas than a gradual drawing out of ideas.[15] Recording an improvised piece of *raga alapana* or *swara kalpana* meant keeping a tight rein on a process that would normally have required considerable repetition and listening to oneself in the very act. It meant making temporality, the senses of motion and duration within the music, amenable to the demands of time.

By the 1940s, a musician could become complete only by means of a peculiar fusion with technology, a combination of 'live' and recorded music. In 1949, the regular music and dance column in the Tamil magazine *Kalki* included comments on radio broadcasts of annual music festivals in Madras. 'The music festivals are recorded daily by the radio station, on the spot. If those *vidwans* who had sung would listen to themselves on the radio broadcasts the next day, they would be astonished. They would ask in wonderment, "Did we actually sing like this?"' (Kalki 1949: 15). The problem was that during a concert, the audience noise, the problems with accompanists, and the deficiencies in the singer's voice were all forgotten in the moment. Some *vidwans* even had the habit of sticking their fingers in their ears as they sang, so as to hear nothing that might distract them. All such practices were fine for concerts. But on the radio, Kalki Krishnamoorthy (Kalki 1949: 15) argued, 'the true form of the music is released. *Mohana ragam* takes the form of a ghost/evil spirit. *Kalyani* takes the form of *Yama* and dances a death-dance. *Shankarabharnam* changes into a snake and hisses. *Bhairavi* takes the form of the great *Bhairavar* and frightens the listeners. When listening to *vidwans* who ordinarily seem to be well in tune, it becomes clear that they are a half or quarter pitch flat. ... Some *vidwans* begin *alapana* with one *sruti* and end with another.'

In order to redress such problems, the Music Academy decided that all *vidwans* doing radio broadcasts should be required to make an electric recording first. 'This is definitely necessary,' wrote Kalki (1949: 15). 'It would give these *vidwans* a chance to hear themselves at least once before the radio broadcast.' Beautiful ragas, brilliant *alapana*, the very foundation of Karnatic music, begin to sound like monsters when recorded by the unhearing ears of phonographs and broadcast through the unspeaking speaker of a radio. Precisely because the gramophone and radio do not compensate, they reveal 'the true form' of Karnatic music. Having heard oneself just once on a recording could change forever the experience of singing or playing live.

## 'I Could Not Believe My Ears'

C. Subrahmanya Ayyar's description of his first experience of recording is so matter-of-fact that it is hard to find in it any amusement or astonishment at the process. He saved his disbelief for the result: hearing the record more than a month later, he reported that 'we were quite delighted with the two sides of the record, played on the fine Table-Grand (large-sized) gramophone, inside the noise-deadened studio, with electrical pickup. I could not believe my ears that it was my own violin record that I heard' (Subrahmanya Ayyar 1945: 27–28). Imagining one's ears to be separate from oneself, the idea of a mechanism apart from oneself that can hear, is a distinctly phonographic notion. Learning to believe one's ears, to connect the disembodied music one hears with one's own body and experience, then becomes a musical skill.

It was precisely to enable listeners to believe their ears that, in the late 1920s, small publishers in Madras began to publish songbooks in Tamil including the lyrics of songs, and their raga and tala, which could be heard on popular gramophone records. Indexed by the first line of the song or by the musician's name, such books provided only the lyrics, not the musical notation, for thousands of songs. With written proof of the song in front of them, listeners could literally begin to believe their ears. The songbooks provided the correct words, while the gramophone itself provided the music. One such set of books, published from 1929 to 1931, was titled *Gramaphon Sangeetha Keerthanamirdam* (The nectar of gramophone music). The editor, K. Madurai Mudaliar (KMM), wrote in his introduction that 'the gramophone is a kind of musical instrument. Is there any doubt that the gramophone, as a musical instrument that gathers the songs sung by famous and successful *vidwans*, and light music by drama actors, gives a blissful feeling to those hearing again and again the sound of it resounding with the sweet voice of those mentioned above? For that reason we have clearly printed in book form the songs arranged by their first line. ... I believe that any listener who buys and reads aloud [*vaci*] this book will attain great joy' (1921: i).

If the gramophone was to be a musical instrument, some suspension of disbelief was necessary. The functions of singing, recording, listening, and hearing had become separated by the gramophone; the songbooks emerged to effect a kind of resynchronization. KMM used the Tamil verb *vaci* to indicate reading aloud or chanting, rather than the verb *pati*, which implies silent reading. In reading aloud the song lyrics, presumably along with the record, the listener would learn to be musical in a new, phonographic way, by learning to match his voice with the recorded one. The convoluted structure of KMM's Tamil sentence reveals a quite technical understanding of the process of learning to listen to gramophone records. One did not attain joy merely by hearing the voice of a beloved singer. One achieved a blissful feeling by hearing the sound of the gramophone, on which one played the record over and over again, resounding with the singer's voice. The blissful feeling, produced by so unbelievable a process, turned to great joy once the listener could safely believe his own ears by substituting himself for the absent singer. KMM used the word *neyar*, meaning radio or record listener, TV viewer, or magazine reader, to indicate a kind of indiscriminate hearing; presumably such listeners could be turned into *racikars* [connoisseurs] if they played the records often enough.

In 1933, E. Krishna Iyer, Madras advocate and music critic, felt compelled to write a guidebook for such listeners. It was getting more and more difficult to keep any standards in music, he wrote, in the face of such a 'letting loose on the public of all kinds of radio broadcasts and gramophone records' (Krishna Iyer 1933: xx). In his sketches of individual artists, he mentioned those musicians with voices 'particularly suited to the gramophone' (Krishna Iyer 1933: 41). In general, women's voices recorded well; however, the male vocalist Musiri Subramania Iyer, possessed of a 'rather high-pitched, sharp' voice that was very speedy and flexible, was particularly successful on record. Voices had become conceivable as combinations of different characteristics that were separable from one another. The gramophone seemed somehow able to compensate for what Musiri's voice lacked: volume. 'If, along with these qualities, [his voice] had only a little more volume and innate resonance, how perfect and enchanting it would be! ... It is more a sharp pencil, best suited to draw thin, minute, and sometimes intricate designs of fancy. ... What a paradox in voice qualities!' (Krishna Iyer 1933: 29).[16]

Not only did gramophones correct the deficiencies of Musiri's voice, they also made it possible to hear the voice of a girl as young as ten. This girl was M.S. Subbulakshmi, who was to become the most famous female singer in India. M.S.'s records became the craze all over South India; indeed, many listeners had their first education in gramophone records and Karnatic music by listening to her recorded voice. The celebrated scientist C.V. Raman (quoted in Kalki 1941: 24) is said to have remarked, upon hearing M.S.'s voice, 'I won't say that [she] is singing; she herself has melted and is flowing forth in a flood of sound!' The conditions of listening to a gramophone record had come to epitomize the ideal listening experience: the best musicians disappeared in their voices. In 1942, in a review of one of M.S.'s records, Kalki himself (1942: 75) remarked that 'if you hear it once, you will have the desire to hear it again and again, a thousand times. Luckily it is a record, and can be played over and over again.' In a review of a record by D.K. Pattammal, Kalki (1945: 47) wrote that 'she finishes [*raga*] almost as soon as she starts it. Why such a hurry? We feel angry. But then—*we* are in no hurry. We can play the record a second time. Indeed, these records are worth hearing many times.' The vanishing and recollection of music enabled by gramophone records afforded a new kind of pleasure that became synonymous with the ideal listening experience. As Theodor Adorno (1990: 38) wrote in 1934 in an essay titled 'The Form of the Phonograph Record,'

> Through the phonograph record *time* gains a new approach to music. It is not the time in which music happens, nor is it the time which music monumentalizes by means of its 'style.' It is time as evanescence, enduring in mute music. If the 'modernity' of all mechanical instruments gives music an age-old appearance—as if, in the rigidity of its repetitions, it had existed forever ...—then evanescence and recollection ... [have] become tangible and manifest through the gramophone records.

The long years of patient discipleship under a guru, the several hours a concert might take, are compressed into this time-as-evanescence. The pleasure of hearing fleeting music is redoubled by the knowledge that one can hear it again (and again). The technology of recording had provided a new metaphor for tradition.

## A Clockwork King

Once listening to gramophone records had become the ideal model for listening to music, it was almost natural that radio, another medium of the disembodied voice, should become the ideal medium for Karnatic music's revival. Lionel Fielden arrived in 1935 to become the first controller of broadcasting for the Indian State Broadcasting Service. But before Indian radio could become truly a sound to be reckoned with, it needed a new name.

> I cornered Lord Linlithgow after a Viceregal banquet, and said plaintively that I was in a great difficulty. ... I said I was sure he agreed with me that ISBS was a clumsy title. ... But I could not, I said, think of another title; could he help me? ... It should be something general. He rose beautifully to the bait. 'All India?' I expressed my astonishment ... [it was] the very thing. But surely not 'Broadcasting?' After some thought he suggested 'Radio.' Splendid, I said, and what beautiful initials. (Fielden in Awasthy 1965: 10)

The name, commanding in its grandeur and ethereal at the same time, seemed to capture the potential power of radio in India, a medium as simple and invisible as the air itself but capable of carrying so much.

In 1957, in a series of special lectures arranged to be read on AIR, J.C. Mathur elaborated on radio's gift to Indian music: discipline. In the absence of paying concerts, musicians, were given a new lease on life by the radio, which became like a modern patron. Yet, unlike the patrons of yore, on whose whims the fortune of music rested, AIR operated by standardized rules. Such a difference 'signified ... concretely the change-over from the feudal concept of the patronage of music to a more modern outlook. No doubt, in the air-conditioned and remote atmosphere of the studio, the professional musician misses the direct presence of an appreciative master. But three decades of the radio habit have perhaps given to most of them a new sense of communication with their larger audience in thousands of homes' (Mathur 1957: 98).

If radio was to bring about a true renaissance in Indian music, its discipline had to penetrate the very structure of the music and the way musicians thought about it. In his *Report on the Progress of Indian Broadcasting up to 1939*, Lionel Fielden claimed that 'listeners who complain of monotony in the programmes are attacking not so much the shortcomings of the station's staff as the structure of Indian music itself' (Fielden in Lelyveld 1995: 52). Musicians needed to learn how to make their art conducive to radio. Narayana Menon (1957: 75), the former director general of AIR, wrote, 'Broadcasting ... will turn out to be the biggest single instrument of music education in our country. ... It has given our musicians the qualities of precision and economy of statement. The red light on the studio door is a stern disciplinarian. Broadcasting has also ... given many of our leading musicians a better sense of proportion and a clearer definition of values that matter in music.' Above all, this sense of discipline came from the musicians' awareness of the duration of their performances. This awareness was different from older North Indian musicians' 'insistence on the so-called time theory of the ragas,' in which time was defined as a quality: time of day or night. The radio treated all time as a matter of duration, or quantity, within which music could be made to fit. When musicians' careful calculation of duration, after decades of radio broadcasting, turned into habit, the appreciative master in the remote and air-conditioned studio, would be Time itself.

It was with such values in mind that radio began to appear conducive to music education. Beginning in the 1950s, AIR stations began broadcasting music 'classes': a teacher teaching a group of pupils a particular exercise. Such classes, thirty minutes or an hour long, were designed not for the pupils but for the radio listeners, who could learn from the pupils' mistakes. Listening to such lessons would 'help the listener to take note of the essential points of each lesson in a precise manner, and to benefit from the hints and suggestions of the teacher as he checks and corrects the faults that appear in the learners' performance' (Mullick 1974: 40). At present, the Madras station of AIR broadcasts a daily music lesson after its morning broadcast of Karnatic music. The lesson lasts about thirty minutes and features a teacher and a single student. One composition is taught in each class, with each line repeated until the student gets is right. These 'lessons' depart from the conventions of the *gurukula* system in multiple ways. To learn a full composition with one's guru would take several days at least, perhaps even a month. Thus the radio classes radically compress the amount of time it takes to learn. At the same time, the focus on one composition from beginning to end is different from the process of learning with a guru, where in a typical day one might learn one line of one composition and a few lines of another, or simply sit listening to the guru sing *raga alapana* for some visitors. The learning process changes from one of inadvertent absorption to one of conscious drilling. The long years of casual, almost unconscious listening are replaced by the punctilious timing and infinitude of radio broadcasting.

At the same time as the radio brings music into the home, the radio classes introduce a peculiar, perhaps comforting, quality of distance. They focus the music on compositions rather than improvisation. Radio makes it possible to learn from others' mistakes instead of one's own; it saves one the socially complicated process of finding a teacher; it spares the student ever having to hear from the guru, 'You are not ready to learn this'. Radio, with its regular schedule of broadcasting, also offers the guarantee that things will come to pass. It ensures that the music class will proceed in a timely fashion and end after the required thirty minutes, whereas a guru might refuse to teach his or her student even the next line of a composition for months if the first line is not perfected. The removal of the radio student from the scene of teaching offers a kind of perspective not available from within it. The student's identity is oddly augmented, for now he or she hears not only the voice of the teacher, but the voice of a student repeating the teacher; it is as if one can step back (or simply stay home) and listen to oneself learn. Radio classes eliminate social distance by substituting an internalized physical distance; they make it possible to learn without being 'in the very act.'[17]

## *Gurukulavasam* Is Dead

'The gurukula system collapsed around 1900,' observed R. Rangaramanuja Ayyangar (1977: 10), musician and scholar, in his autobiography, *Musings of a Musician*. 'I awoke, as if from a dream, to realize that elaborate and scientific notation was the only means. ... For the gurukula system and ear and rote learning had been laid to rest long ago.' The repetition of music enabled by gramophone records was seen as a feature of modernity and science, while the rote repetition associated with the *gurukula* system of learning came to be seen as the opposite of all that was modern and scientific. Indeed, this sort of rote repetition was now seen as a threat to the tradition of Karnatic music. B.V. Keskar, who became minister of information and broadcasting in 1950, wrote in 1957 that rote repetition was responsible not only for the ignorance of music theory and history among Indian musicians, but also for the 'distortion' of the music itself. 'Music was learnt from guru to shishya. This led to a gradual distortion and change which is inevitable when anything has to be handed down through the medium of the human voice which cannot copy anything faithfully. ... In this way, inestimable treasures of music were lost to posterity' (Keskar 1957: 38).

Keskar (1957: 55) went so far as to say that *gurukulavasam* would eventually ruin Indian music. A distinction had to be made, he urged, between performers and teachers. Unlike a performer, who had only to be captivating on stage, a teacher did not himself need to be gifted at performing. But it was essential that a teacher be able to explain and repeat when necessary. 'He must make [the student] repeat musical sequences, point out the mistakes, and make him do it again and again' (Keskar 1957: 17). The ideal teacher sounded, literally, like a gramophone, one who could dispassionately reproduce and explain different styles to the student, without being in the act.

## The High-Fidelity Model

If the technologies of recording and radio promoted a musical aesthetic based on the separability of functions, like the distinction between performing and teaching, it followed that the musician could not be considered the best judge of his or her music. For Keskar (1957: 42–43), this role belonged to listeners, who could judge music precisely because they were not in the act of playing or singing it: 'Good critics and listeners are the foundation of music. ... There is an illusion prevailing today that the musician is the best judge of music. ... But what is music without listeners!' The importance of the listener was such that 'even in ancient books we find that [he] has been given his rightful and primordial place' (Keskar 1957: 26). Listeners could be created by the 'scientific' teaching of music. The true listener observed 'pin-drop silence' so as to hear 'all the nuances' of the music. 'A musical performance is a story in sound,' Keskar (1957: 23) wrote. 'All its nuances have to be heard carefully in order to enjoy it. ... The pin-drop silence, the rapt attention and rigid discipline that one observes in the audience in the West demonstrate that they know how to respect music and the way to enjoy it. Our concerts only show that we have not learned fully or probably forgotten the art of listening.'

The art of listening was the art of hearing without interference. 'Pin-drop' silence set the stage for a transmission free of distortion. Such transmission became the model of *sampradaya*, or tradition. In 1962, in an essay on music, T.V. Subba Rao (1962: 227) translated the Sanskrit/Tamil word *sampradaya* not merely as 'tradition,' but as 'faithfulness to tradition': 'By tradition I mean the rich heritage of compositions and raga renderings as passed on from generation to generation in the authentic *guru-sisya-parampara*. It is impossible to overestimate the importance of learning by ear. Music must be heard as it comes from the mouth of the teacher and the exact form as presented should be grasped.' But if the system of learning by ear was to be carried on at all, recording technology had to be used to ensure against total loss of memory. 'In practical music,' wrote Subba Rao (1962: 232–33), 'the only library worth mentioning is a collection of good recorded music.' Recordings could be made to 'disseminate correct knowledge' in classroom settings.

If authenticity was now seen as analogous to high-fidelity reproduction, it is not surprising that Subba Rao resorted to another technological metaphor to get at the ineffable concept of 'inspiration.' 'The mind of man,' he wrote (1962: 230), 'is like the receiving set of a radio which when properly tuned enables us to hear the transmission from a broadcasting centre. The Eternal is forever radiating knowledge and bliss for those who by self-discipline have made themselves worthy to receive them.'[18]

Far from disenchanting the world of music, then, technology reenchanted it. The singer no longer sang with his or her voice, but with the larynx, 'the divine vocal instrument .. [that] by a profundity almost mysterious is calculated to stir us to our very depths' (Subba Rao 1962: 228). A systematic course of voice culture would have to pay attention to the fact that 'tones are produced by the vibration of the chords in the larynx, but no note can be pleasing unless it is rich in components. To secure this end, the note must be fully resonated. The cavities of the chest and the abdomen should be made to take their part as sound-boxes for the note' (Subba Rao 1962: 228). The possibilities presented by *sruti* boxes and talometers—machines that perform only one function but do so with absolute fidelity—are enchanting because they possess 'a range any vocalist would envy,' as a recent advertisement claims. The concept of fidelity itself comes to be identified with automaticity, with capacities for specialization and repetition that exceed the humanly possible. Always already excessive, fidelity emerges in the very moment that it begins to threaten authority, when technology becomes recognizable as almost human.

## Technologies of the Real

Music lives a curiously double life. It is associated with a technical discourse—the musicological terminology of notes and intervals, the acoustic terminology of frequencies and amplitudes—and with a sentimental discourse that centres on meaning, emotion, and a sense of the ineffable. In fact, the co-existence of these discourses, and their essential incommensurability, seem somehow constitutive of 'music' as we know it. What happens when these discourses—if only momentarily—coincide, when the memory of a phonograph and the memory of a musician or listener seem to become interchangeable?

Coomaraswamy was worried in 1909 that Indians would get so accustomed to listening to copies of Indian music that they would lose the real thing. The *gurukula* method, which, for Coomaraswamy, did not allow the intervention of any mechanism between a guru and his *sisya*, seemed to remain unknowable by and to Western technology. For him, as for others, *gurukulavasam* thus preserved what was Indian about Indian music: its oral tradition. In its memorialization of the voice, discourse on *gurukulavasam* also provided a way of imagining the synchronization of elements that modernity had dispersed: a unification of voice and subject and thus a return to authenticity. But the idea of *gurukulavasam* as a synchronization of different elements could come about only once those elements had been separated, once the voice had become disembodied through the gramophone and imaginable in terms of separate characteristics, once the radio singer learned to sing to an absent audience. Only when *gurukulavasam* is declared dead can it take on a life of its own as the embodiment of 'tradition.'

Perhaps, then, it is not coincidental that at the very moment in the 1960s when the *gurukula* system was about to be declared dead, its processes demystified by technology, a small but steady stream of foreigners began to visit India to revive it in its 'traditional' form, each one staying for a number of years and then returning home—much like the fictional Joseph Om. The tension between intimacy and foreignness, the pleasure of hearing one's voice and music repeated by a foreigner: such are the dynamics of this 'traditional' *gurukulavasam*. The tape recorder, capturing the oral transmissions in their exact form, is an essential part of the scene. Importantly, though, *gurukulavasam* is now experienced as a mode that can be entered and exited, switched on or off like a tape recorder, as an enchanting act that can even be exported to the West, as another, perhaps more spiritual, 'world.' Thus, a 1998 *New York Times* article about Anoushka Shankar, the sitarist Ravi Shankar's daughter and disciple, centres on the idea that Anoushka 'negotiates two worlds.' 'At first glance, she could be a shining example of a modern California girl. ... But one look at her left hand—and the thick, purple-striped calluses on her fingers—reveals that she has another life. ... She may be a Metallica fan, but she is also mastering Indian classical music: the raga compositions and rhythmic cycles that have been passed down through centuries of oral tradition' (Pareles 1998). Anoushka herself describes her other world in mystical terms: 'Everything changes when I walk into the music room. I could be lying with my feet in my father's lap watching a movie, but the second we walk into the music room, I am a disciple. ... It's a situation of utter surrender on the disciple's part, and utter respect. ..... It's spiritual, and then it's my father, and then it's my guru. ... It's just amazing' (Pareles 1998).

What is at stake in such mystical descriptions of the guru-disciple relationship? Anoushka's 'everything changes' seems to mark a disturbance; everything *must* change for her to get into the act, as it were: to access a musical real in the midst of a world where it is impossible to imagine music without mechanical reproduction. And in order for us to believe our ears when we hear Anoushka's CDs, we need to imagine that everything changes; *gurukulavasam* is as much an object of traditionalist desire as it is an object of desire for the consumer of Indian music in the West. *Gurukulavasam* now appears as a sign, a quotation, of Indianness; it confirms the essential difference, figured as oral tradition, that makes Indian music securely Indian (and suitable for consumption in the world market as such). The difference between Anoushka's romantic vision of *gurukulavasam* and Malan's somewhat darker portrayal is seemingly elided here; even the computer Yakshani must undergo *gurukulavasam* in the end. But only after fidelity's ambiguous logic has radically questioned who owns his master's voice.

## Notes

1. Here I am referring to Friedrich Kittler's *Discourse Networks 1800/1900.*

2. The violin was brought to South India by the British and the French in the late eighteenth century and shortly thereafter was adapted by South Indian musicians for use as a solo and an accompanying instrument in Karnatic music. While the instrument itself is the same as a western violin, the tuning, playing position, and technique have been changed.

3. This and the passages that follow are my translations of the original Tamil short story by Malan.

4. *Gurukulavasam* can be translated literally as 'living with the guru's family'; the term is a compound of *kula* (family or lineage) and *vacam* (living). Tamil and Sanskrit words, such as *gurukulavasam*, which appear commonly in English, are transliterated here as they usually appear. Other Tamil words are transliterated according to the Madras University Tamil Lexicon System.

5. *Puja* is prayer and/or meditation performed by Hindus on a regular basis in a home shrine.

6. *Shadjam* is the long name of *sa*, the tonic or first note of the scale. Each note is called a *swaram.*

7. *Bhairavi* is the name of a raga, the melodic basis of Karnatic music, a scale or melodic mode that specifies certain characteristic phrases to be used in both compositions and improvisation.

8. *Raga alapana* is the free-time improvised elaboration of a raga; *kriti* is a type of composition in Karnatic music; here *swaram* refers to improvizations done within the specified time-cycle, or *tala.*

9. *Saralivarisai* are exercises for beginning students.

10. The word *ka<u>n</u>akku*, used here to refer to frequencies of sound waves, is also the word for the rhythmic improvisation, based on calculations, that Karnatic musicians, do. It it thus simultaneously in the realm of music theory and of technology. Therein lies its threat: If a computer can master one aspect of *ka<u>n</u>akku*, can it not master the other as well?

11. Between 1900 and 1910, the Gramophone Company (later to become 'His Master's Voice') made over 4,000 recordings in India, more than in any other single country on its world tours (Gronow 1981: 225). By 1905, the Talking Machine and Indian Record Company had started a branch in Madras (Kinner 1994: 10). Electrical recording was first introduced in India in 1925, and the magnetic tape recorder became available around 1950 (1994: 148–49).

12. *Gamaka*, usually translated as 'ornament' or 'embellishment,' can be thought of as a specified way of getting from one note to the next in Karnatic music. *Gamakas*

are highly individual to different musicians and are not included in printed notation.

13. Kittler, in both *Discourse Networks* and his later *Gramophone, Film, Typewriter*, relates phonography, cinematography, and typing to Lacan's registers of the real, the imaginary, and the symbolic, respectively. The Symbolic refers to the signified of all writing before print, which Kittler, in his description of the discourse network of 1800, calls variously the voice, the soul, the inner self. In a post-print environment, writing is associated with the symbolic (but not the Symbolic) because the typewriter reduces writing to the combination and recombination of a finite set of signs in their bare 'materiality and technicity ... without taking into account philosophical dreams of infinity.' The real, associated with phonography, 'forms the waste or residue that neither the mirror of the imaginary nor the grid of the symbolic can catch: the physiological accidents and stochastic disorder of bodies' (Kittler 199: 15–16). Phonography represents writing without a subject, the ability to record regardless of meaning or intent.

14. This notion of the separability of functions, writes Kittler (1999: 38), underlies the 'discourse network' of 1900. Theories of the localization of brain functions, and the idea of testing humans for speech, hearing, and writing as isolated functions, emerging around 1900, had to model themselves on the phonograph, which performed only the function of 'hearing.' See also Kittler 1990: 214.

15. A recording by the violinist Dwaram Venkataswamy Naidu from the early 1940s features a *ragam-tanam-pallavi*, an improvisational item that in a concert would have taken about an hour at that time, compressed into four segments of exactly three and a half minutes each. The present-day idea that a musician should, when doing *raga alapana*, make the raga clear from the very first phrase, rather than keeping the listeners in suspense, probably gained its urgency first from the demands of recording. Musicians speak of five-minute *alapanas* or twenty-minute *alapanas* as choices they make depending on the amount of time available; the ideal is to carefully plan one's spontaneity.

16. The metaphor of gramophone recording also crept into Krishna Iyer's concept of improvisation. Throughout his sketches, he used the image of 'hackneyed grooves' (Krishna Iyer 1933: 29) to convey the opposite of *manodharma*, improvised music. While the 'grooves' called up the image of a gramophone record with its connotations of automaticity and repetition, the lofty term *manodharma*, a Sanskrit compound translatable as 'pertaining to the mind,' implied a sovereign musician setting forth ideas untouched by such influences as gramophone records.

17. In 'The Voice in the Machine,' Jay Clayton (1997: 226) discusses how technologies for transmitting sound, such as the telegraph and telephone, were perceived in the nineteenth century as 'annihilating distance.' Instead of abstracting and distancing, like media of visual reproduction, the telegraph had an effect of 'intensification and immediacy,' an internalizing of distance, producing in its users 'a split but oddly augmented identity.'

18. Allen Weiss (1995: 32) comments on the status of radio as an 'acousmetric medium,' a medium of the disembodied voice. 'Radio is, *a fortiori*, the acousmetric

medium, where the sound always appears without a corresponding image. ... These features of the disincarnate voice—ubiquity, panopticism, omniscience, omnipotence—cause the radiophonic work to return as hallucination and phantasm; it is thus not unusual to find the radio fantasized as receiving messages from the beyond, serving as a spiritual transmitter in overcompensation for a psychotic dissociation from one's own body.'

## References


Adorno, Theodor. 1990. The form of the phonograph record. *October* 55: 56–61.

Awasthy, G.C. 1965. *Broadcasting in India*. Bombay: Allied.

Clayton, Jay. 1997. The voice in the machine: Hardy, Hazlitt, James. In *Language Machines: Technologies of literary and cultural production*, edited by Jeffrey Masten, Peter Stallybrass, and Nancy Vickers. New York: Routledge.

Clayton, Mark. 1999. A.H. Fox Strangways and the music of Hindostan: Revisiting historical field recordings. *Journal of the Royal Musical Association* 124: 88–118.

Coomaraswamy, Ananda K. [1909] 1981. *Essays in National Idealism*. New Delhi: Munshiram Manoharlal.

Farrell, Gerry. 1997. *Indian Music and the West*. Oxford: Oxford University Press.

Fox-Strangways, A.H. [1914] 1995. *The Music of Hindostan*. New Delhi: Mittal.

Gaisberg, Fredrick. 1942. *The Music Goes Round*. New York: Macmillan.

Gronow, Pekka. 1981. The record industry comes to the Orient. *Ethnomusicology* 25, no. 2: 251–84.

Kalki Krishnamoorthy. 1941. Narada ganam. *Kalki*, 1 October, 24.

———. 1942. Icai virutu. *Kalki*, 1 August, 75.

———. 1945. Icait tattu. *Kalkti*, 1 September, 47.

———. 1949. Atal patal. *Kalki*, 1 September, 15.

Keskar, B.V. 1957. *Indian Music: Problems and prospects*. Bombay: Popular Prakashan.

Kinnear, Michael. 1994. *The Gramophone Company's First Indian Recordings, 1899–1908*. Bombay: Popular Prakashan.

Kittler, Friedrich. 1990. *Discourse Networks 1800/1900*, translated by Michael Meteer. Stanford, Calif.: Stanford University Press.

———. 1999. *Gramophone, Film, Typewriter*. Stanford, Calif.: Stanford University Press.

Krishna Iyer, E. 1933. *Personalities in Present Day Music*. Madras: Rochouse.

Lelyveld, David. 1995. Upon the Subdominant: Administering music on All-India Radio. In *Consuming Modernity: Public culture in a South Asian world*, edited by Carol Breckenridge. Minneapolis: University of Minnesota Press.

Madurai Mudaliar, K. 1929–31. *Gramaphon Sangeetha Keerthanamirdam*. Madras: Shanmugananda.

Malan. 1981. Vidwan. In *A<u>n</u>ru: Terntu cirukataikal 1917–1981*. Vol. 2. Madras: Orient Longman.

Mathur, J.C. 1957. The Impact of A.I.R. on Indian Music. In *Aspects of Indian Music*. New Delhi: Ministry of Information and Broadcasting.

Menon, Narayana. 1957. The Impact of Western technology on Indian Music. In *Bulletin of the Institute of Traditional Cultures*. Madras.

Mullick, K.S. 1974. *Tangled Tapes: The inside story of Indian broadcasting*. Delhi: Sterling.

Pareles, John. 1998. Ravi Shankar's daughter negotiates two worlds. *New York Times*, 24 December, E2.

Rangaramanuja Iyengar, R. 1977. *Musings of a Musician: Recent trends in Carnatic music*. Bombay: Wilco.

Subba Rao, T.V. 1962. *Studies in Indian Music*. Bombay: Asia.

Subrahmanya Ayyar, C. 1939. *The Grammar of South Indian (Karnatic) Music*. Madras.

_____. 1945. *My Musical Extravagance*. Madras.

Weiss, Allen. 1995. *Phantasmic Radio*. Durham, N.C.: Duke University Press.

# 7.

# Things Fall Apart: The Cinematic Rendition of the Agrarian Landscape in South India

Dilip M. Menon

THIS CHAPTER EXPLORES THE TRANSITIONAL DECADE OF THE 1970S IN THE HISTORY OF the southwestern state of Kerala, India, through the films and novels of M.T. Vasudevan Nair, arguably the most important litterateur in Kerala today. After the historic election of a Communist ministry to power in 1957, Kerala then stepped gingerly back from a radical politics and moved towards a restitution of an older masculine, agrarian order. By looking at the shifts in politics and the social order simultaneously with the progression of Vasudevan Nair's own filmic sensibility, the article raises the question of whether historical time and filmic time can be easily mapped on to each other.

From the inside there is no answer to be given; it was simply the way things were.

Arthur C. Danto, *The Transfiguration of the Commonplace* (1981)

## Scene 49

*A village post office. The postmaster stands behind the half-shut door with the letters, looking at them with silver frame spectacles and reads out names. He holds in his hand a copy of the newspaper,* The Hindu. *A crowd of expectant people.*

Kunnathuthodi Velayudhan.
*The man is not there. Puts it aside and calls the next name.*
Mundamvalappil Saithali, son of Mundamvalappil Anthru.
*A man reaches out and takes the letter.*
Melevalappil Chathu.

This article was written and first presented when I was a Fellow on the Programme in Agrarian Studies at Yale, April 2004. I would like to thank Jim Scott and my fellow Fellows for providing a stimulating and provocative audience, and Susan O'Donovan and Lara Jacob in particular for critical readings.

*The Journal of Peasant Studies*, Vol. 32, No. 2, April 2005, pp. 304–34
ISSN 0306-6150 print/1743-9523 online
DOI: 10.1080/03066150500094519 

*The man is not there.*
M.T. Sahadevan.
*A youth takes the letter.*
P.K. Kausalya—west Kattur.
*No one claims it.*
K.N. Brahmadattan Nambudiri, Melekkavu temple.
*The postmaster looks at him and the redirected address and gives him a copy of* The Hindu.
*Unni Nambudiri takes it and steps out.*
*In the background, the reading of addresses continues.*
Ponnumkuzhil Kuttan. Thekkepat Vasu.

*Nirmalyam* [The offering of flowers], (1973)

## I

The village post office: the global in the local. A place where different times, geographies and entities intersect. In the roster of names is a Muslim, Saithali; a Brahmin, the Nambudiri; some lower castes, characterized by the initials and lack of surnames; and a woman of indefinite caste, Kausalya. Some of them are present to collect their letters: the Nambudiri Brahmin at the temple and the Muslim: an embodiment of patrilineal continuity. Chathu, Kuttan and Velayudhan are absent. Have they not been able to turn up or have they left, emigrating as part of the large labour diaspora from Kerala to West Asia and South East Asia? Who wrote these letters to them: someone from an earlier generation of migrants? Is the Muslim Saithali able to ensure his continued presence within this landscape on remittances that come from across the ocean? Or has he returned wealthy, after gruelling years of labour abroad and now with the memory of want effaced, become the hub around whom others congregate in search of riches? We are halfway through the film, *Nirmalyam*. By now the viewer knows that the Nambudiri (the only one among the people assembled at the post office who is a character in the unfolding story) is about to leave this landscape as well. *The Hindu*, in his hands, holds the promise of jobs in a place elsewhere, even if in the dark recesses of some government office, and he is driven by both guilt and a sense of responsibility. The viewer also knows something else about the last name to be called—Thekkepat Vasu—to which no one answers. This is the nickname of Madathu Thekkepat Vasudevan Nair (1934–), the screenplay writer and director of the film.

This spectral, Hitchcockian presence is a signifier of absence. With *Nirmalyam*, MT (as he is popularly known) has finally left the landscape that he had been cataloguing with care in his short stories and novels from the early 1950s. From *Sacred Sword and Anklets* (1954), the story from which *Nirmalyam* was scripted, through to his first novel, *Nalukettu* [The Ancestral

Home] of 1958 and his first screenplay *Murapennu* [The Betrothed](1965), M.T. had been writing stories of the disintegration of a traditional society and order, that in his eyes had been held together by the matrilineal households of the Nairs. The stories were dark, brooding and shot through with metaphors of madness, unrealized loves, and the break-up of families through an excess of greed for property. However, these were the intimate renditions of someone who was implicated in the stories that he was telling. There was sadness, but it was a wry, knowing sadness. *Nalukettu* told the story of the young fatherless boy Appunni, who is rejected by his mother's distinguished and decaying family, and struggles for love and recognition. A Muslim trader, who is believed to have poisoned Appunni's father, and whom he initially sees as his enemy, helps him to get employment. At the end of the novel he buys the Ancestral Home and restores his mother to her rightful estate. *Asuravithu* [The misbegotten one] (1962) was more radical as well as despairing. Govindankutty, regarded as a ne'er-do-well by his Nair matrilineal family, and tricked into a marriage with a woman already pregnant, decides to convert to Islam and finds himself suspended in a space where neither Hindu nor Muslim wants to own him. An epidemic breaks out in the village, and Govindankutty redeems himself but casts himself as the ultimate outsider by burying the dead: 'the dead needed him'. The novel ends with the words, 'My dear ones, it is to return again that I begin my journey.'[1] In *Kaalam* [Time] (1969), Sethu leaves the village and his matrilineal household and enters the vortex of the city and the larger world: unemployment, a job and the shady world of commerce, illicit love with his employer's wife and a final broken return to the village, unable to be present at his mother's bedside as she dies. He crosses the river in an uncertain return to the city; the river itself, 'dreaming of floods even as it grew dry.'[2] In the film *Nirmalyam*, the river has run dry, and the mood is one of cynicism and loss. In one of the most searing endings in Indian cinema, the central character, a temple oracle, repeatedly cuts his forehead with the temple sword in a state of possession and dies in the sanctorum, spitting blood in anger on the face of the deity who has betrayed his devotion to her. It is the character of the young Namboodiri who leaves the temple for the city forever who is the other pivot of the film. So what happened between 1953 and 1973; why had Thekkepat Vasu left the countryside that he had so painfully recorded? Had each of the earlier renditions been in fact, a chronicle of a departure foretold?

Was this a peculiar trajectory? Let us take another contemporary filmmaker, but from the *avant garde* end of the spectrum: G. Aravindan (1935–91), cartoonist, stage director, musician and employee of the Kerala Rubber Board. His life in some senses encapsulates the trajectory of many intellectuals and artists in Kerala, chained to the security of a numbing government job yet living lives of the mind that roamed free. Aravindan worked as a cartoonist for the weekly *Mathrubhumi* (of which MT was the editor between 1968 and 1981) drawing the series, *Cheriya manushyan valiya lokam* [Small humans in the big world] between 1961 and 1979. The lower middle class hero Ramu, with his trademark hair combed back in a puff, is a witness to a changing world of increasing unemployment, faithless politicians, passionate intellectuals, idealistic schoolmasters and occasional loves.[3] The frames are full of incidents, characters and an affectionate, intimate irony about the state of the world. In one of the early cartoons (Figure 1) Ramu's retired father tells him that the postman was enquiring after him. Dreaming of a job interview, Ramu goes through his daily meanderings at the library, the Muslim teashop and the secretarial college (where the then object of his affection sheds tears at his imminent departure). Finally, the postman gives him back the letter that he had posted; returned on account of insufficient postage. By 1978, the mood has changed. If in the case of MT's film, he has left the landscape, Aravindan's later cartoons are evacuated of characters and depth and are tinged with a melancholy sarcasm. Emptiness characterizes the space within the frame and the characters are pushed out to the edges. Ramu himself has lost his cockiness, his iconic puff has lost its buoyancy and the radical intellectual has reinvented himself as an Indo-Anglian writer (Figure 2). The language itself has been corrupted; Ramu and his erstwhile friend speak to each other in a peculiar argot of Malayalam and English. When the writer tells Ramu that he has been residing in the five-star hotels of Delhi and writing the authentic Indian novel, the latter asks him whether the real India is visible in such spaces. The intellectual replies, 'India at all times has been one, brother, *with its poverty, prostitution, superstition, filth, flies*'[4] (the italicized words are in English in the original text). In Aravindan's first feature film, *Uttarayanam* [Tropic of Capricorn] (1974), the hero Ravi, disillusioned with the city, numberless lost job opportunities and surrounded by too corruptible friends, abandons everything to find meaning in religion and a godman. There is a dark cynicism as in the case of *Nirmalyam*—and departure—but a different resolution.

## II

*. . .and everywhere*
The ceremony of innocence is drowned

W.B. Yeats, *The Second Coming*

So what indeed had happened between 1950 and 1973? In 1957, the people of Kerala *elected* the first Communist government to be voted to power anywhere in the world and E.M.S. Nambudiripad became the state's chief minister. This had been preceded by two decades of mobilization that challenged rural

Figure 1: From G. Aravindan, *Cheriya manushyaraum, valiya lokavum* [Little people and a big world] (Kottayam: DC Books, 1996), p. 10.

inequalities as well as caste hierarchies.[5] However, communism in Kerala was far more than just a political movement organizing the proletariat and the peasantry into militant entities pressing for exigent economic concessions. Euphoric visions of a new order and a rampant rejection of past hierarchies found expression in popular songs, literature and films. The iconic play of the

Figure 2: Aravindan, *Cheriya manushyarum, valiya lokavum*, p. 407.

1950s, *Ningal enne kammyunist aakki* [You made me a communist] (1952) written by Thoppil Bhasi (1924–92) and performed by the Kerala People's Arts Club, had as its hero a young Nair peasant revolutionary who converts his uncle, a rich peasant, to communism. However, there were strains evident even then. The move towards an electoral communism in 1952 had been criticized by a radical left as a degeneration into 'parliamentary cretinism'.[6] With the formation of the state of Kerala in 1956, it became necessary to discipline the cadres at the same time as mobilizing them. It also became increasingly obvious that fundamental issues of caste inequality were being brushed under the carpet as a largely upper caste leadership assumed power and defined regional culture in its own terms.[7]

There is another important factor to be considered here. Kerala is different from most other states in India in having a significant and powerful minority of indigenous Muslims and Christians, as well as a heterogeneous group of Jews, Gujarati Muslims and Konkani merchants along the coast. The assumption of power by the East India Company of this region in 1792 had been premised on the decline of maritime commerce in the region and the turn inwards by the Company state towards strengthening the hands of landed elites and realizing revenue from land alone. While a number of the Mappila Muslims continued with their engagement with coastal trade in an age of diminished maritime activity, and the Christians retreated by the late nineteenth century into the niche economy of rubber and coffee plantations, the Hindu landed groups were granted a new hegemony. Colonial discourse rewrote the history of Kerala as a history of land settlement, writing out, in effect, the histories of commerce as much as the groups that had once made Kerala part of the larger world of the Indian Ocean.[8] Social and political activity had depended to a considerable degree on the disintegration of the upper caste Nair matrilineal landed households (*tharavadu*) and the entry of a younger generation of Nairs into the making of a new world. In 1867, the Madras High Court had decreed that the *tharavadu* was an impartible, co-residential unit headed by the eldest male. Demographic pressures generated a discourse of the tyranny of the *Karanavan*, or the eldest male, who was vested with almost absolute legal powers of sale and acquisition of property, as younger men attempted to strike out on their producing tremendous strains within the *tharavadu*. In 1933, the Matriliny Act was passed which stated that the matrilineal system was ended and the 'social stream [was] flowing along more natural channels.'[9] However, matriliny as a system and matrilineal values both were a long time dying. The *tharavadus* with dominant elder males, dependent younger men and women and a system of bilateral inheritance continued till 1973 when matrilineal inheritance was finally abolished. The agitations for the abolition of matriliny also generated a sense of identity among Nairs, and it was not uncommon to come across statements such as the one made by a Nair meeting in 1932 that the Nairs should lead the other communities in the 'creation of the new age'.[10] This Nair universalism, if we may call it that, also allowed for the Oxford educated Nair historian, K.M. Panikkar to say that the central fact of the history of Kerala in the last 400 years was the decline of the power of the Nairs.[11] One finds echoes of this again in Thoppil Bhasi's radical plays. The world of the Nairs is what Bhasi is most comfortable with and there are brilliant portrayals of crumbling households, litigious families, shady land deals and a critique of Nair nostalgia. The Nairs as anchors of the plays undergo transformation towards a universal consciousness while the other castes remain trapped within their stereotypical renditions.[12] M.T.'s novels share the same paradigm. However, there is a radical difference. While there is an implicit universalization of the Nair condition as metaphor for conditions in Kerala, in M.T.'s work the hope of radical transformation that Bhasi espoused has evanesced.

The Communist ministry introduced the Land Relations Bill in 1959, proposing the abolition of landlordism and transferring the land to the tiller—a measure that threatened the hegemony of the Hindu landed households in particular. Christian interests were ostensibly protected under a dispensation that declared the plantations and land reclaimed from the backwaters out of the purview of this legislation.[13] However, the ministry's attempt to regulate private education intruded into a realm in which the Christian church as well as Hindu reform organizations had been historically active. This and other radical measures like preventing the police from intervening on the side of industry in the case of strikes, led to a social movement bringing together conservatives among the Hindus and Christians against the ministry.[14] For the first time since Independence in 1947, the central government in Delhi interfered in 1959 and removed the ministry on grounds of the breakdown of the machinery of law and order. The Communist Party was to return to power again but with its radical sheen somewhat dimmed (Figure 3). A series of coalition ministries of uncertain ideology followed. In 1967, out of power for eight years, the Communist Party was elected in an alliance with the Muslim League, a few socialist parties and an agrarian party led by a Christian priest. The price of alliance with the Muslim League was the carving out of a Muslim majority district in Malappuram, accompanied by a political uproar about opportunist politics.[15] At the national level the late-1960s saw rising unemployment, industrial recession, the perception of a large-scale intrusion of foreign capital, and a slowing down of the rate of agrarian reform. Meanwhile, the national Congress Party flirted with socialism, adopting a swathe of populist measures calling for the immediate extermination of poverty, abolishing the privy purses of the erstwhile princes and nationalizing banks.[16] In this atmosphere of disillusionment, away in north-east India a peasant uprising in Naxalbari, under the leadership of Charu Mazumdar, fanned the spark of hope for those disillusioned with what came to be called the 'neo-revisionist leading clique' which included now the name of E.M.S. Nambudiripad. In 1969, the Communist Party of India (Marxist-Leninist) came into existence, committed to Maoist strategies of peasant revolution. In Kerala, there was one major incident on 24 November 1968, when Kunikkal Narayanan and a group

Figure 3: *Three communist governments later, cynicism descends*...from O. V. Vijayan, *A Cartoonist Remembers* (Delhi: Rupa and Co., 2002), p. 8.

of armed men attacked a police station in Wynaad district. This turned out be more of a symbolic gesture, and the echoes of the Naxalite movement were to be felt in the intellectual realm more than in any fundamental social upheaval.[17]

The 1970s began in a mood of despair with the prospect of social transformation deferred yet again. The oracle spits in the face of god. Ramu regresses into cynicism. From the mid-1970s another option had opened up. It was no longer about staying but leaving. The boom in oil prices in the Gulf region had sparked off a massive need for both labour and technical expertise. Kerala which for a millennium had been incorporated in the rhythms of the Indian Ocean, responded with a massive outflow of labour, a majority of them Mappila Muslims. And a generation later it is possible to argue that Kerala survives as a viable entity purely on the strength of remittances from across the ocean, given its lack of industrialization, high rates of unemployment, and extremely volatile coalitional politics.[18] However, the ocean is not part of M.T.'s world, living as he does beside it. The only novel that he wrote about the sea was *Arabiponnu* [Arab gold] in 1962, co-authored with N.P. Mohammad. The ocean was a threatening presence, bringing in money, gold and illicit wealth that undermined rural values and displaced the natural order of the village. Koya, the central character, having blown his patrimony in gambling, remakes himself through getting involved in the smuggling of gold. Alcohol, greed, prostitution and corruption are the persistent themes in this novel that shows an aristocratic disdain for commerce and money and the Mappila Muslim associated with this.

However, in his other novels, M.T. had worked at a portrayal of the relationship between Hindu and Muslim (and we shall return to this theme later) that ranged from seeing the Muslim as a moral centre (Saithali as the guardian of Appunni in *Nalukettu*) to envisaging dissolution of identities (Govindankutty converting to Islam in *Asuravithu*). In *Nirmalyam*, the experience of the Gulf boom, the formation of the Muslim majority district of Malappuram, and the visible impact of the Mappila *nouveau riches* is reflected but in a chilling image. The oracle returns home at dusk to collect the temple sword and the sacred anklets to prepare himself for a possession in the face of the epidemic that threatens the village. He knocks on the inner door and the Muslim moneylender, Maymunni, sidles out followed by the oracle's wife. Driven by want and the fact that temple ceremonies no longer provide sustenance for the family, she has slept with the moneylender to pay off debts incurred for daily food. It is the last straw. The oracle then goes on to a final, glorious, possessed performance and his death. M.T. too moved on, but into a Hindu world, after the seemingly radical rejection of religion in *Nirmalyam*. His most recent novel titled *Varanasi* is set in the Hindu holy city of Benares, towards which the protagonist slouches after a life of irresolution and personal betrayal. However, can regional or even national history be the template for a discussion of an artwork like film? Is the parallelism that I have sketched between 'events' and 'representation' too easy a resolution? How are we to negotiate the question of 'time' in its plurality: of historical and cinematic 'times'?

## III

Time held me green and dying
Though I sang in my chains like the sea

Dylan Thomas, *Fern Hill*

M.T. has had an enviable record both as a screenplay writer and director. *Murapennu* [The betrothed] (1965 Director: A. Vincent) his first screenplay based on the falling apart of a *tharavadu* and the travails of the protagonist ground down by responsibilities, to the extent of sacrificing the love of his betrothed was a resounding commercial success. *Iruttinte Atmavu* [The soul of darkness] (1967, Director: P. Bhaskaran), based on his own short story of a decade earlier went on to win the President's National award for best film and also recognition for Prem Nazir who played the simple-minded hero driven to an acceptance of his insanity. *Olavum Theeravum* [Waves and the shore] (1969, Director: P.N. Menon), again based on a short story of 1954, about a Muslim boatman and the community of Muslims living off trade and transport on the river, and written in the Muslim Malayalam dialect, won the Government of Kerala's award for best film, director and screenplay. *Nirmalyam* [Offering of flowers] (1973), his first directorial venture and scripted from a short story of 1954 went on to win not only the President of India's Gold Medal, but also six state government awards and the best film award at the Asian Film festival at Djakarta. M.T. went on to direct five more films, the most recent being *Oru Cheru Punchiri* [A slender smile, 2000] and script 60 more screenplays, all of which have enjoyed resounding success.[19] A new film scripted by M.T. is an event in Kerala and an assured box office success. In 1996, he received the Jnanpith, India's highest literary award for lifetime achievement in literature.

*The Encyclopaedia of Indian Cinema* characterizes M.T.'s early films as 'the melodrama of feudal nostalgia'.[20] This definition, though it has the obvious benefits of economy, does not help us move towards an understanding of M.T.'s films beyond a formulaic reduction into a type. At the same time it reduces the space of the films to one genre, one historical time and one affect. In a limited sense, the plots structured as they are around familial relationships, star-crossed lovers, forced marriages, heroes doomed to tragic failure, villains displaying their power through sexual aggression, heroines committing suicide, are amenable to being interpreted as melodrama. There are two kinds of problems with such a reading. Any definition of genre invariably tends towards a circular logic. Certain characteristics are isolated and then the presence of some or all of these characteristics becomes the means of identifying other films as belonging to that particular genre.[21] This poses a problem both of arbitrary definition as well as the fact that the power of most popular films derives from the fact that they borrow from different 'genres'. In the case of Hindi films, in particular, it has been convincingly argued that they belong to a category of 'super genre' which cannibalizes other genres as they emerge.[22] So a film like the classic *Sholay* (1976) could be seen as a melodramatic musical in the style of a western incorporating themes of caste, region, nation and family, with moments of both high comedy and tragedy. Of course, to state this is to get back to the details of the film itself and not allow oneself the lethargy regarding details that Grand Theory induces. The easy resort to genre theory flattens nuance and certainly a case can be made for 'piecemeal theorizing', *a la* Noel Carroll, that allows a dwelling on the details of particular films, instead of receding into a taxonomic exactitude.[23]

The second problem comes from a notion of a transcendent time that determines the reading of the film in terms of the 'empty, homogeneous time' of the Nation, of Modernity or indeed of Incomplete Modernity. The 'genre' of melodrama can then be read as located within 'transitional' moments that exemplify 'the struggle of a morally and emotionally emancipated bourgeois consciousness against the remnants of feudalism', or in a more extreme reading, as 'the drama of capitalist modernisation, framed in such a way as to exclude the very possibility of change in a socialist direction'.[24] However, such analyses of melodrama seem to be theorizing the time in which the film is made and conflating it with the different times *within* the space of the film itself. There is not just one presiding time, or notion of time in a film, apart from the obvious empirical linear time that carries the plot from a beginning to an end. We have Metz's seemingly commonsensical observation that, 'a narrative has *a beginning and an ending*, a fact that simultaneously distinguishes it from the rest of the world.'[25] To which we can counterpose Godard's *riposte* that a film has a beginning, middle and an end though necessarily not in that order. Or indeed, M.T.'s own observation that a story 'may have a beginning, middle and an end'.[26]

The notion of one regnant time under the shadow of which creation takes place finds its best expression in Frederic Jameson's expansive, apodictic formulation, 'all third world texts are necessarily . . . allegorical, and in a very specific way: they are to be read as what I will call *national allegories*.'[27] In such a reading, nationalism comes to be seen as the only authentic cultural attribute of the non-western parts of the world. Moreover, the distinction that Jameson creates between third world and first world literature replicates and carries on the central concern of western Marxism: its nostalgia for totality. The Lukacsian positing of the totality of imagination in the epic as against the fragmented present delineated in the novel is reprised by Jameson but in a curious dehistoricizing conflation. The third world text is equated with the epic: the telling of individual stories in the third world novel 'cannot but ultimately involve the laborious telling of the experience of the collectivity itself'.[28] The influence of this view is obvious in studies of Hindi cinema that reduce 50-odd years of filmmaking to the one theme of the nation.[29] I would rather argue that in any film there is an articulation of several times, the time at which the film is made being only one of the times that is reflected in the film itself.

There are the times in the film and the times of the film, and these are two related, but different, matters to be elaborated in conjunction for a historical reading that also allows for the relative autonomy of the Artefact. Time in the film is embodied in different characters, in objects, in the music (both as background and in songs), in the pace of editing, in literary or cinematic references, and in artifices such as the flashback and voice-overs. Deleuze, in his reading of Dreyer's *Passion of Joan of Arc*, argues that there is 'a whole historical state of things, social roles and individual or collective characters, real connections between them.' At the same time, there is something else, which is 'internal' to the film, though not exactly in an eternal or unconnected sense. 'It is like two presents which ceaselessly intersect, one of which is endlessly arriving and the other is already established.' While the film may be speaking of events and characters in a historical time (present or past), 'one part of it [the events] is profoundly realized in a state of things, whilst the other is all the more irreducible to all realisation.'[30] And M.T. emphasizes one of the senses of an internal time when he writes that it is when 'characters throw open the windows of their minds by unspoken words and *display half-suppressed emotions*, [that] they tend to shine with glowing reality before audiences' (*emphases added*).[31] The use of silence and gesture invites the viewer to read into the discontinuities that they generate in terms of plot, character and cinematic time. Making sense of the discontinuous is rendered possible because the narration is 'fraught with background' to refer to Auerbach's reading of Biblical narrative.[32]

The viewer fills in the details of an already-known history (the time of a society in turmoil and change) in the immediate space of the viewing, through both personal autobiography as well as the revealed life of the character on-screen. The relation between these three times is what renders transparent the 'obscurity' engendered by the unspoken and the half-suppressed that is the staple of M.T.'s films. Let us take the sequence of scenes before the Intermission in the film *Iruttinte Atmavu* [Soul of darkness]. The lead female character, Ammukutty knocks on the protagonist Velayudhan's door. He is a simple-minded man (seen as mad by his family) and has just been beaten for threatening with a knife the family retainer delegated to look after him. Ammukutty is his cousin and according to matrilineal custom, his betrothed. She gives him a plastic toy watch as a gift from the village fair; he gives her bangles that he has bought from the fair as well, having managed to elude his retainer. Their cousin Rajan who is visiting from Singapore, comes up to the doorway, smoking a cigarette and breaks the bangles (a signal of rivalry since he too stands in the position of betrothed to Ammukutty, since she is his mother's brother's daughter). In the next scene, Rajan and his sister Prema are shown in a bedroom. A gramophone record plays music for dancing the 'twist.' Rajan, dressed in pants and shirt is smoking a cigarette and Prema is occasionally dancing and chatting with her female friend. Prema is dressed in a frock with her hair fashionably cut short. Their return from Singapore to stay on in the family home in Kerala is much against their will but compelled by their mother's nostalgia for her native land. Ammukutty enters, dressed traditionally and carrying a tray of coffee cups. Prema turns to her friend (who has taken a shine to Rajan) and asks mischievously, doesn't he have the *cut* of, i.e., a resemblance to, Rock Hudson. [*That is in the screenplay. When the film was made, the director changed the reference to the then Hindi film matinee idol Dilip Kumar*] (scene 49)

In the next scene, Ammukutty carries snacks into a room where her uncle from Singapore sits with his friends drinking alcohol and there are the sounds of loud, unrestrained laughter (scene 50/51a). On her way out, she is accosted on the staircase by Rajan, who flirts with her (scene 51b). Meanwhile, Prema lies on her bed reading *The Actor* by Niven Busch (screenplay writer of *Duel in the Sun, Postman always rings twice* and *Pursued*). M.T.'s screenplay had suggested 'some cheap romance' by Denise Robbins or Hermina Black. Lying on the bed, Prema speaks about a girl in love with three men and marrying a fourth, and sensuously leans back, reclining languidly. She asks Ammukutty whether she would like to get married (scene 52). The camera moves to the darkness outside and then tracks back to Ammukutty in her room putting out the lamp. She begins to sing: a song of moonlight, her dreams and the moon unthinkingly shining down on human pain.

INTERVAL

This sequence is revealing in the cross hatching of times in the film, through the formal, cultural and cinematic references that abound in a relatively short span of viewing time. In an analysis of this sequence, I inaugurate a framework of analysis that I develop in the course of the article and anticipate some of the themes that are explored later in detail. Ammukutty presents a *toy watch* to Velayudhan as he stands under the door lintel (a liminal space), and he gives her bangles, the cultural symbol of prospective matrimony. These are both arrested gestures referring to two stopped times. Velayudhan, significantly the potential successor to family headship but disabled by his simple-mindedness, comes to accept that he is a lunatic and accedes to being incarcerated in his matrilineal home at the end of the film. He represents the dark, brooding, involution of matrilineal families in a time of change, representing like the madwoman in *Jane Eyre*, a space and time out of joint. The time of matriliny is over; hence the stopped watch. Matriliny is also gestured towards in the reference to a woman having to choose between lovers, polyandry having been one of the threatening features of matriliny that was summoned up by male reformers.[33] The breaking of the bangles is also a disruption of the matrilineal line of affect by the cousin who has come from Singapore, the space of modernity, of money and of a linear time oriented towards the future. He wears pants and a shirt, in contrast to the waistcloth and bare body of Velayudhan; the very objects on him (*wristwatch* and cigarette) speak of the time of the modern. The cigarette as much as the bottles of alcohol in the following scene are markers of another, more degraded time (and we shall return to the discourse of objects later).

We move from this juxtaposition to another one: of cinematic times. The reference to Dilip Kumar/Rock Hudson and Niven Busch's book on which the camera focuses is a playful intertextual reference to other cinema industries; a reference to the global within the local.[34] However, these references, riffs are indicative of an intersection of times rather than an example of cinema in the Time of Hollywood. The reference in the screenplay to the cheap popular romances shows how cinema exists within a larger universe of signification where the film viewer is always already in a world of circulating images: literary, the cinematic-literary (screenplay) and the movie-image.[35] And finally, the music that serves both as setting the period ('twist' music of the 1960s) as also serving as an example of simultaneous times. When Ammukutty sings, she locates herself in another time—that of the high literary and classical poetry—with its references to the moon as presiding over the longing experienced by lovers. The song itself is not diegetic i.e.. it does not carry the story forward, it is a hammock of time in which the heroine luxuriates and the lyricist revels in imagery and language quite out of keeping with the demotic. The first line images the white moonlight spread over the landscape as akin to a woman who has emerged from her bath in clothes drenched with water and circumambulating a temple in prayer. This concatenation of times is not random. We can *also* see the spaces of a dying matriliny (the stopped watch gifted to Velayudhan), of a resurgent, decadent modern (Rajan and Prema), and the timeless arena of classicism occupied by all of MT's heroines, representing as they do the ineffable worth of Tradition. And finally, the Intermission/Interval, which bisects every Indian film, creating dramatic suspense as much as allowing the viewer to engage with bodily functions as with the 'consumer economy' in the foyer. This reinsertion into real time is also a form of 'cinematic punctuation' that is a closing strategy for the first half and points towards a narrative that will unfold in the second half. The perceptive viewer seeing Ammukutty singing blithely of romance prior to the interval feels an anticipatory chill, or thrill, at the thought of impending tragedy. As Lalitha Gopalan puts it, 'the interval lies at the bedrock of our comprehension of the structuring of narrative expectation, development and closure in Indian cinema.'[36]

The space of the songs is also the space of the time of a traditional femininity. Songs serve no plot function, as in musicals, but serve to transport the heroine as well as the audience to another time. Male protagonists appear to have no respite from the struggle with the multiple times that they inhabit. Within the space of the song, the women occupy a space that is both timeless as well as uncorrupted. Studies of Indian cinema are shamefaced about the music and songs in the films, since they seem to serve no obvious diegetic function, and are there almost as independent accretions. However, one of the most significant features of the song is that they are rarely, if ever, in the demotic register of the dialogues. With the opening strains of a hundred violins, the viewer is immediately transported to a time of classicism, of metaphor, and of words laden with meaning and affect. If MT's films as noted earlier are fraught with background and rely on silences and gestures to convey meaning, the songs are explicit in their evocation of a lost time. It is to be remembered that established poets who adhered to the exacting rhythm and metre of classical poetry nearly always wrote the lyrics.

And here there is another history awaiting excavation. In the decade of the 1950s, Vayalar Rama Varma, P. Bhaskaran and other poets had worked with radical theatre and invented a whole genre of 'folk music' set to tunes supposedly corresponding to agricultural work rhythms.[37] This variety of socialist agrarian realism—the depiction of the peasant singing in the fields—was also a feminized one, in that it was the women who were generally shown as singing at work. Women were also the repositories of tradition, uncorrupted by the modern, and representing a pure spontaneous adherence to revolution. These very same poets moved to the film industry and while the narratives may have been less than revolutionary in their import, the women continued to sing songs studded with religious and rural images. In *Murapennu*, Bhagi is shown singing two songs: a romantic lullaby (in which the arrival of the boat bringing her lover induces the flush of a rainbow on her cheeks); a deliberately 'traditional' bucolic song about a thousand virgins celebrating the festival of the asterism of *thiruvathira*. This is before the Intermission. She is then forcibly married to the city educated Aniyan and leaves the village for the space of the estate and the modern accoutrements of house, car and furniture. Bhagi never sings again in the 'decorated prison' that her husband has transplanted her in; song was possible only within that agrarian wholeness in which women could properly be women incorporated within the time of ritual and lore.

There is a changing relation too, to the time of the religious. In *Nalukettu*, his first novel, MT describes a scene in which Appunni, the young protagonist witnesses a family ceremony to propitiate the local snake deities. At the heart of the rite are the pubescent girls of the family who are seen as the conduits to the erotic, powerful charge of the serpents. In pages saturated with longing and desire, Appunni sees from behind a pillar his cousin Ammini, seated bare-breasted with her hair cascading like a serpent over her shoulder (Figure 4). The lamplight flickers and wriggles on her body and Appunni enters a reverie of an insurgent masculinity. As in the space of the song, femininity is complete because it belongs both to a cosmic time as well as a not yet disrupted matriliny.[38] In the films, religion is the space of the incomplete. Witness the incomplete ritual of the oracle at the end of *Nirmalyam*, in which what was meant for the greater glory of the deity has been rendered as the despair of the devotee. Rituals are constantly being disrupted. In *Murapennu*, an indigent uncle comes in and pulls down the decorations disrupting a similar serpent

Figure 4: From M.T. Vasudevan Nair, *Nalukettu* [Ancestral home] (Thrissur: Current Books, 1990), p. 48.

propitiation ritual. The incomplete ritual conveys the impossibility of a sacred time. Towards the end of the film, in an echo of the uncle's act, the protagonist Balan pulls down the garlands and streamers in the structure built for his sister's marriage. His sister then commits suicide, fulfillment denied. *Iruttinte Atmavu* shows the inevitability of incompleteness as also the degrading of religion in a time out of joint. A fierce exorcist beats Velayudhan in an attempt to cure his 'madness'; again, Velayudhan turning on his tormentor interrupts the ritual.

The figure of the lamp brings together brilliantly the discourse on the time of religion, gender and objects. The lamp, borne by women, is one of the objects redolent of a time of religion that is also a time of uncorrupted femininity (Figure 5). In the films women are shown lighting lamps at the time of dusk, praying in front of lamps at temples, seated next to lamps in the family prayer room.[39] However, the aura of the lamp frames the dying space of the matrilineal. Either they are trapped in the space of the lamp (an extreme instance being in *Nirmalyam* where Ammini is seduced by the young Nambudiri by the light of the temple lamp in a double violation). Or they leave the lamps behind and move into the harsher, modern space of the electric light as in the case of Bhagi in *Murapennu*, condemned to a loveless marriage in the estate. In *Iruttinte Atmavu*, the 'modern' woman, Prema, who has returned from Singapore is always seen in rooms lit by electric bulbs as

Figure 5: From Vaudevan Nair, *Nalukettu*, p. 88.

opposed to *Ammukutty* who is positioned in relation to the lamp. *Nirmalyam* has a darker rendering of the time of tradition and the space of religion and women. In earlier scenes in the film, the oracle's younger daughters are shown studying by the light of the lamp, and the lessons they learn are ironic both in terms of the materiality as well as social conditions that they describe. For instance, in scene 16, the girls are reading out, 'Mother gives us milk and she will be sad if we do not drink it. I should grow up to be as big as my father. This is what mother desires.' By scene 66, the tempo towards the climax has set in: the temple priest has seduced Ammini and the oracle has driven his son from the house. The girls are shown around the lamp at home reciting their prayers and we never see them at their books again. They have reverted to the time of religion from that of the pedagogic modern.

Another notion of time, less contingent and more transcendental, lies in the background of M.T.'s creations. It is the time of the river: both landscape and metaphor, witness as well as participant, that frames the actions of the characters on-screen. The flowing river is the horizon of all the lives depicted in the films, contrasted with the relative fixity of the land, individual roots and households.[40] The ocean is written out, except in the formulaic references to Singapore and Colombo (or Singaporecolombo as the old grandmother puts it in the film *Murapennu*), which come to stand in for the 'foreign' across the sea, through their very repetition. As we saw earlier, in his novel of 1962, *Arabiponnu*, M.T. had dealt with the threatening aspect of the ocean as that which corroded an existing hierarchy through the possibility of the wrong kind of people making money. In M.T.'s conservative vision, it is significant that characters associated with the oceanic space are generally presented as intruders and disrupters of the moral economy of the rural landscape. In *Iruttinte Atmavu*, the arrival of Madhavan Nair with his wife and two children from Singapore (prefigured by a shot in which the camera zooms in on an envelope that has arrived in the household in Kerala with a postage stamp from Singapore), starts the downward spiral of the film. The matrilineal family is partitioned; Rajan, the Singapore returned cousin attempts to rape Ammukutty the heroine, who then is forced into marriage with a widower; and Velayudhan, the protagonist is exorcized, chained, and finally comes to accept his madness driven by Madhavan Nair's intolerance. In *Nirmalyam*, a Brahmin driven by slim pickings as temple priest, starts a teashop and dreams of going to Singapore to make money. The arrival of Kunhali, who has made money on the other coast in the city of Salem, is the hinge on which Olavum *Theeravum* turns, bringing tragedy into the lives of the protagonists.

The turbulent time of the ocean is replaced by the local, familiar rhythms of the river. In one of the most evocative sequences in *Iruttinte Atmavu*, Velayudhan sits by the well in the compound of his house, next to a large vessel containing water for his bath. As he waits for the retainer to come bathe him, he idly pours the water out on the ground with a scoop. The water flows along a channel and the camera then pans to the river to a dream sequence in which Velayudhan stands on a boat in full sail and his face, otherwise tormented and diffident, is carefree and radiant. Yet another scene has him climb the flexible trunk of an areca nut tree and as he swings from one treetop to the other, the vision of the river transports him. His simplicity is aligned with the time of the river, at odds with the discontinuous and jarring modern. In *Murapennu*, the song *Karayunno puzha, cirikunno* [Does the river weep or does it laugh] frames the tragedy of the central character Balan, as he struggles with the demands of familial duty over his individual needs. The film begins with Balan, his younger brother Aniyan and their male cousin returning from college to their village by boat. Balan never crosses the river again, sacrificing a college education and becoming a farmer so that his brother can have a career. Aniyan journeys across the river, gains a degree and a well-paid job, but by going to the other side, he crosses a moral line as well, treating his family and his duties with contempt. *Olavum Theeravum* is structured by the rhythms of the river; the boatman Baputty likens himself to a log on the river. After losing the woman he loves and the dreams of a land-based domesticity, he returns to the embrace of the river where he can be untrammelled and away from the casual corruption of humanity.

In *Nirmalyam*, M.T.'s bleak film of 1974, the river has run dry. We first see the young Nambudiri, who comes to the village temple to bide his time as a priest while dreaming of a job in the city, as he crosses the desiccated riverbed and approaches the bank. With his entry, from *across* the river, a chain of events is set into motion including his casual seduction of the oracle's daughter. So far, the imagery is in keeping with the river as a moral boundary. However, we have also the powerful metaphor of the oracle's perpetual thirst. He asks for water at the very beginning of the film soon after finishing his ritual performance. As he wanders around in the course of the film, throat always parched, trying to raise money for temple rituals he is shown drinking water from a spout, poured by a kindly woman. Later on he is refused water at the teashop, the parsimonious owner saying firmly that he would have to have tea or coffee. And finally, as we move towards the climactic end, the oracle returns home at dusk, calls for his wife to bring him water, knocks on the door and the Muslim moneylender steps out of the interior. His thirst unquenched, he goes to the temple pond, dips into it, and emerges revived, pulsing and possessed to go to his ritual death. From ocean, to river to pond. From fluidity to the stagnant. The longer, persistent time of the river has run out and the rural landscape is without a moral horizon.

## IV

*The wilderness rose up to it,*
*And sprawled around, no longer wild.*

Wallace Stevens, *Anecdote of the Jar*

Time sticks to people, it inheres in objects. In *Iruttinte Atmavu*, we are introduced to Velayudhan amidst the jumbled disorder of objects and artefacts that surround him. In the opening shot of the film the camera moves across the walls of his room, covered over with childish drawings and then moves in on particulars: wood shavings on the floor, a knife, and a bowl of water. It tracks to Velayudhan, carving a statue. We see him get up and search in his rusty trunk filled with seeds, gilt paper, the burner of a lantern, round stones, pieces of cloth, and old coins. These remains represent not only the lack of wholeness in his life but also stand as a metaphor of his matrilineal inheritance. They are the fragments that he has shored against his ruin. There is a discourse of objects in M.T.'s films where 'things' are no longer ciphers. They circulate within the film adding another layer of meaning. Objects are an integral part of the 'visual economy' of the film. Viewers construct meaning through *what* they see as much as much as *how* what they see is put together through the use of the vocabulary of lighting, editing and other joining effects. Madhavan Nair, the *nouveau riche* returnee from Singapore is shown always clutching a tin of *555 State Express* cigarettes, expresses not only wealth, but a lack of breeding that makes him smoke in the inner spaces of the house and without a sense of decorum and respect towards elders. The impending confrontation between the family head and Madhavan Nair is signalled in a scene where he chastises the *Karanavan*, the head of the family (his brother-in-law and uncle of his children) questioning his right to reprimand his niece. In a reprise of the classic conflict within matrilineal households between older uncles and younger nephews/sons-in-law, Madhavan Nair says venomously, 'Uncles to advise and scold, indeed! Have uncles been of any use to my children?' He throws his lighted cigarette down, mutters, 'Uncles', and spits on the ground. The *Karanavan* stubs the cigarette out with his foot (scene 72). The extinguishing of the cigarette is also the vanquishing of the upstart. Later the *Karanavan* will remind Madhavan Nair that he has known him from the time that he was indigent and used to smoke *beedis* (the local hand-rolled tobacco leaf). From this moment on Madhavan Nair moves towards recognition of how money has blinded him. One episode towards the end of the film that brings him back to his senses is when he wanders into his son's room and finds him smoking a cigarette and looking at photographs of unclad women. Needless to say Madhavan Nair never smokes again.

M.T. writes about the challenge that the screenplay writer has to face when he has to express something on screen where neither word nor action will suffice. He refers to Dudley Nichol's script for John Ford's *The Informer* (1935), in which the mental anguish of Gypo Nolan after informing on his friend is shown through the movement of a poster announcing a reward for Frankie's arrest. The wind blows the poster towards Gypo and entwines the poster around his knees and ankles. He kicks it aside and later as he sits down at a fire with Frankie and Dan, the poster falls into the fire and burns as a horror-stricken

Gypo looks on.[41] By their objects shall ye know them. The externality of the characters and their inner domain are knitted together through their relation to objects. Back to the cigarette. The cigarette is the marker of the modern and the corrupt, as also of a villainy born of a location outside the moral community of the rural landscape. In *Olavum Theeravum*, only the villainous Kunhali smokes cigarettes, while the hero Baputty and the other rustic characters are shown with beedis. When Madhavan Nair in *Iruttinte Atmavu* and Kunhali in *Olavum Theeravum* offer cigarettes, only the comic characters accept; their traffic and friendship can only be with the fool and the marginal. In *Murapennu*, there is a slightly more complicated semiotic in operation. Keshavankutty returns from college and his betrothed, Kochammini ribs him about having given up beedis for cigarettes. This should be enough to ring alarm bells in the alert viewer's mind; we know that he has *changed* in a fundamental sense. As the film progresses, Keshavankutty moves away from his childhood love, after attempting unsuccessfully to seduce her, and consents to marrying a girl from a rich family, where he can enjoy the comfortable status of the son-in-law. The only other person who smokes in the film is Aniyan, the brother who leaves family responsibility behind to make money. In *Nirmalyam*, fairly early on the local madman asks the oracle for a *beedi*; a profane request which establishes the character's madness. The very first time we meet the oracle's ne'er-do-well son, Appu, he enters the compound smoking a beedi, which he throws away only as he is about to step in to his house.

Mirrors play an important role in the economy of the films. They serve as obvious mediators of self-recognition as in *Iruttinte Atmavu*, when Velayudhan walks into his visiting cousins' room and looks at his face in a mirror for the first time. He is displeased by what he sees. Till this moment he has been within the space of his family where there is a recognition of his simple mindedness but softened by love and acceptance. In the very next scene, we see Prema enter the room, see Velayudhan in her bed and she shrieks. Madhavan Nair enters the room and says that madmen ought to be locked up and not allowed to wander around the house. This is the first time that Velayudhan is characterized as 'mad', and the film allows another register for our understanding of him. Ammukutty, the heroine of *Iruttinte Atmavu*, is in her room changing after her bath; when we see in a mirror her cousin Rajan enter after stubbing out his cigarette on the doorframe. Later in the film, he will attempt to rape her, asserting his right over the woman betrothed to him by tradition. In *Murapennu*, Bhagi, who is in love with the hero Balan, is in her room, looking at the gift that he has brought for her. As she stands lost in thought we see the image of Aniyan, Balan's younger brother, who will eventually coerce her into a loveless marriage, in the mirror. She looks up and the first time she sees him is in the reflected image. In *Olavum Theeravum*, Nabeesa goes to the village market and squats as she buys bangles, a sign of love having entered her life and a sense of commitment to Baputty. The villain Kunhali's image appears in the mirror placed on the ground; this is the first time they see one another. She rushes away from the market. The next time they occupy the same frame is in her hut when she sees him in the mirror again as he enters to rape her. Significantly, at the very moment of happiness the women see in the mirror the men—from outside the rural moral economy, and engaged with the modern—who will bring sorrow into their lives. Their own access to the modern and the outside cannot be direct, it is mediated both through objects and the aggressive masculinity that lays claim to them. It is as if any attempt on the women's part to reach happiness, is hopeless; their hopes rebound off the glass.

There is of course, the obvious engagement with the objects that characterize modernity. In *Iruttinte Atmavu*, when Madhavan Nair and his family arrive from Singapore, their attire and accoutrements mark their very bodies. Madhavan Nair has on gold-framed spectacles, rings on fingers, gold bracelet, gold watch, and he wears a silk shirt. His son, Rajan, is wearing pants and shirt and the daughter, Prema, is in a dress with her hair cut short. The good, noble rural characters are always clad in traditional attire and very often the men are dressed in waistcloths with the dirt of hard work in the fields marking their bodies. Again, in the portrayal of spaces, those occupied by the women and older men in the household are characterized by darkness, and very often shots are taken through window bars or shadowed by wooden staircases. However, within the same house, the new entrants have airy rooms that are almost effulgent with light. Dark and light are ironically represented and do not necessarily correspond to bad and good. Two scenes take us to the rooms of Rajan and Prema in quick succession, as seen through Velayudhan's eyes. Rajan's room: shirts on bed, transistor on table, some shoes on the floor. Timepiece. An album lies on the central table with a photograph of Rajan in a suit. It has other photographs of women in swimming costumes. An owl clock on the wall strikes the hour. Velayudhan watches (scene 37A). Prema's room: film stars on one side of door frame, on the other traditional paintings of women by the 19th century Malayali painter Ravi Varma; blouses on hanger, a bed with a mosquito net, photograph of girl with a fan looking at mirror; on one side a big mirror with make-up items (scene 37B). Seeing as we do this profusion of objects through the eyes of the hero Velayudhan, we are cynical of such luxury and are invited to contrast it with Velayudhan's own clutter with which the film began. Simplicity is opposed to a shallow display.

At the turn of the twentieth century most of the novels written by upper castes spoke of the modern inner spaces of homes with desire. The late nineteenth century had inaugurated the move away from matriliny and polyandry to the nuclear monogamous unit of husband and wife. In Chathu

Nair's novel, *Meenakshi* [1890], the interior of the home is done up in the style of the Victorian bourgeois domestic spaces with painted mirrors, expensive carpets, sofas, chairs, glass lamps, and there is a library with two cupboards holding, appropriately, Sanskrit and English books. Again, in *Lakshmikeshavam* (1892), by Padoo Menon, Devaraja Naidu's house has carpets, marble-topped tables; glass panelled cupboards, and oil paintings. Moreover, the home was ruled by a new notion of time, with every passing minute accounted for: 'The sound from the clocks hung in a row on the wall was so loud that one had to talk loudly in order to be audible.'[42] The owl clock that farcically strikes in Rajan's room as if only to please and amuse Velayudhan has replaced this obsessive engagement with the time of modernity. This innocent engagement with the baubles of modernity and the celebration of the domestic space of the nuclear family has given way to a cynicism regarding 'modern' spaces filled with obscure objects of desire. By M.T.'s time, we are in the time of the fragmentation of the matrilineal, and the shine has begun to wear off the great patrilineal hope.

Another object that figures prominently in M.T.'s novels and film is dice. Gambling and dice bring together notions of time, fortune and control. It is about being able to attain the desired number in as few throws as possible; winning is also about being able to control time. And there was a time when time itself was amenable to being held in a fist and rolled. In his first novel, *Nalukettu* (1958), Appunni hero-worships his father, Konthunni, whom he has never seen but who is a village legend: strong, irascible, popular and good at dice. The novel recounts a legendary match in which Konthunni, required to throw 32 to save the honour of the village, throws the dice three times, each time the maximum 12. His defeated opponent swears never to touch dice again. However, in the films, time is out of joint and that wholeness in which men were master of fortune is over (Konthunni asks why he should invoke the bitch-goddess luck before he throws for a win). The novel *Arabiponnu* (1962) begins with the character Koya entering the Café de Paradise where frenetic gambling is in progress and we realize as the story unfolds that Koya was once rich on a patrilineal inheritance that he squandered away through gambling. However, this novel, his only one set beside the ocean, is about the corrupting influence of the ocean and the immoral quality of the money made through illegal commerce. In the films, only the losers, so to speak, play dice. We first meet Baputty in *Olavum Theeravum*, crouched by the riverbank playing dice, and losing. He may have been cheated, but he has no control over the game. Aniyan, in *Iruttinte Atmavu*, squanders the money that he earns at the estate on gambling, never having any for the urgent needs of his family back home in the village. In the case of Appu, the oracle's son in *Nirmalyam*, there is an important twist. He is shown winning at dice, in a sequence where the oracle walks towards cries of 'six, six', sees Appu playing, and the camera focuses on the dice showing six and six respectively. However, lucky at dice... Appu, driven by poverty and anger, attempts to sell the goddess's sword, and is driven out of the house by the oracle. The dice raise the question of a degraded time that we have been exploring. However, we wonder too, whether it is a question of degraded masculinity. In Konthunni's time men were men, what now in the twilight of matriliny?

## V

Remember us—if at all—not as lost
Violent souls, but only
As the hollow men
The stuffed men.

T.S. Eliot, *The Hollow Men*

Let us go back to M.T.'s debut novel, *Nalukettu* of 1958. The novel begins with the words, He would grow up. Yes he would, and become big and strong. His arms would be muscular. Then he need not fear anybody. He would hold his head high and be respected. If anyone asked him, 'Who are you?' he would reply (in a ringing assertion of patrilineal descent) head held high, 'It is I, Appunni, *son* of Konthunni Nair.'[43] The story tells of a fatherless child, who goes back to his matrilineal household, subjects himself to the indignities and insults heaped on him by the head of the family, his mother's uncle, and finally, through hard work buys the family house, the eponymous *nalukettu*. He installs himself as the head and brings his mother back into the house from which she had been cast out for loving unwisely. The tussle between the older order of agrarian masculinity represented by the *Karanavan*, and the newer order of the educated young male has been resolved in favour of the latter. The novel ends with Appunni reminding himself that he was not alone in the world despite the sacrifices that he had to make. 'Chains of obligations' bound him to members of other communities and other generations; he has become the universal representative.[44] This confident assertion of a new masculinity is absent in the films; uncertainty and irresolution has taken its place. All of the films end in the heroes' failure or capitulation to forces beyond their control. At the same time, they stand disencumbered on the edge of a new and as yet unresolved identity.

In all of the films, in keeping with the matrilineal mode, the hero's father is absent. It is the uncle that has to be contended with, presenting a model of authoritarian masculinity under which the hero buckles. The older males, who stand in the relation of father in the films are generally invalid or lost in the glories of another age. In *Iruttinte Atmavu*, the grandfather of Velayudhan lies in his bed under the staircase, framed in shadows, a silent witness to the squabbling and disputes in the family. He is full of stories of powerful *karanavar* of another time, men feared when they were alive, but poisoned in their prime or driven to madness. Similarly, in *Nirmalyam*, the oracle's father is paralysed, and lies in a corner of the house, the camera focuses persistently on his moving eyelids to emphasize his bodily incapacity. We know that both he and his father were oracles to reckon with, capable of negotiating with the goddess of smallpox and stay her hand. A dominant masculinity carries the seeds of its own destruction. The dominant *karanavar* of *Murapennu* is able to bend the wills of those around him but drives them to tragedy. The heroes cannot and do not aspire to the overriding, arrogant and infructuous maleness of the *Karanavan*. It is the villains, so to speak, who also occupy the space of the modern, who possess the will to power, but it is expressed only in relation to the women. Rajan attempts to rape his betrothed, Ammukutty in *Iruttinte Atmavu*, just as Aniyan in *Murapennu* slaps his wife in his desire for control. The possession of education is an ambivalent virtue. In *Iruttinte Atmavu*, the teacher appointed to instruct Prema in English, attempts to woo her through romantic tropes in the poetry that he teaches and even uses Einstein's Theory of Relativity to impress upon her how his longing makes him experience time differently.

The hero stands in between this decaying older trope of masculinity and the resurgent, immoral new one. To be in-between is to inhabit a tragic space: the road to madness as in the case of Velayudhan or to lose everything as with Balan. *Olavum Theeravum*, though it is set in a Muslim community, has the hero Baputty embark on the river once again after having lost the woman he loves. He chooses loneliness. In *Nirmalyam*, the oracle's principled life can culminate only in his death. The options open to him are to leave the rural landscape (as the young Nambudiri priest does) or turn to the profane world of commerce (like the older Nambudiri priest who sets up a tea shop). Loves are structured by the yearnings of matriliny; heroes love their female cousins, the daughters of their uncles. In a time out of joint, these loves remain unfulfilled. The younger women have little option; they enter into unhappy marriages or commit suicide. But this is also a rendering of matriliny that is too conditioned by the history of the crusade against it. Women had once headed households, but that is a narrative that M.T. suppresses. Even the older women are dependent, shadows in the presence of the dominant older males. Women can be only the objects of love and lust, or pity. And we realize that is not against other males that masculinity is created, it is in relation to the female. It is the image of Appunni leading his mother back to the ancestral home that structures the trajectory of malehood.

What is being forged here is the man in the new mode of patriliny. And this cannot be done within the space and time of the agrarian landscape. In *Murapennu*, Balan decides to sacrifice his college career so that his younger brother can have a career in a place elsewhere. Shortly afterwards, he is initiated into rural life through a thrilling sequence in which he takes part in a bullock race and emerges the winner even after falling in the slush of the rice fields. Covered with mud, triumphant, he seems to have been vindicated in his option. However, by the end of the film, every venture of his, including his heroic effort to get his younger sister married has come to naught. The male characters have to leave; every film stands poised on the edge of a future wholeness. And where does that lie? Madhava Prasad has interpreted brilliantly the recurrent theme of how time after time the police always arrive late in films made in almost every Indian language. The state apparatus—the time of the modern—is kept at bay, and it is community justice that is triumphantly meted out through the agency of the hero. In M.T.'s films, the state is significant by its absence and the community is present only in its imminent dissolution. The burden of transformation is on the new man arising from the ruins of matriliny and the structuring of the public domain around a resurgent masculinity.[45] The new man is also the reconstructed agrarian Hindu. Living by the sea, M.T. has also effaced the maritime and its rhythms, silencing of the space of commerce, and therefore the Muslim and the Christian. It is worth remembering that in M.T.'s short story 'Sacred Sword and Anklets' (1954) there is no Muslim character at all. In *Nirmalyam*, the film on this story and made two decades later, we are given the chilling image of the Muslim moneylender who has entered the home of the oracle. It is an icon that summons up the fears of the new politics of Hinduism. From within the heart of a regional progressive poetics and the lapsing dream of a new society, MT has forged a vision that prefigures an emergent national paradigm.

## Notes

1. See Vasudevan Nair (2003: 248).
2. See Vasudevan Nair (1995: 235).
3. It would be a fundamental mistake to see these as 'local' cartoons teeming with the business of everyday life in Kerala alone. As M.T. points out in his introduction to the 1996 edition of Aravindan's cartoons, the justification provided for retailing the adventures of a lower middle class hero came as much from Kingsley Amis's *Lucky Jim* [1961] which was part of their literary imagination. It is also worth remembering that in one of the cartoons a friend tells Ramu, on the basis of his having taught in a local college, that he was a retired Professor of sorts. The schoolteacher retorts that (Federico Garcia) Lorca once remarked that a chameleon is a crocodile of sorts.
4. Aravindan (1996).

5. See Menon (1994).

6. See Damodaran (1984) and also Mallick (1994).

7. For a discussion of these issues see Menon (1998).

8. The first chapter of my book looks at this discursive process. An initial exploration was Menon (2000).

9. For the most incisive historical work on matriliny in Kerala see Arunima [2003].

10. *Mathrubhumi*, 11 May 1932.

11. See Panikkar (1931).

12. See Menon (2002).

13. See Herring (1983) and Baak (1997).

14. There is as yet no comprehensive study of this important period in the history of Kerala in which an alliance of forces came together to bring down the Communist ministry in alliance with the central government. That this agitation called itself the *vimocana samaram*, or the freedom struggle, is rich in implication for a history of postcolonial India.

15. See Fic (1970) and Nossiter (1982).

16. See Frankel (1978) and Rudolph and Rudolph (1987) for excellent analytical overviews.

17. See Bannerjee (1984). A cultural history of the Naxalite movement in India is yet to be written. This is a curious fact given that in almost all the regional languages of India, the engagement with Sartre and French existentialism dates to the Naxalite debacle and the retreat of the young intellectuals into the world of the ephemeral radical literary journals that mushroomed in the decades of the 1970s and 1980s.

18. See the essays in Parayil (2000).

19. See www.mtvasudevannair.com for a list of awards.

20. Rajadhyaksha and Willemen (1999).

21. Tudor [2003: 5] poses this problem well when he observes of the genre of 'westerns' that, 'To take a genre such as a western, analyse it, and list its principal characteristics is to beg the question that we must first isolate the body of films that are westerns. But they can only be isolated on the basis of 'principal characteristics', which can only be discovered from the films themselves after they have been isolated.

22. Prasad (1998: Chapter 3) theorizes the 'super genre' of the Hindi film in his book. Of course, the idea of super genre is an example of having one's cake and eating it too: both genre and not-genre. For a similar idea of always 'hybrid' genres see Berry-Flint (2004). For a reading of Hindi film as blurring genres, see Gopalan (2002).

23. I have benefited much from Noel Carroll's (1988) acerbic readings of the ambitions of certain kinds of film theory. His philosophical engagement with the movies is akin to the idea that god is in the details, a principle dear to the historian's heart.

24. See essays by Elsaesser (1973: 2–15) and Willemen (1993) for two characteristic readings in two different contexts.

25. See Metz (1978: 17).

26. See Vasudevan Nair (1998: 453).

27. Jameson (1986: 69).

28. Ibid., 85–86.

29. See for instance the punning on imperso (nation) in Chakravarty [1993] and Virdi (2003).

30. Deleuze (1986: 106). Deleuze's text as ever is dense and provocative and elliptical, and my use of his ideas is as yet a very tentative one.

31. Vasudevan Nair (1998: 459).

32. See Auerbach (1968: 11–12), who writes: 'the externalisation of only so much of the phenomena as is necessary for the purpose of the narrative, all else is left in obscurity; the decisive points of the narrative alone are emphasized, what lies between is nonexistent; time and place are undefined and call for interpretation; thoughts and feelings remain unexpressed, are only suggested by the silence and fragmentary speeches.'

33. As of now, the jury is out on the question of polyandry under matriliny. While there was no formal institution of marriage prior to the Marriage Act of the late nineteenth century, and the Malayalam word *sambandham* was variously read as relationship and liaison, serial monogamy rather than polyandry may have been the norm. See Arunima (2003).

34. The cinephile could argue here that the reference to Rock Hudson is itself a gesture towards the Hollywood melodrama of Douglas Sirk who juxtaposed Hudson's wholesome masculine persona against themes of failure, impotency and blindness. In fact, there may be a parallel also in the fact that Sirk's films have been interpreted as 'the history of the congealed disintegration of society'. See Halliday (1972) and also Klinger (1994).

35. M.T. observes in his essay on cinema that it is through references to what lies outside the film, but is within the realm of the viewer's imagination, that the writer contributes 'a literary dimension and depth'. For instance he refers to Wajda's film *Kanal* (1957), set in the last days of the Warsaw uprising: 'The cranky character who spouts lines from Dante in *Kanal* provides this literary dimension: it is Dante's *Inferno* that reminds is of the hell in which unfortunates are consigned to live' (Vasudevan Nair 1998: 459).

36. Gopalan (2002: 71). Her book is the first to work with the structure of Hindi films and the conditions of their viewing rather than subject them to the theoretical conditions of viewing framed in much film theory. She proposes a cinema of interruptions in opposition to the idea of continuous viewing and consequent subject-formation; beloved in particular of what Carroll terms the 'Althusserian-Lacanian paradigm'.

37. P. Bhaskaran (1924—) was associated with the radical cultural movement of the 1940s and the 1950s, and composed more than 3,000 lyrics in the invented tradition of romantic agrarianism. M.S. Baburaj (1921—), the composer of the music for *Olavum Theeravum*, also came from the theatre movement, and was one of the first to introduce

north Indian classical music into Malayalam film, incorporating a slower beat, minimal orchestration and a music that was more melody rather than rhythm based.

38. See Fig. 4 for the illustration by Namboodiri in *Nalukettu*.

39. See Fig. 5 for a 'prototypical' representation of the woman with the lamp. Sanil (2002: 70–81) argues that Namboodiri who has done the illustrations for most of M.T.'s novels, revels in 'prototypes' as opposed to 'stereotypes', the former being more future oriented and open in their nature than the latter which are congealed forms of social perception.

40. See the dense, suggestive section in Deleuze (1986: 76–80) in which he discusses the significance of running water in the films of Renoir and the French school.

41. Vasudevan Nair (1998: 457).

42. See Menon (2004) and Kumar (forthcoming). 43 Vasudevan Nair (1999: 1).

44. Vasudevan Nair (1999: 189).

45. Exploring this paradox of a state where the physical well-being of women is far superior compared to other states in India while at the same time men dominate the public sphere in a strongly patriarchal mode of functioning is just beginning to be explored in recent studies. For the classic study of Kerala as a model for the equality of women, see Jeffrey (1992). For the emerging new paradigm see Devika (1999) and the ongoing doctoral work by Ratheesh (2004).

## References

Amis, K., 1961 [1954]. *Lucky Jim*, Harmondsworth: Penguin Books.

Aravindan, G., 1996 [1978]. *Cheriya lokam valiya manushyan*, Kottayam: D.C. Books.

Arunima, G., 2003, '*There Comes Papa': Colonialism and the transformation of matriliny in Malabar, 1850–1940*, Hyderabad: Orient Longman.

Auerbach, Erich, 1968. *Mimesis: The representation of reality in western literature*, Princeton, NJ: Princeton University Press.

Baak, P., 1997. *Plantation Production and Political Power: Plantation development in southwest India in a longterm historical perspective, 1743–1963*, Delhi: Oxford University Press.

Bannerjee, Sumanta, 1984. *India's Simmering Revolution: The naxalite uprising*, London: Zed Books.

Berry-Flint, Sarah, 2004. 'Genre', in Toby Miller and Robert Stam (eds.), *A Companion to Film Theory*, Oxford: Blackwell.

Carroll, Noel, 1988. *Mystifying Movies: Fads and fallacies in contemporary film theory*, New York: Columbia University Press.

Chakravarty, Sumita, 1993. *National Identity in Indian Popular Cinema, 1947–1987*, Austin, TX: University of Texas Press.

Damodaran, K., 1984. 'The Tragedy of Indian Communism', in Tariq Ali (ed.), *The Stalinist Legacy*, Harmondsworth: Penguin.

Deleuze, Gilles, 1986. *Cinema 1: The Movement-Image,* Minneapolis, MI: University of Minnesota Press.

Devika, J., 1999. 'Engendering Individuals: A Study of Gender and Individualisation in Reform Language in Modern Kerala, 1880–1950', Unpublished PhD dissertation, School of Social Sciences, M.G. University, Kottayam.

Elsaesser, Thomas, 1973. 'Tales of sound and fury: observations on the family melodrama', *Monogram*, No. 4.

Fic, Victor M., 1970. *Kerala: Yenan of India—The Rise of Communist Power, 1937–1969,* Bombay: Nachiketa Publications.

Frankel, Francine, 1978. *India's Political Economy, 1947–1977: The gradual revolution,* Princeton, NJ: Princeton University Press.

Gopalan, Lalitha, 2002. *Cinema of Interruptions Action Genres in Contemporary Indian Cinema*, London: British Film Institute.

Halliday, Jon, 1972. 'All That Heaven Allows', in Jon Halliday and Laura Mulvey (eds.), *Douglas Sirk*, London: British Film Institute.

Herring, Ronald J., 1983. *Land to the Tiller: The political economy of agrarian reform in South Asia*, New Haven, CT: Yale University Press.

Jameson, Frederic, 1986. 'Third world literature in the era of multinational capitalism', *Social Text*, Fall.

Jeffrey, Robin, 1992. *Politics, Women and Well-Being: How Kerala became a 'model'*, Basingstoke, Hampshire: Macmillan.

Klinger, Barbara, 1994. *Melodrama and Meaning: History, culture and the films of Douglas Sirk*, Bloomington, IN: Indiana University Press.

Kumar, Udaya, 2016. *Writing the First Person: Literature, history and autobiography in modern Kerala,* Delhi: Permanent Black.

Mallick, Ross, 1994. *Indian Communism, Collaboration and Institutionalisation*, Delhi: Oxford University Press.

Menon, Dilip M., 1994. *Caste, Nationalism and Communism in South India: Malabar, 1900–1948*, Cambridge: Cambridge University Press

_____. 1998. 'Being a Brahmin the Marxist Way: EMS Nambudiripad and the Pasts of Kerala', in Daud Ali (ed.), *Invoking the Past: The uses of history in South Asia*, New Delhi: Oxford University Press.

_____. 2000. 'Houses by the Sea: State experimentation on the South West Coast of India, 1760–1800', in N. Chandhoke (ed.), *Mapping Histories: Essays Presented to Ravinder Kumar*, New Delhi: Tulika.

_____. 2002. 'Lost Visions: The Imagining of a National Culture in the 1950s', in Alice Thorner (ed.), *Land, Labour and Rights: Ten Daniel Thorner Memorial Lectures*, London: Anthem Press.

_____. 2004. 'A Place Elsewhere: Lower Caste Malayalam Novels of the Nineteenth Century', in Vasudha Dalmia and Stuart Blackburn (eds.), *India's Literary History: Essays on the Nineteenth Century*, Delhi: Permanent Black.

Metz, Christian, 1978. *Film Language: A semiotics of the cinema*, New York: Oxford University Press.

Nossiter, T.J., 1982. *Communism in Kerala: A study in political adaptation*, Berkeley, CA: University of California Press.

Panikkar, K.M., 1931. *Malabar and the Dutch (Being the History of the Fall of Nayar Power in Malabar*), Bombay: D. Taraporevala Sons & Co.

Parayil, Govindan (ed.), 2000. *Kerala: The development experience—reflections on sustainability and replicability*, London: Zed Books.

Prasad, Madhava, 1998. *Ideology of the Hindi Flm: A historical construction*, Delhi: Oxford University Press.

Rajadhyaksha, Ashish and Paul Willemen (eds.), 1999. *The Encyclopaedia of Indian Cinema*, Delhi: Oxford University Press.

Ratheesh, R., 2004. 'Masculinities and the Restructuring of the "Public Domain" in Contemporary Kerala', Centre for the Study of Culture and Society, Bangalore.

Rudolph, Lloyd I., and Susanne Hoeber Rudolph, 1987. *In Pursuit of Lakshmi: The Political Economy of the Indian State*, Chicago, IL: Chicago University Press.

Sanil, V., 2002. *'Kandukondain Kandukondain': Namboodiriyude chitramezhuthine kurichu* ['Transfixed by the Look': On Namboodiri's Drawings], Paccakuthira, July–September.

Tudor, Andrew, 2003. 'Genre', in Barry Keith Grant (ed.), *Film Genre Reader III*, Austin, TX: University of Texas Press.

Vasudevan Nair, M.T., 1995. *Kaalam* (trans. Gita Krishnankutty), Hyderabad: Disha Books.

——. 1998. [1978], 'Visual Literature' (trans. V. Abdulla), in *The Demon Seed and Other Writings*, Delhi: Penguin Books.

——. 1999. *Nalukettu* , Trichur: Current Books.

——. 2003. *Asuravithu*, Kottayam: D.C. Books.

Virdi, Jyotika, 2003. *The Cinematic ImagiNation: Indian Popular Films as Social History*, Brunswick, NJ: Rutgers University Press.

Willemen, Paul, 1993. 'Negotiating the Transition to Capitalism: The Case of Andaz,' in Wimal Dissanayake (ed.), *Melodrama and Asian Cinema*, Cambridge: Cambridge University Press.

# Contributors

Rustom Bharucha, Independent writer, director, dramaturg and cultural critic, Kolkata, India

Sumita S. Chakravarty, Associate Professor of Media Studies, The New School, New York

Ramachandra Guha, Historian, public intellectual and independent scholar, Bengaluru

Dilip M. Menon, Mellon Chair in Indian Studies, University of Witwatersrand, South Africa

Tanika Sarkar, formerly Professor of History, Jawaharlal Nehru University, New Delhi

Amanda Weidman, Associate Professor of Anthropology, Bryn Mawr College, Pennsylvania

Patricia Uberoi, Chairperson and Honorary Fellow of the Institute of Chinese Studies (ICS), Delhi